GLOBALIZAT

INSTITUTIONS &
GOVERNANCE

SAGE Series on the Foundations of International Relations

Series Editors: Walter Carlsnaes *Uppsala University, Sweden*

Jeffrey T. Checkel *Simon Fraser University, Canada*

International Advisory Board: Peter J. Katzenstein *Cornell University, USA*; Emanuel Adler *University of Toronto, Canada*; Martha Finnemore *George Washington University, USA*; Andrew Hurrell *Oxford University, UK*; G. John Ikenberry *Princeton University, USA*; Beth Simmons *Harvard University, USA*; Steve Smith *University of Exeter, UK*; Michael Zuern *Hertie School of Governance, Germany*.

This series fills the gap between narrowly focused research monographs and broad introductory texts, providing graduate students with state-of-the-art, critical overviews of the key sub-fields within International Relations: International Political Economy, International Security, Foreign Policy Analysis, International Organization, Normative IR Theory, International Environmental Politics, Globalization, and IR Theory.

Explicitly designed to further the transatlantic dialogue fostered by publications such as the *SAGE Handbook of International Relations*, the series is written by renowned scholars drawn from North America, continental Europe and the UK. The books are intended as core texts on advanced courses in IR, taking students beyond the basics and into the heart of the debates within each field, encouraging an independent, critical approach and signposting further avenues of research.

GLOBALIZATION, INSTITUTIONS & GOVERNANCE

James A Caporaso & Mary Anne Madeira

SSFIR | SAGE Series on the Foundations of **International Relations**

⊛SAGE

Los Angeles | London | New Delhi
Singapore | Washington DC

First published 2012

SAGE Publications Ltd
1 Oliver's Yard
55 City Road
London EC1Y 1SP

SAGE Publications Inc.
2455 Teller Road
Thousand Oaks, California 91320

SAGE Publications India Pvt Ltd
B 1/I 1 Mohan Cooperative Industrial Area
Mathura Road
New Delhi 110 044

SAGE Publications Asia-Pacific Pte Ltd
33 Pekin Street #02–01
Far East Square
Singapore 048763

Library of Congress Control Number available

British Library Cataloguing in Publication data

A catalogue record for this book is available from the British Library

ISBN 978-1-4129-3492-3
ISBN 978-1-4129-3493-0 (pbk)

Typeset by C&M Digitals (P) Ltd, Chennai, India
Printed in India at Replika Press Pvt Ltd
Printed on paper from sustainable resources

CONTENTS

LIST OF FIGURES AND TABLES

ACKNOWLEDGEMENTS

As with most things we produce, a book is a social product, the result of connections and debts too numerous and too invisible to recount. The curiosity and stimulation of students, at both the undergraduate and graduate levels, were crucial for the senior author. But the biggest debt of both authors is to the academic editors of this series, Jeff Checkel and Walter Carlsnaes, as well as to Sage editor David Mainwaring. Jeff and Walter not only convinced us to write the book but also guided us through at least two rounds of revisions. Their comments got us to think about the book in different ways and led to serious revisions, revisions which we think resulted in a much better book. While the readers will not be able to do the comparison, we hope they agree that it was worth the effort.

INTRODUCTION

Globalization: A Rapidly Changing Field

Globalization confronts all of us, even casual observers, with a bewildering range of observations. One does not have to go far to take notice of these events. At the time of this writing, the European Union (EU) contemplates the rescue of Greece from its budgetary troubles; Iceland, as close to sovereign bankruptcy as a country can get, is struggling with repayment of its huge external debt to the Netherlands and Great Britain; and the hugely successful private company, Google, is considering pulling out of China because of Chinese censorship and human rights violations. German and American fiscal authorities do battle with individuals who would escape the control of national taxation systems by putting money outside the reach of their own governments. In addition, riots continue between migrant workers from Africa and Italians in Calabria, and the Swiss People's Party votes in favour of a referendum to ban the building of minarets by Muslims in Switzerland. State and non-state actors are important, and motivations range from principled concerns about human rights to attention to the bottom-line profits and position in the international distribution of power.

The Italian and Swiss examples are telling. The town of Rosarno in Calabria (at the tip of the boot in Southern Italy) relies on migrant labour from the Maghreb and sub-Saharan Africa to pick its citrus fruit. The workers live in very poor conditions and receive perhaps 25 euros a day as their wages, of which they must hand over a portion to the local mafia called the 'Ndrangheta. Reports indicate that two of the workers were shot by locals while they were in their camp. Riots ensued in which many were injured. The result was that well over a thousand African workers either left voluntarily or were removed by the police (*Economist*, Jan. 19, 2010: 1). The situation was brought to a point by the fact that it appeared not profitable to pick the fruit at all, since the Italian economy had been flooded by cheap Spanish oranges and Brazilian orange juice. It seems that even the low agricultural wages of southern Italy were not low enough, in the sense that competition both inside and outside the EU could undercut local prices. While tariff protection may be an option in some countries, it is not viable within the EU owing to the free movement provisions of the Lisbon Treaty (the governing Treaty of the EU), and tariffs against Brazil are heavily discouraged by the World Trade Organization (WTO). Thus, from the standpoint of local producers, workers (domestic and migrant workers), and consumers, there are few options. The constraints implied by Thomas Friedman's 'golden straitjacket' are all too prevalent here but the gold (symbol for the economic benefits) is hard to find (Friedman, 2000 [1999]). Indeed, both Italians and African workers could ask 'what's so golden about this straitjacket?'

The situation in Switzerland is interesting because it demonstrates a significant anti-immigrant movement in an environment where the immigrant presence is not very pronounced. There are approximately 340,000 Muslim immigrants in Switzerland, about 4 per cent of the population, and most of them are from the Balkans and Turkey, two of the more liberal (non-fundamentalist) Muslim countries. Furthermore, the issue on which the Swiss referendum was held had to do with the building of minarets, of which there are only four in all of Switzerland. Yet, the xenophobic Swiss People's Party, which is one of the largest parties in Switzerland, succeeded in leading the campaign against the building of minarets. This campaign relied on a sophisticated approach focusing not on television advertisements but on the power of a fixed image. One of the two most important posters showed minarets positioned as ballistic missiles emerging out of the Swiss flag, an image which was shown in conjunction with another poster of a woman in a niqab, a full-length garment, with the word STOPP in large red letters. Underneath, at the very bottom of the poster, was a large green JA, along with 'zur Minarett-Verbots-Initiative'. In other words, stop the building of minarets. Say 'yes' to forbidding the building of minarets (*New York Times*, Jan. 17, 2010: 1).

All of these examples are culled from reading the newspapers of one week (Jan. 14–21, 2010). If one wants to extend the time frame back a bit, we can think of the French and Dutch rejection of the proposed constitutional treaty by the European Union in May 2005 (events partly motivated by anti-globalization fears); the rise of far-right political parties, which are often anti-immigrant in Europe as a whole; the recent conference on the environment and global warming in Copenhagen; enforcement of stronger controls on airplane travel motivated by fear of global terrorism; and the diffusion of regulatory and legal practices across national borders, in areas such as food labelling, criminal law, and anti-trust laws. Microsoft and Boeing must worry not only about the anti-trust division of the United States Justice Department, but also about the General Directorate for Competition in Brussels.[1]

---

[1] The General Directorate for Competition of the European Union is responsible for enforcing competitive practices among economic entities in the European Union.

Just about every imaginable aspect of modern society has been globalized. The economy gets the lion's share of attention, with trade, capital flows, technology transfer, and migrant labour occupying centre stage. However, much the same could be said for social and cultural practices and services, such as American and Indian movies, Italian fashion, hip hop culture, blues from the Mississippi delta, and so on. Food has definitely been more and more globalized: Turkish kebabs in Lucca, Italy, one of the most culinarily resistant countries in the world; northern Italian food everywhere in US cities; Korean and Ethiopian food in Washington DC; and the influences of Vietnamese food on French cuisine. It is difficult to think of many areas which are untouched by globalization. We may think that mental illness is at least a private affair, in the sense that it is rooted in individual personality structure and at most conditioned by the family or by society more broadly. Yet, in *Crazy Like Us: The Globalization of the American Psyche* (2010), Ethan Watters argues that identifying, understanding, and treating mental illnesses are processes that are shaped by global forces. The therapeutic communities and big pharmaceutical companies, along with those who control the content of the Diagnostic and Statistical Manual (DSM), are in the business of constructing categories of mental illness. Contact among these professional communities (within universities, professional meetings of psychiatric, psychological, and social work associations), along with the interest of drug companies to market pharmaceutical solutions widely (i.e. globally) and without respect to borders, accounts for the export of US understandings of mental illness. Illnesses such as anorexia nervosa, attention deficit disorder, bipolar disorder, borderline personality structure, and bulimia have been on the increase in many parts of the world. Part of the increase is no doubt due to the identification of illnesses that were in some sense objectively 'there', but part is also due to the social construction of illness and the diffusion of Western understandings of illness across borders.

Finally, no description of the importance of globalization in the modern world would be complete without mention of the contemporary global financial crisis. The ups and downs of an economy, its periodic swings in terms of output, inflation, unemployment, wages, and salaries, are of concern to all of us. Perhaps there was a time when we could think of these cycles in terms of closed national economies, ignoring the influences of trade and capital flows. In today's globalized setting, the reliance of most countries on the external sector (trade, foreign direct investment, migrant labour, outsourcing, etc.), makes closed economy analysis[2] all but impossible. Because of the multiple channels that link countries, economic activity that starts in one place is likely to be quickly transmitted elsewhere, whether for good or ill. One striking example comes from Krugman's *The Return of Depression Economics* in which he notes that in 2007, on the eve of the financial crisis, the US had overseas assets equal to 128 per cent of GDP and liabilities equal to 145 per cent

---

[2]The phrase 'closed economy analysis' refers to a type of economic analysis in which the national economy is assumed to be insulated from the outside world, i.e. insulated from trade flows, capital flows, and economic disturbances.

(2009 [1999]: 177 [1999]). These assets (and liabilities) make for a strong coupling of economic interests and in a sense they create a non-territorial economy. As a result of these links, a financial crisis that originates in one country can become contagious and quickly spread to other countries. Not only are business cycles not dead, or moderated; they have become synchronized and globalized. This is why the present financial crisis, far from over at the time of this writing, is a global phenomenon affecting many parts of the world, though with more severity in some places than in others.

The financial crisis of 2008–10 began as an asset bubble in the housing and banking sectors. Cheap credit (real interest rates near zero to one per cent in Europe and the US) and lax rules in banking and finance more generally led to a situation where housing in most parts of the United States was greatly overvalued. As with all bubbles the one in housing was ripe for bursting, and when it did, the consequences quickly spread. Similar bubbles in France and Spain led to regional versions of the sell-off in the United States. North America, Western Europe, the advanced capitalist world, Eastern Europe, and the less developed world were all gradually and not so gradually drawn in.

The crisis was in the housing and banking sectors only in a narrow sense. In reality, the bubble was in the financial system as a whole. At bottom, the problem was the under-pricing of risk and the highly leveraged nature of investments, often with other peoples' money. While perhaps not technically a Ponzi scheme, individuals, banks, and financial institutions were making risky bets that were 'covered' only by the hoped-for appreciation of assets, not by a stream of income from productive investments. After the price of assets fell, as in the housing market, many creditors called in their loans and wanted to be paid off, thus setting off a downward spiral. Investors, including home owners, were now in possession of assets which in many cases were worth less than the value of their loans (they were 'underwater').

Responses to the crisis may have been slow, partly because policy-makers went from denying the crisis, to asserting that it was contained to the housing market, then to admitting to a liquidity problem but not an insolvency problem, to finally recognizing its full import and severity. Once the problem was recognized, governments at many levels and in many countries and international organizations sprung into action. In the US, the Troubled Asset Relief Program (TARP) attempted to provide help to banks and financial institutions to rescue both from financial ruin. Indirectly, TARP should help home owners too by improving liquidity and encouraging banks to make loans again. In addition, the Obama administration allocated hundreds of billions to stimulate the economy to get the virtuous cycle of investment, jobs, and economic growth going again. In Europe, both the EU and national governments set up spending programmes though most of the money came from national treasuries and was allocated by national authorities to solve problems at the national level. The EU, which is weak in terms of fiscal powers, did put together a package but the biggest part of it involved the European Central Bank drawing down interest rates even lower. A spirited debate ensued in Europe regarding the strengths and limitations of *Le modèle Français*, *Modell Deutschland*, and the Anglo-Saxon model. European leaders touted the way their economies adapted because of the automatic stabilizers (state expenditures that kicked in automatically), while in the United Kingdom and the US, political authorities had to fashion economic policies out of new cloth.

Once the crisis erupted, there was no shortage of explanations for why it occurred. Rapacious bankers, naïve, gullible, and disingenuous home buyers, lax (or overly zealous) regulators, and speculators interested in 'making a killing' by placing bets with their own or other people's money. Each time a financial crisis occurs, it is as if it falls out of the sky with no warning. The Mexican debt crisis of 1982, the Tequila crisis of 1994–5, the Argentine inflation crisis of the late 1980s (3,000 per cent inflation), Japan's lost decade of the 1990s, and the Thai (and Asian) currency crisis of 1997. The list could go on and on. As Kindleberger and Aliber put it (2005: 1), financial crises are 'hardy perennials'. While post-hoc explanations abound, the analytic skills of those involved in the making of financial crises seem blunted during the process. Few of these crises are predicted and part of the reason is that mania and euphoria abound in the run-up to the outbreak of the crisis. In a sense, the factors that make for crises, particularly euphoria, are the same ones that prevent us from seeing them coming. We are having too much fun, making too much money. Why not enjoy it, reap the benefits, and do the analysis later? We are not suggesting that this is an accurate description of the mental processes of the participants in the making of a crisis. What we are suggesting is that financial crises have a structure and that they originate, develop, and play themselves out in surprisingly coherent ways. The participants may or may not see this structure but their behaviour nevertheless conforms to a pattern. There are causes that operate 'behind the back' of the actors as well as those that are 'in their heads'.

Guideposts to Navigate a Complex Terrain

The preceding discussion suggests a bewildering variety of influences in today's world. We can introduce some order into this confusing picture by identifying three guideposts or clues about how to analyse global relations. We illustrate each with an extended example. The first guidepost is that globalization often takes us outside the state-centric paradigm. It forces us to view the world from multiple perspectives and institutional contexts. There are many political and cultural groups that exist outside the state and barely recognize state borders in their daily transactions. As a shorthand, think of this as the 'multiple arenas' principle. The second point has to do with the importance of private (non-state) actors, particularly economic actors. The third point has to do with the interdependence of actors (private, state, cultural) across the globe. Think of this as the interdependence principle related to the decline of economic sovereignty in our globalized world.

We analyse each of these guideposts with a telling example. The war in Afghanistan shows the futility of capturing the relevant action within a state-to-state framework. The second example, the current struggle between Google and the People's Republic of China, illustrates the importance of private actors in world politics. The third example, the 'Greek debt crisis', illustrates just how interdependent countries and private actors are in the modern global system and how difficult it is to contain economic disturbances to a limited area.

First, let us turn to the point concerning the multiple arenas in which globalization takes place. In making the case for sending additional troops to Afghanistan, President Obama, in his televised address, repeatedly mentioned Afghanistan and Pakistan as the sites of the war. But is this really accurate? And war against whom? Interestingly, the US is not at war with either Afghanistan or Pakistan. It is at war in Afghanistan and Pakistan. The enemies are the Taliban (in Afghanistan) and al-Qaeda (in Pakistan). Fighting al-Qaeda is particularly problematic since al-Qaeda is a non-state actor whose activities are not confined to any one country. Indeed, its ability to cross borders and to use the resources of the global system (telecommunications, finance, computers) makes it a formidable foe.

A *New York Times* article (Dec. 6, 2009: 1, 4) suggested that President Obama refer to the area where the war is being pursued as Pashtunistan. Of course, Pashtunistan does not exist on any geographical map. It is not a member of the United Nations, it does not enjoy diplomatic status, and it doesn't send and receive ambassadors. But it is a definite area in terms of the distinctiveness of the people (ethnic Pashtuns), their language (Pashto), and the coherent cultural and moral code which they share, as well as 'a centuries-long history of foreign interventions that ended badly for the foreigners' (*NYT*, Dec. 6, 2009: 1). Pashtunistan is fictional from the legal standpoint of the modern state system. But it is a reality in economic, cultural, social, and political terms and its importance calls attention to one of the blind spots of a state-centric approach to international politics.

The conflict between Google and China calls attention to the importance of private economic actors. In January of 2010 Google Inc. threatened to pull its business and search engine technology out of China in response to computer attacks on its operating systems as well as to efforts by the Chinese government to censor the content of searches in China. Search efforts in China directed toward 'Tiananmen Massacre' and 'Dalai Lama' will turn up no results (*NYT*, Dec. 6, 2009: 1). In making its protests, Google made clear that it was motivated by its business interests in China as well as by human rights and free speech concerns. While the outcome of this conflict is not yet known, it seems likely that companies like Google (who at present don't have a huge investment in

China) stand to lose out in a lucrative and growing market for the internet and mobile services (*NYT*, Jan. 13, 2010: 1, 3).

Our third example, the 'Greek debt crisis', illustrates the decline of economic sovereignty in today's world. The phrase is in quotes not because we believe there is no debt crisis in Greece; there most assuredly is one. However, despite Greece's role in the crisis, the forces which gave rise to it are global and the consequences of the crisis will extend beyond Greece. Indeed, there is a concern that the crisis will spread to other vulnerable countries such as Italy, Portugal, Spain, Ireland, and Lithuania.

The narrative is a familiar one: government overspending, a bloated state which employs a huge percentage of the population, unsustainable budget deficits, a huge public debt, and non-transparent accounting procedures which in turn mask the severity of the debt. While the core of the crisis is economic, elements of the human drama are ever present in dubious accounting procedures and the profligacy of political and economic actors who neglected to discipline themselves by adhering to the budgetary standards set by the European Union. Indeed, since membership in the Euro in 2001, Greece has never complied with the debt limits set by the Stability and Growth Pact (Bastasin, Dec. 16, 2009: 1).

While Greece has undoubtedly played a role in bringing about the debt crisis, a look at the broader picture brings into focus the importance of other factors. Since the euro was introduced, for accounting purposes in 1999 and in currency form in 2002, members of the euro area have shared a single currency. Thus the inflation experienced by Greece, Spain, Ireland, and Portugal could not be corrected by traditional means, namely by devaluing the currency. A major policy tool was lost when monetary sovereignty was transferred from national capitals to Frankfurt (the seat of the European Central Bank). In addition, with free capital mobility in all EU countries (regardless of euro membership), money could move in and out according to investor desires. In the case of Spain, capital from all over Europe fuelled a speculative boom. Spain's finances were sound; it ran no huge deficits nor engaged in suspect accounting practices. Nevertheless, the speculative mania that fuelled Spain's real estate market hit a high point and then plunged downward, causing further erosion of investor confidence. In short, the combination of capital mobility and excess credit which found an outlet in real estate markets damaged the Spanish economy and also added to Greece's woes. The true story was not exclusively one of profligacy and debt but also one of a speculative boom fuelled by the newly found capital mobility.

These three vignettes illustrate three important principles of the global system. The war against al-Qaeda in Afghanistan and Pakistan is not easily thought of as a traditional war against a country whose leadership has control over what takes place within the borders of that country. The case of Google resisting censorship of its searches in China illustrates the clash between a private company and a government over conflicting priorities – freedom of searches on the internet and the right of a government to control access to information within its territorial borders. And the Greek debt crisis illustrates just how far we are from a world where an economic crisis can be thought of solely in national terms, both in terms of the origins of the crisis and its potential consequences.

Definitions

Despite the fact that the terms 'global' and 'globalization' are widely used, the exact meanings are unclear. Moving toward greater precision with regard to definitions is a first step toward clearer and more effective analysis. Let's start with a commonsense notion of interdependence. People in different parts of the world are affected by the actions of others outside their own borders. We are affected by the range of choice of consumption items, by technology that is available from other countries, and by the pools of labour and capital that one can either directly import or access directly in a foreign country. We are also affected by undesirable things such as pollution, crime, drugs, trade in pornographic material, the tax structures and interest rates of other countries, and by the regulatory styles, political institutions, and customs of other countries. The present global financial crisis brings home the point about interdependence painfully. We are all vulnerable to the economic downturns that occur outside our own national boundaries. And while a heightened sensitivity to these troubles may cause any country to draw back within its own borders and to search for external scapegoats, long-term withdrawal from the global system is likely to be a recipe for poverty, as the histories of Burma (present-day Myanmar), Albania, and China during the Great Cultural Revolution (1966–76) suggest.

When do we think of these interdependencies as globalization rather than simple interdependence? In one sense, globalization is just interdependence (economic, cultural, or political) on a global scale. We can think of national interdependence between countries, regional interdependence within a region (e.g. East Asia, Western Europe, sub-Saharan Africa) and global interdependence beyond the regional level. Keohane and Nye define globalism as 'a state of the world involving networks of interdependence at multicontinental distances' (Keohane and Nye, 2000: 2). These networks can be filled with goods and services, capital, power, ideas and information, germs and diseases, etc. That is, globalization is not limited in its content. It applies to many different things. Globalization refers to the increase (or de-globalization the decrease) of globalism (Keohane and Nye, 2000: 2).

In comparison to interdependence, globalization has two additional characteristics, one referring to the number of actors involved and a second referring to the spatial scope of interdependence. We do not call a relationship global if it involves only two countries, or for that matter, even if it involves the set of all bilateral relations in the world (which would be almost 18,000 pairs of countries). So US–Canadian relations are not global, nor are US–South Korean relations, even though in the second example the countries are on different sides of the globe. While we do not think it is productive to set a minimum number of countries (or other actors) that must be involved, we do think it is necessary to go beyond looking at the world dyadically, that is, in terms of pairs of countries. A global orientation is more a question of outlook than a focus on an exact number of countries.

The second definitional requirement has to do with the scope of interactions. We do not think of something as global if it does not reach outside its immediate region. If we analyse economic relations among Canada, the US, and Mexico within NAFTA, we do not call these relations global. Similarly, if we analyse economic or political relations among the members of the European Union (EU), we do not think of this as global, though as we shall see, we might do just that if Turkey is admitted to membership. The scope of interactions requires that the interdependencies reach outside their immediate region. So relations between members of the NAFTA and MERCOSUR (Common Market of the South) can be considered global, as can transatlantic relations between the EU and the US. To some extent definitions are arbitrary. Nevertheless we have to set some boundary conditions for the terms used in this book, even if we contest these terms later.

In sum, globalization implies more than interdependence in terms of the number of actors and the scope of interactions. Globalization implies interactions between more than two actors at multi-continental distances. The focus is not just on states but on a variety of actors, such as multinational corporations and transnational pressure groups.

Actors

There is a tendency to equate globalization with internationalization. They are close to one another but not the same thing. Internationalization implies increasingly close relationships among nation-states. States are the important actors and the basic relationships are government to government. Representatives of governments meet and negotiate over an arms agreement or environmental treaty, or to coordinate economic policies, or to do more mundane things like set standards for foods and other products. These activities are indeed part of what we mean by globalization but they are not the whole story. Nation-states are only one type of actor in the globalization picture, and some say not even the most important one. In addition, there are multinational corporations, international governmental organizations such as the United Nations and the Association of South-east Asian Nations, international non-governmental organizations such as Amnesty International and Greenpeace, terrorist groups such as al-Qaeda, international movements such as the women's movement which launched the Women's Decade (Berkovitch, 2000), pirates (which do not form a recognized organization but are nevertheless important), and private individuals such as private money managers who move money from country to country looking for the best investment return.

For some analysts, the proliferation of multinational corporations and international non-governmental organizations (INGOs) signals the decline of the nation-state as the most important actor in the modern world. This viewpoint is evident in the titles of several books: *Sovereignty at Bay* (1971) by Raymond Vernon; *Le Défi Americain* or *The American Challenge* (1968) by Jean-Jacques Servan-Schreiber; and K. Ohmae's *The Borderless World* (1990). It is not usually Greenpeace and the Red Cross that are seen as the major challengers but rather MNCs and corporate interests at the global level. On the other side of the debate are the realists of international relations theory who argue that it is only where powerful states have paved the way (by providing physical security, freedom of the seas, stable property rights) for capital that capital has been able to become multinational. Reflecting on the rise of modern piracy, a realist might point out that should piracy become widespread it could significantly affect global commerce. States are the most likely organization to eradicate pirates. States have numerous tools at their disposal to affect the globalization of commerce and production, including the ability to tax subsidiaries of corporations in foreign countries or to patrol the high seas in order to secure shipping lanes. A change in either taxation or security policies could easily affect the incentives for doing business in a foreign country.

While states structure the environment of non-state actors, we should not minimize *a priori* the importance of non-state actors. True, states can make it unattractive for corporations to do business abroad, but only at considerable cost. Subsidiaries of corporations in foreign countries generate a lot of wealth and some of that wealth finds its way into both national income and the financial coffers of states. Also, while most countries are politically sensitive to export of jobs that occurs when corporations locate in different countries, people and governments are reminded that additional investment also flows into the home country through foreign direct investment. Thus, while Michigan congresspersons lobbied for a bailout of the auto industry in the US, politicians from Alabama – where Toyota plants are located – were not so enthusiastic.

In addition, corporations are not the only important non-state actors. Private advocacy groups can be important, as were environmental groups at the protests in Seattle in 1998. Particular individuals such as Jody Williams were important in getting the treaty against landmines passed in the face of resistance by powerful countries, including the US. Amnesty International has been important in raising consciousness about political prisoners and victims of torture. All of this leads Thomas Risse, a student of non-state actors, to argue for a trifocal view of global governance that includes states, firms, and advocacy groups (Risse, 2002: 268).

We don't attempt to settle the debate about which actors are most important at the start of the book, because one of the most interesting things about globalization is the debate over precisely these sorts of issues. How important are multinational corporations? Indeed, how multinational are multinational corporations? Is global capital really footloose and outside the control of governments? Has the internet given new powers to private actors in civil society or is the internet also under the thumb of governments? We attempt to explore these debates in the book.

Questions

Globalization raises many questions, and we attempt to address the most important ones in this book. A first question has to do with how significant borders are in a globalized world. This question arises because the forces of globalization – technology, economic specialization, trade, and movement of factors – seem to seek out the most attractive opportunities regardless of location. A profit-maximizing firm with a global reach will search worldwide not only for markets in which to sell its goods, but it will also strive to find the cheapest sources of capital and labour as well as the most efficient techniques for combining the factors of production. Such a firm will not be bound by territory and will be open in principle to operating within many different political jurisdictions. Given the presence of economic actors with a global outlook, what is the role of territorially fixed borders?

A little background may help to put this issue into historical perspective. Borders – particularly national borders – took on a special relevance as nation-states emerged and developed. States wanted stable populations, both to identify individuals for purposes of taxation and conscription, as well as to target them as beneficiaries of citizenship rights (the vote, welfare benefits). The implicit political exchange was between economic benefits and political support. States taxed their populations and used the revenue to engage in redistribution. In this way, capitalism as a system of production could remain private (i.e. ownership could remain in private hands) while the benefits could be effectively socialized. The large working classes, who made up the bulk of the population, could thereby acquire a stake in a system that produced an incredible amount of wealth, thus lending a degree of stability to a situation in which there might otherwise be potential for unrest and violence.

If the development of the modern welfare state rested on the ability to tax and spend, this in turn required a stable population, one that did not move to and fro across borders, and one whose transactions were identifiable. Forum shopping for social benefits, unreported earnings, and shifting of assets within and across borders so as to hide their value were activities intensely disliked by governments (Bartolini, 2005; Ferrera, 2005). As both duties and privileges of citizenship developed, borders took on added significance, not just the physical borders on the surveyor's map, but also the economic borders so crucial to the capacity of state officials to control economic activity. Thus, we saw the development of customs officials, border police and patrols, immigration and emigration officials, food inspectors, and so on. Yet, with the rise of globalization, many have questioned whether borders are weakening, either as a result of political decisions, as in the EU's decision to allow mobility of labour across its 'internal' borders, or as a result of the inability to control movements of goods, people, and capital.

One way of approaching this issue is to pose the hypothetical question and ask what the world would look like if borders did not exist, i.e. if the only factors affecting production, prices, and trade were economic ones. Jeffrey Frankel (2000) points out a simple fact. The US accounts for 25 per cent of world production. If the US were indifferent between domestic and foreign sources for its consumption, buying only on the basis of price and quality, it would have an import to GDP ratio of 0.75, instead of the roughly 0.12 which it in fact has. To be sure, the 0.75 is based on the assumption of no borders, no political barriers, and zero transport costs. Still, the difference between what the US actually imports and its 'expected' import ratio, based on the no borders assumption, shows how far we are from a borderless world.

The economic significance of borders can also be assessed in terms of the ease or difficulty with which goods, services, people, and ideas move within versus across national boundaries. The same may be said for price movements. In a well-functioning market, prices should converge toward one another for the same goods. If prices (say for consumer goods) on one side of the border are 20 per cent higher than prices for the same goods on the other side, this is likely to reflect political distortions (tariffs, quantitative restrictions, regulatory differences). In the absence of these political distortions, market forces would result in movements of capital, labour, and resources that would in the final analysis equalize prices.

Finally, the significance of borders can be assessed by noting the difference in the productivity of labour in two countries with shared borders. A migrant worker who crosses the Rio Grande to enter the United States immediately acquires a level of productivity dramatically higher (perhaps over 50 per cent) than previously possessed, a fact that can only be attributed to the differences in capital, knowledge, infrastructure, and institutions on either side of the border (Olson, 2000: 52–3). Since this increase in marginal productivity is nearly instantaneous, it can't be caused by acquisition of human capital (training, education) or socialization to a new system of values, both of which take a considerable amount of time. We will take up this issue in Chapter 2 on theories of globalization.

A second question has to do with the possibility of pursuing national goals in a globalized world. Friedman's metaphor of the 'golden straitjacket' raises the frightening prospect that globalization has put all countries in the same economic bind. One concrete implication of globalization –the ease of movement of capital across countries – is that the freedom of national authorities to control interest rates and money supply is sharply curtailed. But if this is true, then it follows that national spending priorities, the crucial tradeoffs between inflation, growth, and employment, and a variety of national goals also cannot be independently pursued.

While it is easy to reify states, we must acknowledge that they usually rest on distinctive communities of peoples with their own social purposes. To be sure, to a significant extent, nationalism and collective identity are endogenous to state practices. However, this does not change the fact that different countries have different conceptions of their interests and purposes. To carry out these purposes requires some kind of structure and this usually implies separate political institutions, or statehood. It would seem to be impossible, with either a world state or no state at all, to formulate and realize a distinctive political project. In short, only through statehood can groups of people pursue their collective goals.

Yet there are limits to national sovereignty and these limits become particularly acute when states themselves, or members of their societies, transact with others inside different borders. Whose rules apply? Whose national traditions are respected? Whose courts have jurisdiction in case of disputes? What if production in one country results in downwind pollution in another country? Or what if Swedish auto safety standards keep Portuguese or Italian cars from legally entering Sweden? What happens when Chinese labour policies result in cheaper goods that cause unemployment in a country which imports Chinese goods? And what happens when the universal logic of efficient production and profits runs up against aspiring standards of human rights, as currently represented by the clash between Google and government of the Peoples' Republic of China?

The preservation of distinctive national goals would be easy, or at least easier, if every country were self-sufficient. This would mean that its interactions with other countries would be minimal, and therefore conflicts would be minimal. But in a world of increasing interdependence, pure autonomy becomes next to impossible. How do governments balance the benefits of globalization with the desire for autonomy with regard to economic, political, and cultural goals? We explore these questions in greater detail in Chapter 3 on domestic institutions and globalization.

A third question concerns global governance. Two distinct questions come to mind regarding the governance of globalization. First, will there be robust global governance structures or will globalization be a show run mostly by private interests, corporations, pressure groups, consumers, workers, and employers? Globalization may involve a shift from the public platform to the private sector. Activities previously carried out within a regulatory framework provided by national states might be 'set free' to operate within a transnational framework with considerably less regulatory content. Second, assuming the answer to the first question is that there will be some form of global governance, what kind will it be?

In response to the first question, it is difficult to imagine that some form of governance will not emerge at the global level to manage the conflicts that inevitably occur. Globalization brings actors in contact with one another and creates situations where they may both profit, both lose, or one profits at the expense of the other. The latter two situations do not appear stable. If actors in different countries respond to conflict by trying to take all the winnings flowing from the relationship, they will soon enter a downward beggar-thy-neighbour spiral. Without institutions, they may not be able to manage conflicts. Institutions may provide the information, the long-term setting, and the transparency (about underlying preferences and strategies) that are required to make cooperation work.

Second, what types of governance institutions are likely to take shape? A single, centralized world government is the least likely outcome, since one size clearly does not fit all in the global system. It is more likely that global governance will be quite a bit messier, more *ad hoc*, and less globally comprehensive, both in terms of members and the number of issue areas addressed. And institutions as well as policies are likely to vary more as the preferences of members (states and other actors) diverge and as economies of scale of institutions lessen. It is more likely that, instead of comprehensive global governance, we will see different groups of countries responding to different problems: the G-8 for major problems among the eight major industrial countries; the G-20 for issues related to international financial stability; the United Nations Conference on Trade and Development (UNCTAD) on issues related to development and the Third World; the EU to manage trade, capital markets, and monetary policy for its twenty seven members, the Association of South-east Asian Nations (ASEAN) to govern trade and trade conflicts among its member states, and so on. Bilateral governance relationships are likely to retain importance as well as pluri-lateral (some countries), and multi-lateral relations. In one metaphor, the global system will be characterized by 'islands of transnational governance' (Shapiro and Stone Sweet, 2002).

Will these institutions and practices be democratic, or will they follow the lines dictated by a hegemon? If these institutions are democratic, how will we judge democracy? In the same way we judge it at the domestic level? If so, then global democratic institutions should mirror domestic ones and look pretty much like a presidential or a parliamentary system. We should find strong executives, disciplined political parties, independent judiciaries, and representative legislatures. Political processes of representation, participation, and political competition should therefore be highlighted. Some analysts (e.g. Keohane, 2001) have argued that these criteria for assessing democracy are not relevant for the international level, where it is impractical to hold elections, form coherent party positions, create representative legislatures, and mobilize people to vote. More appropriate criteria for legitimate international governance might have to do with transparency, accountability, and persuasion (Keohane, 2001: 13). We will take up the issue of global governance in Chapter 4.

A fourth question has to do with whether globalization is mostly a win–win process or one that primarily involves winners and losers. This question is part of a heated debate between those who see overall net gains from globalization (Bhagwati, 2004; Wolf, 2004) and those who see the effects of globalization as deeply divisive (Klein, 2000; Stiglitz, 2003). Not surprisingly, economists line up in favour of the view that globalization, since it is based on comparative advantage, specialization, and exchange, inevitably brings benefits to participants. The backward areas of the world are those that are left behind and ignored, not those which are densely involved in the world economy. Yet, it is easy to identify specific groups who have been harmed by globalization. In a chapter of *The Lexus and the Olive Tree* titled 'The Backlash', Friedman identifies some labour unions, environmental activists, anti sweat-shop protesters, and those concerned with the ill effects of genetically modified foods (Friedman, 2000 [1999]: 334). Along similar lines, Suzanne Berger (2002: 1–2) speaks of the attacks on globalization in *Le Monde Diplomatique*, often centring on US films and the desire to preserve cultural autonomy, as well as the wave of strikes in the late nineties, and the trashing of a McDonald's in Southern France as examples of anti-globalization in France (see also Berger, 2000). At a slightly more abstract level, we can identify those who do not share the fruits of globalization, those who oppose a widening inequality, and those concerned about loss of identity and traditional way of life. Still more abstractly, Kenneth Waltz (1999: 694), a globalization sceptic, argues that most of the resistance to globalization comes from economic nationalists who want economic autonomy, particularly where jobs are concerned, cultural traditionalists, rent-seekers (who use anti-globalization rhetoric as a cover for economic gain), and religious fundamentalists, who often see modernization as a threat to their religious traditions.

Developing explanations for opposition to globalization is a more difficult task than identifying the anti-globalization groups. While we discuss these explanations in the chapter on winners and losers in globalization, it is worth pointing out some of the theories that might help in this effort. The Stolper–Samuelson theorem (1941) predicts that groups in society which are endowed with relatively abundant factors (such as labour in a labour-rich economy) will benefit from economic openness while groups with relatively scarce factors will lose. Thus, if trade between two countries is expected to increase, owing say to the initiation of a free trade area, we expect the country relatively well endowed with capital to benefit the capitalist class while the country relatively well endowed with labour will benefit the working class. One country may have an absolutely larger supply of both labour and capital but that is not what counts. It is the relative supply of labour and capital that counts. The United States may have a larger labour supply than Mexico but an even larger supply of capital by comparison. So when the two countries trade, the US will specialize in capital-intensive goods and Mexico in labour-intensive goods.

Other theories are pitched at the sectoral rather than the class level. Jeffry Frieden (1991), for example, argues that who gains and who loses from trade has more to do with the properties of specific economic sectors (automobiles, metallurgy, insurance, textiles) rather than the overall factoral composition of the economy. He expects those sectors to gain which have assets that are mobile and not specific to particular kinds of production. Thus, if international trade or capital mobility increases, we expect the sectors which are most mobile to do better. Finally, we should at least entertain the proposition that it is not necessarily those countries or groups most exposed to globalization that are the most resistant. Perhaps those left out will protest against a global order that does not include them. Countries in Eastern Europe and the Balkans enthusiastically applied for membership in the EU, an organization that is a regional engine for economic integration, thus casting their votes for a regional form of globalization. Countries in sub-Saharan Africa, by contrast, often have few choices in terms of entering the global economy.

Particular groups in all countries may have lost out because of globalization. However, countries from the global South (i.e. LDCs) argue that there are entire parts of the world which have suffered. This is particularly true of sub-Saharan African countries where many of the world's poorest countries are located (Chad, Benin, Burkina Faso, Niger, Republic of Congo) though the recent earthquake in Haiti demonstrates that extreme poverty exists in the Western hemisphere not too distant from the United States. Given the improvements in productivity and standards of living in many parts of the world, as well as the opportunity to purchase many mid- to low-level technologies, it is interesting to ask why there are still numerous countries that are miserably poor, living on a few dollars a day, with a low life expectancy, and without access to the simple requirements for human existence such as clean drinking water and access to basic medical services. Are these countries ignored, exploited, victims of poor governance, or cursed with unfavourable natural endowments (poor land, unskilled labour, lack of capital)? Any discussion of problems of the global political economy must take these countries into account. We take up the issues of who wins and who loses from globalization in Chapter 6.

The preceding introduction suggests how the rest of the book will be organized. Chapter 2 will provide an overview of different theoretical approaches to globalization. Theories pose certain questions and make them central while relegating other possible questions to the background. They are like a searchlight which focuses a beam on certain aspects of the terrain while leaving other parts of the terrain in the dark. We attempt to develop the most important of our globalization theories so as to clarify the relationship between each approach and our subject matter. Chapter 3 moves to a discussion of domestic institutions. Here the central issue is how different countries can shape, adapt, and control processes of globalization. Central to our approach is the notion that states are not just passive in the face of impersonal global forces. Indeed, they shape these forces and are very active in responding to these forces once they are in operation. Chapter 4 deals with questions of global governance at an abstract level where governance and government institutions are treated as separate. It is the first of two chapters on global governance. Chapter 5 sets out to finish what Chapter 4 initiates, but here we describe and explain specific global institutions such as the World Bank and International Monetary Fund. Finally, in Chapter 6 we turn our attention to some of the more divisive issues in globalization. Who wins, who loses in this complex process? This is where the debate over globalization becomes most heated, as one would expect, since it is here that we assess the gains and losses of globalization and the groups that reap the profits and shoulder the burdens. The spirit of our analysis here is not so different from the one initiated at the domestic level by Harold Lasswell some years ago in his classic book, *Politics: Who Gets What, When, and How?* (1971 [1958]).

2

THEORIES OF GLOBAL POLITICAL ECONOMY

Introduction

Globalization presents us with a wealth of information about the global system. Yet, without theoretical guidance, it is difficult to know where to begin our analysis and where to end. Consider the following pieces of information. Trade is very high as a proportion of gross domestic product (GDP) and it has been growing, though not nearly as fast as capital mobility across borders. From 1980 to 2003, the stock of foreign direct investment (investment in physical plant, machinery, factories, etc.) as a share of GDP increased 240 per cent (Guillen, 2006, cited in Alcacer and Ingram, 2000: 3). While these figures just catch up to or marginally surpass the levels achieved in 1914, the comparison is based on the volume of trade and capital flows and misses the scope (product areas), speed, and connections among national governments and their economies (domestic and international). A given quantity of international trade or capital flow today is likely to become more politically salient than the equivalent share a century earlier since governments are much more involved in the economy, and mass electorates hold their governments more accountable for macro-economic performance today. In addition, short-term capital movements (e.g. portfolio investments) are much more important today and foreign direct investment (FDI) is much more diversified, in contrast to the early twentieth century when it was concentrated in mining and agriculture (Kahler and Lake, 2003: 5).

The global economy operates on a daily basis to transfer goods and services, capital and labour, to all parts of the world. A clothing product purchased at the local mall may be so globalized that it is difficult to tell where it is produced because the product is the result of numerous part-processing steps in many different countries. For a shirt, the wool may have come from England, the design may have been created in New York or Paris, the laser-beam cutting may have taken place in Hong Kong, the sewing in India, packaging in Thailand, the shipping on a Panamanian carrier, and all of it insured by a firm in New York

City, Chicago, or Los Angeles. The simple question of where a product is made has no simple answer. Part-processing activities and global production chains raise not only theoretical issues but also ones of great practical significance, such as whether to put the label 'made in the USA' or 'made in China' on the shirt.

The daily operation of the global economy, including its beneficial effects, should be seen along with increasingly frequent disturbances. We could list the Japanese real estate and stock market crises of the eighties, the Mexican peso crisis of 1994–5, the South-east Asian financial crisis of the mid-nineties, the current worldwide financial crisis that centres on real estate and financial markets, and the Greek financial and budgetary crisis that threatens the Euro area. Many of these crises seem to be linked, as Kindleberger and Aliber argue is the case for the Japanese, Mexican, and South-east Asian crises (Kindleberger and Aliber, 2005 [1978]:6 [1978]). With the current (2009–10) crisis, governments are responding with a mix of policies, ranging from doing very little to massive fiscal stimulus packages and more stringent regulatory policies. There are even discussions, though only that at the moment, for labour market reforms and structural reforms to make markets more competitive.

In short, on its face, globalization presents costs and benefits, sometimes very substantial costs and benefits. Thus, it is not surprising that globalization has its ardent defenders (Bhagwati, 2004; Wolf, 2004) as well as its vocal critics (Stiglitz, 2002; Klein, 2004). Many tout the economic benefits of free trade and capital mobility while others just as strongly argue that cultural identity and political autonomy are sometimes victims of the pressures of globalization. We see widespread support for free trade among the economic and political elites but also protesters in Seattle, Genoa, and meetings of the World Trade Organization (WTO). We see academics and activists announce the end of the business cycle at the same time that we witness increasingly frequent economic crises and volatility in financial markets. We hear claims of experts that people have rational expectations that are, on average, correct about the performance of markets at the same time that we witness wild swings in many indicators of market performance.

What are we to make of this contradictory evidence? While there are people at the extremes who would like to brush aside the evidence of conflicting trends, we argue from the start that many of these costs and benefits are real and any attempts to wish away the conflicting data or speak in general terms about 'bottom lines' and 'net effects' will not satisfy either defender or critic. There are indeed winners and losers. Recognizing this should not be interpreted to mean that globalization necessarily should be stopped, restrained, or even channelled. But it would be equally misleading, indeed wrong, to claim that globalization is all good or all bad. We will carry out a more detailed analysis of winners and losers in Chapter 6.

The sheer volume, speed, and diversity of globalization present a dizzying challenge to our understanding. What is important, central, and enduring and what is unimportant, marginal, and ephemeral? How are we to understand complex phenomena having to do with rich and poor countries or regions, growth and stagnation, an increasingly specialized division of labour, and global production chains? Are trade and investment across borders necessary to the healthy functioning of the global economy or can they be dispensed with, at little loss, at least for the countries with larger domestic markets? Are domestic notions of democratic governance, organized around representation, participation, and policy-making easily transported to the international level or do we have to develop completely new criteria of democratic governance such as transparency, accountability, and third-party dispute resolution?

The above are key questions with no obvious answers. To make a beginning we need some vantage point to provide leverage so that the right questions are asked. This is where theories come in. We can ask innocently, 'what are theories for?', 'why do we need them?' Our first answer is that they provide criteria of relevance and importance. Out of the infinite number of events that one could single out, theory will suggest which ones are more important. Of course, different theories will have different answers to this question, and, in a sense, this is where the fun starts. Indeed, this is what makes theories controversial. Second, theories suggest hypotheses which can be tested in principle. Extensions of neoclassical economics suggest that exposure to international trade should increase the wealth of certain productive groups in the economy more than others. This is essentially what the Stolper–Samuelson theory says (1941). Drawing out the implications of Marxian theory would lead us to expect that capitalist exchange and production relations will expand into different parts of the globe, a process that really defines imperialism. Also, according to Marxian theory, the search for cheap labour should extend beyond national borders and assume global proportions. This flows out of the theory of capital accumulation and is not simply an *ad-hoc* response on the part of firms to expand operations abroad. By way of contrast, realist theory suggests that economic blocs, even those promising large gains from trade, should form around natural allies and not extend to potential enemies. So security competition, uncertainty, and multi-polarity should all decrease international economic integration. Third, and perhaps most importantly, theories function as explanations. All theories embody generalizations which form the foundation for explanations.

Our choice of theories reflects our prior beliefs and commitments. In this chapter, we focus on neoclassical economic theory (sometimes referred to as liberal economics), structural theories such as Marxism and dependency theory, realist theory (sometimes dubbed mercantilism), institutional theory, and constructivism. While not exhaustive, we hope these broad theoretical approaches will provide a good understanding of the questions asked and answers given by global political economists.

Neoclassical Political Economy

Before developing a framework for neoclassical global political economy several obstacles have to be overcome. To see why this is so, consider the economic core of neoclassical economics – the market. Neoclassical economics provides a theory about how markets function, how they set prices, how they provide answers as to what to produce, with what technology, and how supply and demand interact. The reach of markets is quite extensive. There are markets not only for goods and services but also for productive factors such as land, labour, and capital. A market is a system of voluntary exchange among numerous participants who may or may not know one another. There is no market leader, no central figure who makes choices about production and consumption. The market is decentralized and agents decide for themselves how they should transact with others.

Markets are institutions to manage the problem of allocation under scarcity. Economists claim it is the most efficient system for doing so. A central dictator, a committee of wise persons, or some abstract principle such as equality will not do as well (i.e. be as efficient) as the market principle. This is true from the producer's standpoint as well as the consumer's. From the producer's standpoint, there is a variety of ways in which one can combine land, labour, and capital to produce goods and services. This process of combining and reshuffling resources will continue until it has reached a point where the additional cost equals the additional benefit. The same is true for the consumer who will continue to trade (goods or money or labour) until his or her lot cannot be further improved without harming someone else (Dasgupta, 1985: 78–9). This may be a good time to call attention to the assumption that individuals and firms will exchange up to the point where they can improve their welfare without harming the welfare of others. This is certainly a powerful assumption and one that seems often violated in the real world. We come back to this point later. If a market works well, i.e. information is abundant, property rights are well specified, and a competitive economic structure exists (i.e. no monopoly), then the costs and benefits of transactions will be fully internalized, meaning that the parties to the transaction will pay for production costs and receive the economic benefits.

There is one striking result of a well-functioning market in economic theory. If markets perform perfectly, then there is no need for politics.[1] Why so? If market transactions do not have consequences for others, and if all market transactions are voluntary (as they are by definition), we can think of them as private. Limited constitutional governments usually reserve a private sphere that is in principle free from government interference. Thus, the important question is to what extent real markets approach these idealized characteristics. Many would argue that market imperfections are the norm rather than a deviation from perfectly functioning markets, and that even the most elementary transactions transmit costs and benefits to those who are not parties to the transactions.

---

[1] We recognize, as would nearly all economists, that market transactions require a number of political goods prior to any economic transactions, e.g. public order, security, and well defined property rights to name a few.

Firms which produce autos and paper products also pollute the air and water. High-technology companies not only produce goods to be sold on markets but also see their products imitated (knocked off) by other firms, often in other countries, who can produce the products cheaply once the technology is available. When examples such as these exist, we speak of externalities, i.e. there are external effects which go beyond the immediate market participants. Externalities provide one way of connecting economics and politics within the neoclassical framework.

These examples illustrate something about economic theories. Linking politics and economics is not a simple matter. If we take markets seriously, as economists do, the ways in which we can connect economics and politics are limited. Theories provide opportunities but also constraints in comparison to a free-wheeling empirical approach. The main opportunity, the main analytical bridge connecting economics and politics in neoclassical economics, is provided by the master concept of market failure. When markets fail to function properly, for whatever reason, then politics can be brought in to correct or supplement the market.

Neoclassical political economy starts with an idealized market and asks what happens when markets break down. These breakdowns are referred to as market failures, a general category that includes externalities, public goods, asymmetric information, transaction costs, increasing returns (leading to monopoly), and so on. One could ask why we should start with this model, admittedly unrealistic, and treat political processes as secondary. Why not start from more realistic assumptions where politics is important from the start, e.g. by establishing property rights and providing courts and a legal system to secure contracts? This is a good question but we will not attempt to answer it here. Since our goal is to explore the four theories mentioned, we start by accepting each framework on its own terms. Thus, we accept the initial assumptions of neoclassical economics and pursue their political implications to see where they lead. The three types of global political economy examined here are international externalities, public goods, and strategic trading.

International Externalities

Externalities refer to the effects on third parties of transactions carried out by others. These effects are beyond those transmitted through the price system. For example, if A invents a new technology and sells it to B, and C gets wind of it and buys a licence to develop that same technology, no externality has occurred. All parties have been compensated. But if A invents a technology and sells it to B, and C gets wind of it and engineers a similar version that reduces its cost because the research and development were carried out by A, and then sells these goods, an externality (a positive one in this case) has taken place. We should note that there is no distinction (economic or ethical) between a positive and a negative externality. Both are in a sense 'bad' in economic terms, the latter because an uninvited cost has been inflicted on someone (e.g. suffering pollution caused by someone else) and the former because an uninvited benefit has spilled over from the original transaction. The case of positive externalities requires some comment. Why are positive externalities simply not a bonus to society that results from someone else's behaviour? Isn't nearly any behaviour 'public' in the sense that it could affect the well-being of others? I don't like the way you are 'wearing' your hair today, nor the way you chew your food or for that matter the baseball team you just 'happen' to support. However, the economic case for scepticism toward positive externalities flows quite logically from the basic economic model. Something which is good (i.e. wanted by someone) will tend to be produced more if people pay to consume it and less if people consume it without paying. Beautiful flowers and fountains in public squares may be desirable and yet appear in quantities far below what people would pay for if there were a perfect market for flowers in public squares. In a sense, this is one of the drawbacks of the public opposed to the private, namely that the public realm is defined as that 'place' where benefits are diffuse and recovery of payment for goods produced is difficult or impossible. The global system presents the problem of recovery and contract enforcement in spades.

What are some examples of international externalities? High technology goods that require substantial spending during their research and development phase can create positive externalities since other countries can often imitate them by reverse engineering or more complex chemical analysis. A car or computer can be literally taken apart, analysed, and 'remade'. A pharmaceutical company may produce drugs which can be chemically analysed and mimicked. This is not always easy to do and the basic science behind many pharmaceuticals is guarded more closely than many state secrets. Negative externalities include the depletion of the Brazilian rain forests, which are a carbon sink for the rest of the world, leading to global warming. Related, the use of CFCs (chlorofluorocarbons) further depletes the hole in the ozone layer. These externalities have consequences for everyone, though admittedly global warming is not bad for all countries. Countries in the northern latitudes may gain by global warming. Nevertheless, we are still talking about externalities, whether positive or negative.

Since the global system lacks a single public authority, we can ask how externalities can be managed at the global level. One response, favoured by some economists inspired by Coase's article 'The Problem of Social Cost' (1960), is to let private agents bargain with one another to attempt to arrive at a market solution. At one point, the Japanese suggested that the Western industrialized countries purchase Brazilian rights to deplete their own rain forests. This is an interesting idea but how much would it cost, how would that cost be determined over future generations, and who would enforce such an arrangement? These are difficult questions to answer. The same solution could be offered for transnational pollution carried in the air or by our main waterways. However, unless property rights are well specified and parties to the conflict submit their case to the same body of law, the polluter may just take the view that it is his/her right to continue to pollute as before.

A second solution is to submit conflicts about externalities to international judicial bodies. Many of them exist, some quite specific and others more general. The European Court of Justice (ECJ) has been quite active in resolving disputes that are at bottom international externalities. Take for example the social security laws of the member states of the European Union (EU). These laws can be considered international policy externalities in the sense that they are responsible for failed exchanges at the international level. A law in one country has the effect of discouraging an economic activity in another country. One such case in the EU involved a British citizen (Mr Cowan) who was on holiday in France and was mugged on the streets of Paris. His lawyers argued that there was a French law which compensated French citizens in such cases with the proviso that such compensation was an expression of the solidarity between the French state and its citizens. Cowan argued that limiting compensation to French nationals constituted economic discrimination and if it were allowed to stand, the tourism industry would suffer. Cowan's lawyers in effect argued that the French law had an international externality and deterred the operation of the tourism market. The ECJ agreed with Mr Cowan.

A third potential solution is to create political zones that correspond to the scope of the externality, somewhat in the same way that metropolitan districts create special purpose authorities. Of course, not all externalities among a given set of countries have the same scope. Water pollution may affect just the people living close to a certain river or sea. Non-coastal people may not be affected much at all. Air pollution may have a completely different 'constituency', i.e. its basic pattern may be quite different. This argues in favour of highly specialized authorities that deal with a particular problem or with a set of highly connected ones. Such a pattern would lead to a mosaic of disparate, sometimes overlapping, sometimes disconnected authorities. The Basel Committee of Central Bankers deals almost exclusively with monetary questions while the European Central Bank specializes in monetary affairs but is tangentially involved in broader issues related to economic growth, unemployment, and fiscal affairs. When a set of issues is tightly coupled, such as labour mobility, border control, asylum, drug trafficking, and market making in the EU, a regional authority can and has been created with authority to deal with a variety of complex issues. While some disparage the EU as a 'constitution of bits and pieces' (Curtin, 1993), we can see the coming together of disparate authorities in one regional organization as an adaptive response to a highly complex set of issues that are functionally interconnected but also separate in some important respects.

Global Public Goods

What are global public goods? They are public goods that are wide in scope, wide enough to be called global. A pure, global public good would be one that affected everyone in the global system. If there were a global regime for preventing the planet from being hit by asteroids, this regime would be supplying a global public good. Less fanciful, though perhaps less global, examples might be a regime that rids pirates from the high seas or terrorists from the airways or pollution from the oceans.

Public goods have two characteristics, whether or not they exist at the global or local level. These two characteristics are non-excludability and non-rivalness. Non-excludability means that once a good (or bad) exists, there is no way to avoid its beneficial (harmful) effects. Clean air or foul air is simply there for everyone in an area to breathe. There is no way to avoid it and no known technology for channelling it, privatizing it, and selling it, although putting the problem this way does suggest that what is public and private is dependent on technology. The same goes for deterrence. If a nation's policy of deterring another works, then all those in a certain area will be affected, whether or not they cooperate in producing this policy. Non-rivalness implies that if one actor consumes the good, the consumption of others is not affected. Money is a rival good. If I use $10, you cannot use the same $10. But a stable monetary regime, if it provides order, reduces uncertainty, and provides insurance against financial crises, has non-rival properties. My consumption of these characteristics doesn't diminish yours. Table 2.1 may be helpful in illustrating these characteristics.

According to some analysts (Kindleberger, 1973; Gilpin, 2001) the supply of global public goods is dependent on the presence of a strong leader, a hegemon, who is willing, sometimes at great cost, to supply public goods for the global economy. This is a controversial subject since public goods create free-rider problems. Since public goods are non-excludable, some actors can enjoy their benefits without paying the costs. This requires a calculation on the part of the would-be free-rider that if one does not contribute, the public good will be produced anyway. This may seem risky, and indeed there are many cases where public goods are not produced, precisely for this reason. However, if the country or actor in question is small in relation to other actors in the system, this self-interested calculation is likely to be correct. Luxembourg can safely calculate that its cooperation or non-cooperation is not likely to affect NATO's defence and deterrence policies, and Cyprus and Malta may conclude that their participation is not crucial to an anti-piracy regime. This calculation leaves open the question of whether the hegemon forces beneficiaries to pay.

Large countries or small groups of allied countries with similar interests are conducive to the supply of global public goods. In *The World in Depression, 1929–1939* (1973) Charles Kindleberger argued that the severity and duration of the Great Depression were heightened because of the absence of a powerful state to serve as a market for distressed goods and as a lender of last resort. Even in normal times, for the global economy to function, certain fundamental public goods must be in place. The global system must be open to the flow of goods and services and to the orderly flow of capital. Adequate liquidity must

Table 2.1   Public and private goods

| | | Rivalness | |
		Yes	No
Excludability	Yes	Private goods	Toll goods
	No	Common property resources	Public goods

be provided. Governments must respect the existence of foreign capital within their borders. Currencies must be aligned or coordinated in some way, and macro-economic policies of different countries can't be carried out with complete disregard for the policies of other countries. Even more fundamental is freedom of the high seas for goods in transit, a goal which requires the elimination of piracy and terrorism. In short, public goods at the global level are not just embellishments that affect international economics at the margins. They are necessary for the functioning of the global economic order.

The provision of global public goods is made difficult not only by the free-rider problem but also by disagreement over whether a policy is beneficial or harmful to particular actors. In other words, there may be disagreement on the answer to the question whether or not something (say a trade regime or monetary order) is a public good. This question presents more difficulties than at first meet the eye. If we consider the provision of deterrence by the US against the Soviet Union as a public good (at least for those the policy intended to protect), then where is the controversy? If those in NATO are protected by such a policy, as was clearly the intent of the US, this seems like a clear-cut case of public good provision. In practice, things are more complicated since the policy of deterrence changed quite a bit over time and some of these changes were opposed by European allies. The doctrine of massive retaliation, terrifying as it was, was actually more comforting to European NATO members than the doctrine of graduated deterrence and flexible response. Europeans asked, quite naturally, 'what does flexibility mean?' and 'what threats are and are not being deterred in a strategy of graduated deterrence?' The same goes for the distinction between theatre war (presumably fought in Europe) and strategic war (presumably between the US and the Soviet Union). So when Europeans were asked to pay through NATO contributions, they could well have questioned whether countries on either side of the Atlantic were in the same boat, which is another way of asking if the same public goods were at stake on both sides of the Atlantic.

While hegemony may facilitate public goods provision in the global political economy, it is by no means necessary. What is required is cooperation among a sufficient number of actors, a 'minimal group' as it is sometimes called. It is possible that these actors are of roughly the same size but because of similarity of values and interests, they are able to cooperate. Since a public good by definition implies common interests, this puts the burden on the structure of values, the existence or non-existence of trust, and the institutional structure within which individuals act. A lack of trust, a fear of being double-crossed (cooperating while others do not), or giving in to a wishful 'let George do it' temptation can still prevent cooperation from taking place. But how exactly to provide for trust and a willingness to bear a fair share of the burden are questions not yet answered.

In *After Hegemony* (1984), Robert Keohane decoupled global public goods provision from a hegemonic distribution of power. An open trade regime and stable monetary order were possible even after the decline of the hegemonic power. Elinor Ostrom (1990) joined the effort by showing how problems associated with the global commons could be mitigated by international governance structures. For both, the role of international institutions was seen as crucial in bringing actors closer together, making their aims (preferences and strategies) more transparent, allowing a closer monitoring of compliance with regime norms, and in general increasing the confidence of all parties that the others were willing to cooperate. There was nothing magical about institutions. They simply made it more likely that states and other actors could successfully pursue their own interests.

Strategic Trade Theory[2]

We know a considerable amount about why countries and firms trade with one another but quite a bit less about how they conduct their trade relations. Countries trade with one another because, by doing so, they are able to specialize, produce more, sell more, and consume more. In one sense it would seem natural that firms and states act strategically when they figure out their trade policies. Couldn't firms do better by taking the likely trade policies of other actors into account? Conventional trade theory teaches us otherwise. Orthodox trade theory suggests that governments should do very little beyond providing a healthy domestic and global environment for international exchange. In addition, trade should be non-strategic. There is a best trade policy to follow regardless of what other actors do. It is precisely this assumption of non-strategic

---

[2]This section draws on James A. Caporaso, 'Global Political Economy', in Ada Finifter (Ed.), *Political Science: The State of the Discipline.* Washington, DC: American Political Science Association, 1993.

trade policy that is being questioned by strategic trade theory. In the orthodox view, firms operate under a set of constraints that make it next to impossible to devise a coherent trade policy based on the intentions and strategies of many others. Nearly all the important pieces of information for making trade decisions are givens: the world labour pool, the stock of technology, the natural resources, and the structure of demand. Each of these quantities does not change much in the short run and is not likely to be responsive to policy interventions of governments. Thus, firms should produce and sell in accord with one's comparative advantages. For neoclassical economists, this is the soundest trade policy advice.

The above view that underlying factors of production determine successful trade patterns is questioned by strategic trade theorists. Human capital (or skilled labour) can be seen as a malleable productive factor. Educational policies and work training programmes may be used to cultivate skills that can become the basis for comparative advantage. Much the same can be said for technology, research, and development. Instead of the standard view that technological advantages quickly disappear (because they are either bought or imitated by others), strategic theorists consider whether technological superiority in certain defined areas can be sustained. The fact that there are technological spillovers across sectors may also argue in favour of capturing them at the national level. Global production and global welfare may be damaged but this rent-seeking (profit shifting) activity may improve the income of actors at the national level. There are shades of mercantilism in strategic trade theory, which is perhaps one reason that neoclassical economists are inherently suspicious of it.

Strategic trade theory is built on a foundation that recognizes substantial market imperfections, which is to say that if markets work well, opportunities for strategizing about trade will be nil. These market imperfections include increasing returns to scale, learning by doing effects and technological spillovers. Increasing returns to scale imply monopolistic firms which can indeed strategize. Think of Airbus and Boeing as two airplane companies struggling to increase world market share. One or the other might do better by figuring out what its competitor planned to do. Learning by doing raises some of the same issues as the infant industry argument since it presumes there is some sort of learning curve at work. The longer one does it, the more successful one becomes. A firm in its early stages might not be competitive but after a trial period, it can move up the ranks. And the technological spillover argument rests on the notion that the economy is an interlinked set of activities and that a breakthrough in one area might spread to other areas. Why not advance those areas where these spillovers can be captured? Once market imperfections are allowed into the economists' model, the way is open to the related notions that governments can underwrite policies to create comparative advantages and can intervene in economic sectors where there are economies of scale, learning effects, and spillovers. These suggestions are in strong contrast to normative trade theory where the role of government is minimal.

Realism and Global Political Economy

Realism is a major theory of international relations. Its 'home domain' is national security within an environment of anarchy. However, a major theory of how states compete in international politics cannot avoid economics. Production, growth, taxation, and revenue are at the bottom of military expenditures, arms competition, and the projection of national power.

Realism and mercantilism are often treated as interchangeable frameworks or at least very similar to one another. Both approaches focus on states, both accept the anarchy of the international system, and both understand that anarchy creates a security dilemma for states. However, the two frameworks are also different in significant ways. Realism does not accept the discredited balance of trade theory of mercantilism, according to which true wealth derives from a favourable balance of trade and the resulting inflow of gold and precious metals. There is no reason why realists cannot accept modern theories of growth and trade while at the same time worrying about the implications of the distribution of gains from trade. However, even if realists focus on relative gains from trade (how much A gains compared to B), they can still recognize that the way to economic superiority lies with economic growth and profitable trade with allies. A state that cuts itself off from large swaths of the international system – in the extreme case full autarchy – is likely to be both poor and non-influential.

While nearly everyone agrees that economics is relevant for politics and power at the global level, it is more difficult to specify precisely how politics and economics interact. We explore two linkages out of a larger set of ways in which economics and politics interact in realist theory: the political determination of exchange relations; and economic sources of interstate influence.

State Power and Determination of Exchange Relations

Economists argue that the pattern of international economic exchange is a product of the underlying supply of factors (land, labour, and capital) along with technological forces. The relative supply of factors is fixed in the short run while technology is more variable. Demographics and patterns of economic growth alter the supply of factors so neither factor supply nor technology is fixed in an absolute sense but they are relatively stable in the short term. Firms and countries strive to increase their production and income but the causal direction is overwhelmingly from comparative cost considerations and changes in technology to trade relations. Decreases in transportation and communication costs, improved shipping, and containerization all reduce the costs of international trade. As transport costs fall, the relative incentives for trade as opposed to domestic exchange improve and countries naturally trade more.

Realists note that observable trade patterns follow political divisions in international politics rather closely. Countries in NATO and the EU traded very little with Soviet bloc countries from 1945 until 1990, the years of the Cold War.[3] This strongly suggests the importance of political and military rivalries in shaping trade relations. A strict focus on endowments of factors of production and comparative advantage misses these political influences.

The importance of politics in shaping trade relations can be generalized by turning the causal arrows around. Instead of seeing the state as a diminished actor trapped by technologically driven economic relations, realists argue that these economic relations are themselves the product of policies actively pursued by states, usually powerful states. States supply the initial conditions for exchange to take place (security, freedom of the seas, and secure property rights for goods in transit as well as foreign capital). Without these politically provided goods, there would be very little international exchange.

While basic economic factors may be important and can be ignored only at great cost, states still have a good deal of discretion deciding how to engage the global economy. Some countries such as Albania and Burma (Myanmar), as well as China during the Great Cultural Revolution (1966–76), chose minimal involvement for extended periods of time. Others such as the member states of the EU chose intense forms of economic interdependence with a substantial amount of that interdependence directed toward other members within the region. Japan has pursued the selective building up of trade relations within East Asia and a vigorous export position in global markets at the same time that it has carefully controlled the inflow of foreign capital and technology. Part of Japan's strategy has been to regionalize as a way of buffering itself from the shocks of globalization (Hatch, 2010). In short, we can say that the level and type of economic involvement are still subject to state control while recognizing at the same time the costs of complete autonomy evident in Albania, Burma, and China prior to its decision to re-enter the global economy.

Economic Sources of State Power

One textbook definition of economics is the efficient allocation of scarce resources among alternate ends. Another more classical definition is that economics has to do with material provisioning of human needs. All the activity of human society – artistic, philosophical, leisurely activity – is built on a material economic base. Without food, clothing, and shelter we would not be free to pursue other activities, some higher-order and some not. What is true for art and leisure is also true for military activity. The recruitment and training of a military force and its equipment and provisioning, from the simplest rifle to the most complex anti-missile missile, are costly activities. The use of military force in open warfare is an extreme case of the attempt to project power on the world stage. International influence has many facets, all of them requiring an economic base.

---

[3]NATO came into existence in 1949. The European Economic Community (EEC), the forerunner of the EU, came into existence in 1958, as a result of the Rome Treaty signed in 1957.

In *National Power and the Structure of Foreign Trade* (1945), Albert Hirschman recognized that a country's involvement in the global economy was a two-edged sword. Involvement *per se* surely limits autonomy but it also provides opportunities – not only opportunities for acquisition of wealth but also opportunities to influence others. How so? If we start from the assumption that any international exchange confers benefits on all parties, it follows that termination of these relations also brings a termination of benefits. Of course, both actors are hurt, the one being denied and the one doing the denying. This logic follows inescapably from the assumption that the relevant parties are both benefiting from the exchange. Nevertheless, costs and benefits are rarely equal, a fact that will prompt leaders of countries to ask themselves about the influence potential of their respective exchange positions. What if A supplies B with a crucial good such as oil and alternate suppliers are scarce? If B does not supply A with a good of similar qualities, then A should have some leverage over B. A full specification of the conditions for A's influence over B includes:

- the importance of A's supply of goods to B
- the existence or non-existence of alternate suppliers
- the existence or non-existence of substitute goods, and
- the opportunity cost of shifting to the next best source of supply, including domestic production.

In addition to the above, B's influence over A would have to be taken into account, making it clear that the influence effect of international trade (or exchange more generally) is the balance of A's dependence on B and B's dependence on A. Thus, in international trade, it is not only important to control the level of trade, but also the content of crucial imports such as energy, food, and high technology products. It is also important to take into account the diversification of trade partners. In general, countries will want to avoid trading for goods that they intensely need, can't easily substitute, and can't easily (within acceptable cost) produce domestically. In short, they don't want to be vulnerable to foreign sources of supply.

Of course, one country's vulnerability is another country's influence potential. International ties are the levers by which actors exert influence over one another. Thus a country with a large market such as the US can cultivate exchange relations which are diversified and not heavily influenced by any one country while the opposite may be the case for smaller countries reliant on the US. Indeed, the large country may not even have to consciously strive to create these influence structures. They are, to a certain extent, a natural consequence of size differences among countries.

Economic sanctions and economic warfare are extreme cases of international influence attempts. While the literature on economic sanctions emphasizes the lack of success in most cases, at least in terms of achieving the stated political goals of the sanctioning country, sanctions surely raise the costs to the target country (Baldwin, 1985). Cuba and North Korea may not yield to Western attempts to alter their policies but the costs of not doing so are undoubtedly high. The US boycott of Cuba did not lead to a change of Cuba's policies, let alone to a change of their socialist economy, but it certainly did hurt Cuba economically. Similarly, the OPEC cartel's oil policies did not alter the position of the US on Israel but the US had to absorb the economic costs of staying the course. Klaus Knorr in *The Power of Nations* (1975: 152) examines twenty two cases of sanction attempts, of which only four can be called a success by his reckoning. In *Economic Statecraft* (1985: 147–8) David Baldwin criticizes Knorr's methodology because Knorr ignores the cost aspect of international power relations. Altering outcomes is not the only way to exert power. The capacity to raise costs in an asymmetric fashion, so that A's efforts to alter B's behaviour result in high costs to B, but little cost to A, is also an example of economic influence. In addition, there are other goals that actors have when carrying out sanctions. They may be trying to communicate resolve as in the Arab League's boycott of Israel in 1955 or in the efforts of the Reagan administration to prevent the Soviet Union from building a pipeline and supplying gas to Western Europe. It was not likely that this pipeline would make Europe excessively dependent on the Soviet Union but it was possible that depriving the Soviet Union of Western European markets would weaken it.

In summary, the importance of economics in global politics cannot be denied. Whether we consider state-building, war-making, sanctions, or simply the strategy of inflicting costs, the economic dimension of global politics cannot be ignored.

Structural Approaches to Global Political Economy

What defines a structural approach to global political economy? Structural characteristics are those that change less rapidly than the more variable features of the global system. They are what the French historian Fernand Braudel (1980) refers to as *la longue durée* (the long duration), in contrast to short-term events and cyclical phenomena such as periods of stagnation and periods of inflation. Trade policy may change quite rapidly, even overnight. The World Trade Organization (WTO) may decide to lower tariffs on certain types of goods but the overall trade patterns between rich and poor may not budge much. Policy changes are events. Enduring trade patterns, such as exporting food and raw materials and importing manufactured goods, are structural.

Structural theories tend to emphasize global inequalities and the multiple ways in which these patterns are reproduced. The economic basis of these theories is not worked out as well as in neoclassical economics, and the connections between power and wealth are not as explicit as in realist theory. Some scholars, such as Andre Gunder Frank (1968), believe that wealth and poverty at the global level are closely linked, that is, rich countries are rich because poor countries are poor. This is quite a strong thesis which has come to be known as 'the development of underdevelopment'. As the rich countries developed, they did so partly as a result of their contact with, and exploitation of, the poorer countries of the periphery. As they expanded their trade and production relations into the Third World, they helped to reproduce the unequal structures.

Most students of global inequality do not subscribe to the views of Frank or to his questionable practice of calculating the amount of capital that flows into LDCs and the amount that flows out, as if the net of these two figures, when it is negative, allows the inference that the poorer country is being impoverished. Presumably no wealth is being created within the country. Poor countries are just black boxes into which foreign capital flows in and out. This is an unrealistic way to figure out the influence of foreign direct investment. The reason for the investment is to create wealth, i.e. to invest money into some profitable enterprise so that the initial investment yields some returns. If investments are successful, then the amount of new wealth created must be added to what flows into and out of the country in question.

A different group of scholars began to write under a different banner of the 'dependency school'. Dependency theorists focus attention on the ways that linkages between rich and poor – or between core and periphery in their language – shape overall development patterns. Cardoso and Faletto (1979) argued that the presence of foreign capital in the periphery, particularly when supplied by multinational corporations, leads to a pattern of dependent development where the host country will grow according to the dictates of the MNCs. The host country (in the periphery) might be used as a convenient market for finished goods or as a source of cheap labour, or as a source of intermediate input goods. In each case, the needs of core capital dictate the nature and pace of the production process. Foreign capital will be controlled by the stockholders and executives of the core country; subsidiaries in the less developed country will be enclaves of foreign capital with few ties to the rest of the economy; and only the less-skilled parts of the production process will be open to locals – not the higher-paying positions occupied by managers and technicians from the core. A certain kind of economic growth might occur in the periphery but this growth is likely to be marked by a series of distortions: uneven growth associated with the places where foreign capital is concentrated, marginalization of key sectors from the overall development pattern, and lack of integration of key economic activities in the 'domestic' economy. Indeed, many dependency theorists (e.g. Sunkel, 1973) believe that transnational capitalist integration and domestic disintegration go together. The integration of the local economy into the global economy implies a weakening of links among various sectors of the local economy. This is a plausible claim that is likely to be true for any country, rich or poor, but it is more likely when a country is smaller and when linkages among sectors are not yet well developed.

Other scholars (Prebisch, 1950), closely related to dependency theorists, attempted to explain growing world inequality by reference to the exchange relations (primarily trade) between rich and poor. These structuralists, primarily from Latin America, relied heavily on the terms of trade theory to explain the large gaps of wealth separating rich and poor. According to this theory, adverse terms of trade, deeply rooted in the international division of labour, give rise to unequal trade relations among countries. Rich and poor countries differ in terms of their domestic production structures, level of research and development, potential for technological change, profit margins, and the type of demand for the goods they produce. This last factor – the structure of demand – forms the basis for one argument about adverse terms of trade.

What are the terms of trade? The terms of trade refer to the ratio of one country's export prices to the prices of imports from that country. If we think about this in barter terms – the pure barter terms of trade – we can think of how many bushels of wheat trade for one computer or one car. If the quality of the goods is constant, if the technologies for producing these goods stay the same, and if one country has to give up more wheat for one car (the same wheat, the same car), then that country has suffered a decline in its terms of trade. When expressed in monetary terms, the terms of trade is simply a ratio of export prices to import prices. If a country pays more over time for what it imports, or receives less for what it exports (again, *ceteris paribus*), its terms of trade have declined. Neoclassical economists can also talk about terms of trade. Indeed, prices are central to neoclassical economics. The problem is that there is no long-term hypothesis about which way the terms of trade will move. Food prices will not necessarily go down (relatively) and prices of manufactured goods will not necessarily go up, especially if we take productivity improvements into account. It all depends on relative demand for food and manufactured goods. So neoclassical economics is agnostic about relative price movements, which is after all what we mean by terms of trade.

Structuralists argue differently. Only three assumptions are really needed to generate an adverse terms of trade for poor countries. The first is that poor countries tend to produce food goods and raw materials while rich countries produce manufactured goods.[4] The second is that world income rises over time. And the third is that as income rises, a larger share of that income is directed toward purchase and consumption of manufactured goods. There are 'natural' levels of satisfaction with regard to food goods that come into play more quickly than for manufactured goods. If all three of these assumptions are fulfilled, and they do seem reasonable, then poorer countries will suffer from a declining terms of trade over time. Notice that a decline in the terms of trade does not imply absolute impoverishment. A country suffering a worsening of its terms of trade may still be better off trading than not trading. It simply implies that most of the gains from trade go to the producers of manufactured goods. Nevertheless, if there is a

---

[4]We can relax this assumption and say that when poor countries produce manufactured goods, they are usually in low-technology industries where there is a high level of competition, which naturally depresses prices.

systematic long-term decline in the terms of trade, it will contribute to a growing inequality among countries. The terms of trade hypothesis has been hotly contested on both theoretical and empirical grounds. Many LDCs are now producing manufactured goods, albeit goods that are at the low-technology end of the spectrum. This creates complications since the inequality predicted by structuralists depends on a division of labour between certain parts of the world economy (rich and poor, North and South, core and periphery). The shift from manufacturing production to services among the advanced capitalist countries creates another complication for terms of trade theory, since most advanced countries are evolving into service economies, some of which are exportable, some not.

Institutional Approaches

Institutions are rules and norms that serve as guides to human behaviour. They can be black-letter rules (written down, formal) or they can be informal and customary. They may be enforced by third parties (e.g. courts) or they may be self-enforcing. Rules can constrain or enable behaviour. For example, a rule that coordinates social security schemes across national boundaries may make it easier for workers to work in different countries. A rule that harmonizes job credentials across borders will have the same effect. Thus, not all rules are of the 'do not do' variety. Some rules are necessary for action to take place. Rules designed to make a market function are of this type.

There is an inescapable case for rules in the neoclassical economic model. To see this, let us imagine a state of nature in which there were no rules. What would this look like? There would be no language (since language contains rules about both meaning and syntax), no mutual comprehension of property rights (who owns what), no ability to signal intentions, and so on. The absence of mutually recognized and agreed-upon rules basically implies that the 'other' is incomprehensible to us and hence not someone with whom we can have normal relations. This scenario would describe nothing familiar to us as human beings, since we are rule-bound individuals. Thus, this is one case for recognizing rules, namely, that without them, the most elementary kinds of human intercourse are not possible.

Another case for rules can be formulated in a more utilitarian framework. To see this, let us examine the main components of the neoclassical economic model. The standard model has three components: the preferences of the relevant individuals; the opportunities available to them; and the technology (knowledge) for acting on their preferences given the constraints.

Douglass North (1981) recognized that this model was inherently incomplete in that it eliminated rules from the choice process, and hence from economic exchange. Property rights are needed to specify ownership and the rights that come with ownership. Ownership turns out to be a bundle of rights to use property in certain ways. One might use the back yard to plant a garden but not to build a factory or even to light a fire. Also, certain exchanges, such as buying or selling child labour, are likely to be illegal in most settings. For a long time, even in advanced capitalist countries in Western Europe, there were strict controls on the movement of capital across national lines both for commercial and personal purposes. In short, without specifying the rules, many basic economic transactions would not be able to take place.

If rules are everywhere, how do institutionalists get leverage in terms of explaining their importance? We can attempt to answer this question by focusing on areas where institutions are relevant for global political economy. There are three areas in particular worth examining: the role of institutions in the process of economic growth; international institutions for fostering cooperation; and national institutions in their capacity for managing and structuring globalization.

Institutions and Economic Growth

Growth theory and economic development have traditionally drawn on the supply or balance of the factors of production. Thus, a country's supply of land (fertile and otherwise), its capital stock, and its skilled and unskilled labour supply are the underlying determinants of economic growth. Sometimes the balance among the factors is offered as a determinant of economic growth. A country's sophisticated capital is only useful to the extent that a skilled labour force is available either inside or outside the country. A country's land available for agricultural production is more efficient if joined to an entrepreneurial agricultural class with access to agricultural machinery. Factors of production are seen as exogenous, i.e. as given by nature and 'history', and therefore not very subject to human manipulation.

Economists have more recently come to realize the importance of institutions as crucial determinants of economic growth. An early model, developed in the forties and fifties by Evsey Domar (1946), basically hypothesized that GDP growth is expected to be directly proportional to the amount of investment spending in total GDP (Easterly, 2001: 29). Despite the fact that Domar disavowed his own model, it continued for a long time to serve as the standard for growth models, probably because it offered a very simple prediction about the sources of economic growth. Growth theory also changed of course and by the 1950s Robert Solow set out a new growth model in which he argued that it was not the level of investment in machinery that counted but rather the rate of productivity of labour. While we cannot go into the details of these growth models here,[5] we mention them to establish that these models did not rely on institutions as determinants. They relied on economic factors – machines, labour, investment, the productivity of labour, and so on.

In *Structure and Change in Economic History* (1981), Douglass North argued that a substantial amount of economic growth lay outside the framework of

---

[5]See Easterly (2001) for an overview of these growth models.

productive factors. Institutions, particularly property rights, accounted for much of the variation in rates of growth across countries. The differences among sub-Saharan Africa, North-east Asia, and Western Europe could not be accounted for by differences in factor endowments. The biggest differences were and continue to be those associated with institutions. North singled out property rights (ownership, exchange) and transaction costs as most important. In some countries, the costs of transactions were simply too high to encourage entrepreneurial activity. These costs might include the paper work needed to start a business, the bargaining and organization costs of hiring a labour force, the informational difficulties of accessing needed capital, the necessity of giving bribes to foster acceptance of permits, and so on. North reasoned that the state, not just individuals, was also a rational maximizer, and the state would attempt to accrue revenues, status, and power. Thus, a system had to be devised which gave incentives to the state to produce necessary public goods, such as security, public order, a legal system, roads, a publicly supported educational system, at the same time that it prevented the state from excessive predation and taxation.

North was on to something, as other economists quickly noted. Easterly, in *The Elusive Quest for Growth* (2001), argues that property rights and transaction costs were only part of the institutional story. Easterly notes that the International Credit Risk Guide identifies four aspects of the institutional environment that are relevant for business units: 'rule of law, quality of bureaucracy, freedom from government repudiation of contracts, and freedom from expropriation' (2001: 250). These factors are related to one another in such a way that, as one worsens, others are also likely to worsen, and when one improves, the others are also likely to improve. If, for example, there is a high risk of expropriation, then people will either not invest or will attempt to make payments to those responsible for making decisions about their property (2001: 251). In a closely related vein, Baumol et al. argue that many of the factors emphasized by Easterly are important to the encouragement of entrepreneurial activity (2007: 7).

The importance of institutions in economic development seems to be widely recognized by economists and political scientists alike – so much so that we refer to it as the new orthodoxy in economic development. In an extensive overview of the literature, Mancur Olson (2000) notes that the sizeable differences in GNP per capita cannot be explained by access to the world's stock of productive knowledge, to its stock of capital, or to differences in land/labour ratios or even to human capital. He concludes, 'The only plausible remaining explanation is that the great differences in the wealth of nations are due mainly to differences in the quality of their institutions and economic policies' (2000: 56).

Institutions and Global Cooperation

When acting globally, states, firms, and other actors are technically operating within anarchy. In short, there is no world government. While anarchy does not prevent cooperation, it does make it more difficult to achieve, especially when it is not directed against a third party such as a common enemy. Realists and liberals would subscribe to this proposition though of course realists argue that cooperation is much more difficult to achieve. Earlier, we examined hegemonic stability theory and saw that cooperation is facilitated by the existence of an international hegemon, a country or group of countries powerful enough to produce international public goods on its own and then attempt to elicit others to underwrite the costs, either by persuasion or coercion. However, much global cooperation seems to have little to do with the ups and downs of hegemonic power. We witness many issue-specific areas in the global political economy that are marked by high levels of institutionalization and cooperation. We observe regimes (as institutions are sometimes called) in the areas of trade, finance, monetary relations, development, telecommunications, the environment, fisheries, and many others. How do we account for the levels of cooperation in these areas?

The theory of liberal institutionalism attempts to explain the role of institutions in the mentioned issue areas as a functional response to the inability to reap the gains from cooperation without institutions.[6] In one sense, this approach has all of the limitations of functional explanations generically; in particular it attempts to explain the emergence of institutions as a response to a need. Yet, rational actors, with foresight of their environment, can plausibly anticipate the gains from cooperation and make the pursuit of these gains part of their conscious strategies. If states engaged in trade wars, or acted on the basis of their short-term interests with regard to exploiting common property resources, they would lose in the long run. Still, the mere hypothesis (however plausible) that there are gains from cooperation does not logically imply that actors will cooperate. If distrust is high, behaviour difficult to monitor, and the time frame is short, actors may choose to pursue non-cooperative strategies in the hope of being able to outwit, or outmuscle, their partners. Predation and aggression are not even required for cooperation to fail. An actor may simply be trying to minimize losses and choose a defensive (defect) strategy that ensures the failure of cooperation. Institutions are important because they make the preferences and strategies of others more visible, they enhance the capacity to monitor and perhaps punish, and they lengthen the time frame for expected interactions, thus making cooperation a more rational strategy. Actors who expect that they will be punished in the future if they defect (don't cooperate) in the present are more likely to cooperate.

The fact that regimes foster gains from cooperation does not imply that institutions spontaneously emerge every time there are gains on the table. In 'Big Bills Left on the Sidewalk' (2000) Mancur Olson demonstrates that national economies often operate far below their technological frontiers, and

---

[6]The most thorough and compelling case for cooperation is made by Keohane in *After Hegemony* (1984).

by inference are far from realizing all the gains from cooperative exchange implied by their endowments and technology. Less recognized, not every institution implies the existence and exploitation of cooperative gains. The existence of the Economic and Monetary Union (EMU) in the European Union does not necessarily mean that the member states are better off. True, there is likely to be a reduction of transaction costs due to single currency but this may be more than offset by the loss of national autonomy in terms of controlling inflation, unemployment, and growth. The current financial crisis in Greece and the Eurozone more broadly has raised questions about the desirability and viability of the EMU.

On the role of institutions and cooperation in global politics, one gets the feeling that liberal institutionalism (relying on neoclassical economics) is too nice and realism is too nasty. Liberals tend to see the world through rose-tinted glasses and are better at explaining common gains than the redistributive effects of institutions. Realists, on the other hand, have a hard time knowing what to do with institutions at all since it is power which counts and institutions are simply reflections of power considerations. As Przeworksi reminds us, if institutions are completely endogenous to power, then they do not have an independent role to play (Przeworski, 2004: 10). While this is a strong view, it helps to clarify the logic at the extremes. If the institutions are completely a function of power considerations (say a powerful class of rulers), and if those rulers seek only to reproduce their own power, then the effects of institutions will be redundant with the conditions that power would have produced. While Przeworski is not writing in the context of international relations debates, there are realists such as Mearsheimer who come very close to arguing that international institutions are merely reflections of the wishes of the most powerful states (1994–5).

Thankfully, there is a middle ground between deterministic versions of realism and cooperative theories of institutions. This middle ground allows us to accept that power shapes institutions and that common gains are also reaped by institutions in certain circumstances. Krasner's 'Global Communications and National Power: Life on the Pareto Frontier' (Krasner, 1991) attempts to integrate both efficiency and distributive concerns within a single analytical framework. He accepts the thinking and analytical devices of Pareto efficiency and the Pareto frontier.[7] These concepts are useful in helping us to think about the ways that cooperative exchange can make both (all) parties better off than the status quo. But he departs from the liberal institutionalist approach by asking which point on the frontier is chosen and what determines the selection of the outcome. Different locations on the frontier, while all Pareto efficient, nevertheless may be better for one actor than another. It is better to have a shipping

---

[7]The Pareto frontier refers to all possible outcomes that make both parties better off. Not all choices are possible. There are constraints due to resource scarcities and to knowledge. However, out of those choices which are possible, only some of those make both parties better off. Those which fit this description are the outcomes which define the Pareto frontier.

regime which allocates lanes to different shipping companies, rather than none at all, but there are some shipping lanes that are better than others (more direct, less traffic, easier currents to navigate). Getting to the frontier is a task best explained by liberal institutionalism. Deciding where to locate on the frontier is best explained by power oriented approaches (Krasner, 1991: 365). This approach is more satisfying because it comes closer to our understanding of institutions in real life. We understand that institutions solve problems and provide common benefits but we also have a hunch that power is relevant and that the important states, those with the power and money, get a larger share of the pie. Krasner's approach allows us to deal with both concerns within a single model.

Domestic Institutions and Globalization

The world is globalized and yet populated by nation-states whose geographical reach is of a much smaller scale. Yet, these states represent the highest level of both authority and focus of loyalty in the world today. How do we reconcile these contradictory forces? We are not saying that all levels of activity have to be congruent with one another (economic, social, cultural, and political). A globalized world in economic terms may respond to economic pressures (specialization, scale, and efficiency) while political organization may be more tuned to forces associated with identity, community, and a desire to preserve national traditions and privileges. As a result, the geographic scale of the economy will be larger than that of the community. The former is global while the latter is national and even sub-national. Political authority is located at still a different level, that of the state. There is nothing inconsistent about these multiple levels of activity but it does mean that states have to negotiate both with communities of identity that are sometimes smaller and sometimes larger than states, and with a global economy that lies outside the boundaries of any state. The question is how states adapt and manage their affairs given the economic constraints of the global system.

While we spend an entire chapter on domestic institutions and globalization, it may be helpful here to give a brief overview in theoretical terms. Few would deny that the global economy places economic constraints on economic policy-making. The mobility of capital, in particular, puts pressure on states to change policies in favour of capital as opposed to labour. This could mean a variety of things: a tougher stance toward unions; lower levels of taxation on capital, especially mobile capital; looser regulation of business; and cutting back on welfare state expenditures. Collectively, Friedman refers to these policies as 'the golden straitjacket' which he calls the 'defining political economic garment of the globalization era' (1999: 104). It may be worthwhile to quote Friedman at length:

> To fit into the Golden Straitjacket a country must either adopt, or be seen as moving toward, the following golden rules: making the private sector the primary engine of its economic growth, maintaining a low rate of inflation and price stability, shrinking

the size of its state bureaucracy, maintaining as close to a balanced budget as possible, if not a surplus, eliminating and lowering tariffs on imported goods, removing restrictions on foreign investment, getting rid of quotas and domestic monopolies, increasing exports, privatizing state-owned industries and utilities, deregulating capital markets, making its currency convertible, opening its industries [and] stock and bond markets to direct foreign ownership and investment, deregulating its economy to promote as much domestic competition as possible, eliminating government corruption, subsidies, and kickbacks as much as possible, opening its banking and telecommunications systems to private ownership and competition and allowing its citizens to choose from an array of competing pension options and foreign-run pension and mutual funds. When you stitch all of these pieces together you have a Golden Straitjacket. (Friedman 1999: 105)

Friedman's book *The Lexus and the Olive Tree* (1999) popularized an idea that also exists in the academic literature, namely that globalization forces states to adopt neoliberal economic policies that privatize economic production, limit the role of the state, and loosen regulations in a business-friendly direction (Kahler and Lake, 2003: 16). Fritz Scharpf, a prominent European analyst, refers to capitalist democracy as 'a precarious synthesis' (1999: 29), especially in the context of the European Union (EU), since the European Commission and European Court of Justice (ECJ) have both privileged market-making activities and in so doing have 'reduced the capacity of democratic politics at the national level to impose market-correcting regulations on increasingly mobile capital and economic interactions' (1999: 3). Scharpf's concern is about the pressures on market regulation and regulatory competition. Others worry that globalization and regional integration are resulting in a loosening of national boundaries with problematic results for national welfare systems. According to this line of thought, national welfare systems emerged in the late nineteenth and early twentieth centuries when the nation states provided for the selective closure of national borders (Ferrera, 2005: 2).

Given these global pressures, how do we explain the ability of nation states to remain intact and even to advance their distinctive national goals? This is a difficult question to which the variety of capitalism literature addresses itself. One answer is that there is no single path of greatest efficiency that is associated with the institutions of any particular country. The Anglo-Saxon economies (mainly the US and the UK) may stress flexible labour markets and lower social overhead costs. Germany may stress coordination among banks, firms, labour unions, and the state. The corporatist states of Northern Europe, particularly Sweden and Norway, may rely on centralized bargaining among the social partners (labour, business, and the state). And France, which doesn't fit neatly into any category, may rely on an expensive welfare state which nevertheless redistributes very little (Prasad, 2006), weak unions, and a state which is less interventionist than it once used to be (Gordon and Meunier, 2001).

In short, distinctive national styles and policy mixes are able to survive. Governments of different ideological colours have been able to put in place policies that favour the right or left of centre, depending on the political coalition in power (Garrett and Lange, 1991: 543). Mosley finds convergence in monetary and fiscal policies but continued difference 'in such areas as government consumption spending, government transfer payments, public employment, and the level of government tax revenues' (2000: 739). These results seem to make sense since we expect globalization to create some bottom line pressures toward low inflation, low budget deficits, and efficient firms. However, there are several ways of reaching the same bottom-line standards thus allowing for national political and institutional differences.

Constructivism and Global Political Economy

Constructivism is a relatively new approach that has taken root in political science in the last twenty years. One of the earliest applications of constructivist theory was an effort to explain the collapse of the Soviet Union. Against a variety of materialist accounts that stressed the steep tradeoffs among defence spending, consumer spending, and industrial investment, scholars such as Jeff Checkel (1993) and Matthew Evangelista (1999) advanced arguments about the role of ideas relating to changing conceptions of security and new ideas about global economy. Soviet thinkers came to accept the idea of interdependence and a single differentiated world economy rather than a dualist economy with a capitalist and a socialist sub-system. Another idea that came to be accepted was the idea of common security between East and West, rather than the objective antagonism that supposedly existed between capitalist and socialist countries. Common security was introduced to Soviet institutchiks and foreign policy experts by the Independent Commission for Disarmament and Security (Palme Commission), as early as the 1980s (Risse Kappen, 1995: 198) Later, within the field of European integration, constructivist contributions became commonplace (Waever, 1995; McNamara, 1998; Checkel, 1999; Parsons, 2003), so much so that it can be considered as part of the mainstream within European integration studies.

More recently, in *Constructing the International Economy*, Abdelal, Blyth, and Parsons (2010) have made significant contributions in establishing the theoretical foundations for constructivism as applied to global political economy. Their claim is that ideas are not related to material interests in any simple way and therefore cannot be eliminated without loss of explanatory power. Ideas are neither reflections of material interests, nor simply rationalizations, nor solutions to coordination problems that require focal point attention. Simply put, just as societies may vary in terms of objective conditions (say the supply of labour), they may also vary in terms of cultural conditions (e.g. legitimacy of the market economy, or tolerance of inequality) (2010: 2).

In one sense the central claims of constructivism – that identities and beliefs are important – are not so controversial. It is indeed hard to motivate any serious theory of human behaviour without presupposing that agents have some sense of self and some beliefs that certain actions will lead to certain outcomes. Even the sparest account of human action requires individuals with stable preferences and some capacity to represent the environment in terms of means–ends connections. This of course does not mean that the beliefs are accurate or that they are not characterized by distortions and cognitive biases that may result from greed, fear, panic, or excessive optimism. The current financial crisis allows a generous role for all these emotions.

The claim that identities and beliefs are important is a starting point, somewhat related to the claim that institutions are important. To see how this general proposition might acquire more bite, it may be useful to ask about the counterfactual condition: under what circumstances would beliefs and identities not be important? Let us restrict the question to beliefs; identities admittedly pose the more difficult issues. One condition under which beliefs would not be important would occur when information is abundant in the economic sense, i.e. not scarce. In this case, then, anything we needed to know about the consequences of alternative courses of action could easily be provided by the costless acquisition of information. A second condition where beliefs are less important occurs when beliefs and material conditions are related in some deterministic way, e.g. certain material conditions always lead to certain beliefs. In this event, one need only pay attention to the existing material conditions, which are more readily observable than beliefs. If a certain distribution of military power always (and only) leads to specific beliefs about the balance of power, then these beliefs are in principle dispensable.

One philosophical debate about constructivism centres on whether it offers a causal-explanatory model or whether it aims for something else, e.g. an understanding of the constitution of agents and their attempts to make sense of the world, in other words meaning. How do states, multinational corporations, banks, and labour unions come into being? How do they acquire their capacity to act, their legal and sociological credentials, and their recognition by others in their social field? There are elaborate procedures for recognizing states that are organized around the question of sovereignty in both its internal and external aspects. Does a state have the capacity to make laws, implement them within a definite territorial area, control its borders, and exclude external authority structures? The question of 'constitution' has broad application. It refers not just to actors such as states but also to institutional arenas, such as markets. Caporaso and Tarrow (2009) have studied the emergence of a transnational labour market in the European Union (EU) and have noted that the first stage involves some very practical considerations, such as the definition (constitution) of a worker. This process of definition turned out not to be simple, since it involved legal, political, and sociological considerations.

One aim of Abdelal, Blyth, and Parsons is to facilitate the engagement of constructivism with other approaches to global political economy. To do this, they must make room for genuine debate, a task that involves putting some ontological questions to the side and bringing into focus serious theoretical differences about how the global political economy works. As Fearon and Wendt (2002: 52–3) argue, much of the field has been ontologized, with questions about the ultimate building blocks of reality (individuals, social relations) and the ultimate nature of reality (ideas, material facts) occupying centre stage. These questions, while important, need to be supplemented by more pragmatic yet theoretical explanations about how global politics and economics work, and questions relating to growth, regional centres of power, development, equality and inequality, and jobs and economic crises, just to name a few of the most important topics on the intellectual agenda today.

One central question about constructivist global political economy is whether it lies on the same analytical plane as Marxism, neoclassical, structural, and institutional approaches. Neoclassical economics, applied to the global level, offers a theory of how things work based on the supply of factors, price movements, supply and demand, the specification of property rights, the type of good in question (based on considerations of rivalry and excludability of benefits), the degree and type of information, and the framing of choice. We should note that there are some ideational elements (framing, information) present in the neoclassical agenda as well as institutional elements (property rights) and some components that are more nearly materialistic (e.g. factor supply), though of course factor supply also has to be constructed, if only by professional economists. If constructivism is an approach based on constitutive theorizing and the search for meaning, then it has little in common with the other approaches. As recently as 2002, two prominent scholars, one a rationalist and the other a constructivist, argued, 'Let there be no mistake up front that when it comes to the content and nature of international politics, constructivism is not a "theory" at all, any more than is rationalism' (Fearon and Wendt, 2002: 56). Our sense is that constructivism has come a long way toward developing a theory, or theories, of global political economy.

Our Approach

As this section makes clear, our approach is eclectic and emphasizes several theoretical strands. We consider ourselves Keynesian institutionalists whose focus happens to be on global relations. Our debt to institutional theory is most evident in that we see markets as constituted politically and subject to ongoing political regulation. In economic terms, we owe a great deal to the Keynesian perspective and its emphasis on the self-disorganizing aspects of capitalism, an emphasis directly at odds with the equilibrium focus of economic theory. Capitalism and the capitalist state are prone to periodic crises, as the last two decades clearly show: inflationary and deflationary crises, crises of overinvestment (e.g. in real estate), crises in government spending, financial crises and so on. The market, particularly the global market, is not self-regulating. It overheats and needs to be cooled off, and it sometimes operates well below capacity and needs public expenditures to stimulate borrowing and investment. The institutional and Keynesian approaches provide tools for thinking about the intersections between the political system and the economy even at the global level.

The institutional–Keynesian focus does not mean that we ignore the other approaches. Realism presents a sharp analysis of states within anarchy and the power balancing and search for security that occur while states cautiously cooperate with one another. For realists, the economic concepts of comparative advantage, specialization, gains from trade, and Pareto efficiency are seductive but can never be pursued without constant worry about the security implications of economic exchange. Realists are 'cooperative misers' who constantly miss out on economic opportunities for fear that their opponents will gain more than they do (relative gains), with possible implications for the power balance. Economic exchange, for realists, applies only to countries that have solved their basic security concerns. That is why successful economic integration always occurs within an overarching security community.

Neoclassical economics is admired for its elegant descriptions of equilibrium processes in product and factor markets, its defence of specialization and division of labour, and the idea that efficiency derives from specialization and exchange. Markets are powerful institutions in their own right and it is to economists that we look when we want to understand how markets work. Indeed, even a basic reading of the newspaper takes us into the world of trade, capital flows, currencies, foreign direct investment, development, and financial crises. An understanding of markets is absolutely essential to grasp the meaning of globalization.

The structural perspective is critical too. It is easy, but wrong, to lapse into the fiction that the advanced capitalist world (Europe, East Asia, and North America) is the entire world, or at least the world where most of the economic action lies. Such a viewpoint leaves out most of the world in demographic terms as well as in terms of number of countries. The vast populations of South Asia, China, South-east Asia, and Africa are important too, not just in moral terms but also economically and politically. Major players such as India, China, and Brazil are economic actors in their own right and are expected to play an important role in combatting the current financial crisis.

The institutional and constructivist perspectives constantly remind us of the importance of rules and ideas. The material world, whether described in military or economic terms, is not simply 'out there' for us to observe and analyse. It must be constructed and this is a process that involves the application of our subjective (and intersubjective) understandings. In this sense, ideas, frames of references, discourses, and modes of interpretation matter a great deal.

While there is much on which to draw from these perspectives, we bring a distinct outlook in two ways, though in both cases what is original is the emphasis. First, we do not see a silver bullet in any of the approaches which we discussed and do not adopt any of them 'off the shelf', unmodified, as it were. As helpful as they are, they do not by themselves or in combination provide a complete picture. We are not transfixed by markets; we think they are characterized as much by disequilibrium and self-disorganization as by equilibrium and self-organization. And we see market failures not as abnormal departures from a pattern where markets function in nearly perfect fashion. They are pervasive, endemic, and an inherent part of the way markets work. We could almost as easily start with the absence of markets and theorize the special conditions for their operation as with the functioning of markets and the special conditions under which they break down. Neither are we in thrall to state power, national sovereignty, and the tragic logic of interstate competition under anarchy. While states are clearly powerful political animals, they also struggle with regard to control over borders, engage in daily attempts to exclude external authority structures, and constantly attempt to project laws from the central government to peripheries within their own borders. We see the 'problem of cooperation', much like that of market failure, in that cooperation has been singled out, received its own brand, and been dramatically problematized while at the same time resources are mobilized to show decisively that the defects of the international system can be overcome. Cooperation is deeply implicated in international politics, part of its warp and woof, and not some minor patch-up operation within an otherwise cruel Hobbesian world.

Second, we see in the institutional perspective a powerful idea that cuts across the other areas. Markets, states, North–South relations – none of these topics can be addressed in isolation from an institutional approach. An analysis of markets requires attention to property rights, the legal and political underpinnings of exchange, and the conditions under which one deals with, or ignores, international externalities. The realist approach requires an understanding of the ways in which anarchy, defined as absence of central rule, still requires institutional channels and practices with which to carry out the most elementary actions across borders. And the structural approach soon leads us into the global institutional architecture, North–South relations, the World Bank, etc. While economists have traditionally emphasized the distribution of economic factors as crucially important for development, they have more recently turned to the role of institutions for growth and development. A study by Dani Rodrik et al. (2004: 131–65) demonstrates that institutions are the most important factor behind economic growth. They account for more than factor endowments and integration into the global economy. And the impact of conventional geography measures disappears when institutions are taken into account. Finally, most of the effect of trade is endogenous to institutions themselves.

Conclusion, States, and Markets

At the heart of globalization debates lies the relationship between states and markets. Markets are systems of exchange usually analysed in terms of production and efficiency. States are institutionalized systems of authority usually analysed in terms of power and control. One question that repeatedly emerges from the study of globalization is whether globalization will undermine the state, in effect making it obsolete. This line of questioning arises out of the intuition that states are determined to regulate economic activity, to control its flows within and across borders, and above all to tax such activity for its own treasuries which in turn are often used for unproductive consumption. These activities, so the argument goes, are harmful to markets. The awesome power of markets cannot be denied. There is an undeniable dynamism in billions of people taking up specialized positions in an extended division of labour covering the entire globe, producing with little idea where the goods will end up. This division of labour is not one solely based on trade, with individuals in country X producing for sale to individuals in country Y. It also includes foreign direct investment, part-processing, vertically integrated production chains, and outsourcing.

We concede the power of the market at the same time that we think the opposition between markets and states is misplaced. Markets and states are co-constituted. And we also agree, though it is contestable, that in a shootout between markets and states, such as we periodically witness when a government attempts to defend its currency against speculative attacks, it is markets that usually win. In the current financial crisis centring on Greece and the European Union, it has taken nearly one trillion dollars to calm markets, and we are not yet sure that this goal has been reached. Whether more will have to be done to prevent further decline of the euro and the downgrading of national debt remains to be seen.

Nevertheless, we maintain that the opposition of states and markets is wrong-headed and encourages us to think of a contest between two institutions which, for all their friction, are quite symbiotic with one another. Markets and states are co-dependent. They need one another and profit from the activities of one another. States want the wealth and productive revenue of markets, and they get this through tax revenues. To produce any public goods (roads, health and safety, education, defence), states need to pay for them through tax revenues. Markets, for their part, could not exist in a state of nature, as we have already argued. The large impersonal systems of exchange require not only networks of transportation and communication but also laws, private property, courts, a system of weights and measures, a common currency, and freedom from violence. Of course, states are not benign either. Just as in markets, the government official is a self-interested person with his or her distinctive goals. Thus, predation, self-seeking, corruption, and graft are not only possible but likely. The regulations that are put in place to control the excesses of market agents also have to be put in place to control government agents.

Another reason for treating markets and states in one framework is that markets are not, despite some arguments to the contrary, self-regulating. It is of course true that some markets have self-regulating properties. If someone doesn't like the produce from the corner grocer, he or she can take their business elsewhere. In this sense, the interest of the grocer in good products is also in the interest of the consumer. Departures from this standard can result in signals to the vendor to bring quality and price more in line with the interests of the consumer. But markets on a global scale don't have the same degree of transparency and responsiveness that our corner grocery market has. The land of credit default swaps, financial derivatives, and securitized mortgages is far removed from the average person, even those who have a large stake in how they operate. A home owner in a small Midwestern town may have a mortgage which has been sliced, repackaged, and sold to many different persons around the world. And the prospects of that loan going bad or the value of the house plummeting are dependent on forces outside the knowledge perimeter, let alone control, of the owner. If markets worked perfectly, if individual stakeholders had perfect knowledge, and if risk were priced at realistic levels, all would be fine. The geographic scope of the exchange, the number of participants, and the complexity of the financial arrangements would not be a problem. But of course, all the 'ifs' in the sentence are highly problematic which is why when the financial crisis hit, so many people – not just the innocents in our Midwestern example – were truly shocked. The moral of this story is that markets don't perform best when unregulated. They do require regulation to function properly, though whether they need 'more or less regulation' is not the issue so much as what kind of regulation.

At the end of the day, globalization is not fate; it is a choice (Wolf, 2001: 182–3), but it is a choice no matter if one decides to stay out, keep a low globalization profile, or be an enthusiastic joiner. Globalization has its ardent defenders, its critics, apologists, ideologues, and moderates (and ideological moderates). To us, this is as it should be, entirely understandable, and from the standpoint of democratic values, which are always pluralistic, discursive, and conflictual, even desirable. Globalization raises a roster of issues that is every bit as rich as those that dominate the domestic political agenda.

DOMESTIC RESPONSES TO THE PRESSURES OF GLOBALIZATION

Introduction

This chapter will focus on the ways that domestic actors and institutions respond to the pressures of globalization. The globalization of trade and capital puts pressure on states around the world to open their markets to foreign competition, reduce barriers to trade, and subscribe to other neoliberal economic policies favoured by the World Trade Organization, International Monetary Fund, and other international economic institutions. States vary greatly, however, in the benefits they will reap from globalization as well as the costs they will face. This is because globalization creates winners and losers – some have much to gain, while others are marginalized or are left worse off. States also vary in their national goals and purposes. Some states are motivated more by autonomy, some by stability, some by achieving a high level of equality in their society, some by achieving maximum economic efficiency and growth. The type of government and economic system in a state also matters greatly to its response to globalization. Democratic governments face drastically different domestic political environments than autocratic governments do; capitalist countries differ greatly in economic policy preferences than do countries with centrally planned economies. Even among capitalist democracies, there is a wide range of policy preferences with respect to how much exposure to globalization is desirable, what sectors should be protected or allowed to wither, and who should bear the burden of the inevitable dislocations caused by involvement with the global economy.

If a state's market behaviour depends at least partially upon its social and political institutions, as many political economists argue, how do states with different state-societal arrangements vary in their responses to the pressures of globalization? How do they work to achieve more desirable outcomes? Do the social market economies (SMEs) of Europe respond differently than liberal market economies (LMEs) like the US? What are the challenges faced by developing countries, and how are those different from the challenges faced by developed countries? In this chapter, we argue that national capitalist institutions remain quite distinct even in the face of competitive pressures in the global economy. Firms and institutions are not the same across all nations and they do not react the same way to similar challenges. Instead of converging to a single 'best practice' economic model, scholars find that national capitalist economies are strengthening their institutions in ways that serve their unique national comparative economic advantages (Hall and Soskice, 2001: 56). In social market economies, this means that firms will be more supportive of social policies such as education and labour protections because of their reliance on a highly skilled, stable workforce. In liberal market economies, government will often face greater pressure from business interests for deregulation, since this strengthens the market mechanisms around which firms in LMEs are organized. Without this deregulation, firms in LMEs are more likely to relocate abroad than are firms in SMEs, because they face competition from developing countries that also offer largely deregulated markets and cheaper labour. Evidence also suggests that developing countries face different types of globalization pressures than developed countries, and they often adopt different types of policies in response.

Before assessing the ways states respond to globalization, we need to establish the problems and opportunities that globalization poses for governments. The conventional wisdom holds that globalization is a process that results in a flattening and *convergence* of societies and government policy. Both trade and capital mobility bring pressures to bear on countries and the groups within them. Trade brings foreign goods and services to domestic markets, thus exposing local (domestic) groups to the labour, capital, technology, and regulatory structures of foreign countries. In one sense, this is desirable and says no more than what is implied by the principle of comparative advantage.[1] Capital mobility allows capital to move from country to country in accordance with the search for the most productive location. This applies to many forms of capital, including portfolio capital and financial capital. The mobility of goods and productive factors brings pressures for convergence among different countries.

Convergence could refer to prices as well as to factor returns.[2] The famous economist Paul Samuelson (1948) argued long ago that open trade borders between two countries will drive the prices of the goods they trade to the same level (the single price theory) and will also equalize the returns to different factors of production. Convergence could also apply to factors that are not

---

[1]The principle of comparative advantage was first elaborated by the economist David Ricardo, in *The Principles of Political Economy and Taxation* (1817). Basically, comparative advantage states that countries should specialize in goods in which they have a relative advantage in productive efficiency and import goods where they have a relative disadvantage. Comparative advantage implies that countries should specialize (and therefore import and export) even if they produce all goods more efficiently than other countries.

[2]Factor returns refer to the monetary rewards that go to labour in the form of wages, capital in the form of profits, and land in the form of rent. All the income in a society should ultimately be traceable to one of these three productive factors.

strictly economic, such as the policies or regulatory structure of a country. One of the things we are most concerned about in this chapter is the way in which governments may or may not be pressured to cut public spending. For example, governments operating in a globalized environment may have to avoid policies that result in long-term welfare commitments and also adopt 'lean' regulatory structures that are less effective at regulating private actors with regard to a variety of social objectives such as a clean environment, health and safety regulations, and worker rights. We point out that the regulatory 'race to the bottom' is not the only direction in which convergence may work. True, this is the fear of many groups within the advanced countries but the direction might be just the opposite, generating a 'race to the top' where standards are aligned around the norms of the strictest countries (Vogel, 1995). Less developed countries might see this possibility every bit as threatening as richer countries see the possibility of a race to the bottom.

Despite the recognized homogenizing power of global forces, convergence among countries has not occurred in a clear way. The jury is still out as to what effect globalization has, and will have, on domestic economics and politics. We are witnessing a tug of war between global economic forces and national (and sub-national) political forces. To understand the interaction between globalization and national political forces, it is helpful to set the stage by posing two questions. First, why is globalization seen as a homogenizing force; what is it about globalization that leads us to expect outcomes to be the same across different countries? Second, how do national governments, resist, shape, manage, and, seemingly at least, defy globalization's homogenizing impulses?

Let us take up the first question: What is the basis for expecting globalization to produce similar outcomes everywhere? To understand the answer to this, it is necessary to understand how global capitalism works. Two things are central. First, capitalism is a system of production by private firms (or individuals). 'Private' in this sense means that the production of goods takes place in firms that are owned by individuals (organized as corporations) rather than by governments. Private individuals – not public officials – make decisions about investments, wages, business strategy, and what to produce. Second, these firms produce and sell within impersonal systems of exchange called markets. If firms produce goods sold on markets, they must compete by finding cheap sources of capital, labour, and other factors of production. They must be able to pay labour (wages), buy land on which to produce (rents), and purchase the required capital to run their firms, for which they pay interest. After paying for all production and distribution costs, firms must find the cheapest way to produce in order to turn a profit. What does all this have to do with globalization? If cost-cutting is essential to production, then it follows that firms must search for the cheapest sources of labour, capital, and technology, wherever the location, and they must become the same lean and productive firms wherever they happen to be located. Whether a worker is in Ireland, Pakistan, the Czech Republic, or Germany should not matter so long as this worker contributes in the best and least expensive way to the process of production. Firms have to make these decisions in an unsentimental way, without taking patriotism or solidarity with the welfare of domestic workers into account.

If this view of globalization as a technological necessity is taken to its conclusions, it would seem to result in policy convergence across countries at the expense of national autonomy. Thomas Friedman has popularized this loss of autonomy by referring to the 'golden straitjacket', which he calls 'the defining political economic garment of this global era' (Friedman, 1999: 104). The straitjacket refers to a set of policies that must be followed if a country is to become wealthy. Countries must privatize, deregulate, control their interest rates and money supply, maintain price stability (control inflation), preserve a balanced budget, and open the economy to international competition. Once countries do all these things, they will become wealthy (the 'golden' part). To sum it up, if countries are all part of the same global economy, they must don the same straitjacket, resulting in convergence among government policies, economic performance, and perhaps even institutions. To take just one example of institutional convergence, the arrival of Economic and Monetary Union in the EU has resulted in more countries creating independent central banks modelled along lines of Germany.

The second view of globalization, the *divergence* perspective, argues that there is much more room for different mixes of policies and domestic institutions than recognized by the convergence school. This perspective stresses the continued autonomy and distinctive goals and institutions of different countries. The argument here is that globalization is not the product of blind economic forces but is itself the result of political decisions taken by governments. After all, the modern global economy is the result of the political architecture put in place by leaders in different countries (chiefly in the United States and Western Europe) after World War II. The International Monetary Fund (IMF), World Bank, and United Nations are all the product of political choices. Even in the face of intense globalization pressures, there are numerous adaptive (efficient) responses ranging from flexible labour markets in Great Britain, to Germany's high-skilled economy with investment in human capital, Italy's reliance on industrial districts (Berger, 1996), and Denmark's mix of economic openness and highly active labour market policies. Scholars emphasizing the continued divergence in the economic policies of states around the world cite evidence that these distinctive national differences are not disappearing as economies become more globally integrated.

The rest of this chapter addresses the second question posed above: how do national governments resist, shape, manage, and, seemingly at least, defy globalization's homogenizing impulses?

Responses to Globalization in the Advanced Capitalist Economies

How do governments in the developed capitalist countries respond to the competitive pressures of the global economy? The Varieties of Capitalism approach to studying the different forms of national capitalism provides us with one way to compare different national responses to globalization. The press and popular literature would have us believe that globalization is driving countries around the world toward a common, market-based model with no room for social, labour, and environmental protections or culture-specific values. The principal hypothesis about globalization has been that transnational economic competition will erode national policy-making autonomy, leading to a convergence of national forms of production, regulatory frameworks, and macro-economic policies. As mentioned earlier, Thomas Friedman's 'golden straitjacket' metaphor captures the constraining and homogenizing aspects of globalization. States will be forced to trim their budgets, cut social spending, relax their regulatory frameworks, and privatize their publicly owned enterprises. Governments will be forced to turn away from welfare spending in the interests of creating a political framework for capitalism that encourages efficiency and competitiveness.

However, recent research has shown that this convergence toward liberal economic 'best practices' has not materialized. The Varieties of Capitalism literature challenges the conventional globalization hypothesis by emphasizing the continued *divergence* of national capitalist economies and the deepening of institutional differences (Hall and Soskice, 2001; Thelen, 2001; Boyer, 2005). This divergence of domestic economic policies is explained by the persistence of national institutions and domestic demands for compensation in the face of economic disturbances caused (or perceived to be caused) by globalization (Mosley, 2003). Scholars working within the Varieties of Capitalism approach draw distinctions between models of capitalist economic governance, and they have found that there are a limited number of models around which the majority of advanced capitalist countries cluster. Through comparing these types of capitalisms, we can better understand whether there has indeed been convergence around a 'best practice' model or whether the distinct national traditions of capitalist countries around the world are persisting in the face of the pressures of globalization.

Several different typologies of capitalist economic models have been proposed, a well-known one being Peter Katzenstein's liberal, corporatist, and statist economies (Katzenstein, 1985). More recently, scholars have preferred distinguishing between just two types of systems – liberal market economies and coordinated, or social, market economies (Hall and Soskice, 2001; Pontusson, 2005). Pontusson characterizes social market economies (SMEs) as being host to strong unions, institutionalized collective bargaining systems between firms and labour, generous social welfare provisions, and employment protections (Pontusson, 2005: 17). Proponents of the social market economic model take issue with the belief commonly held by economists that there is an inherent trade-off between societal goals of equality and economic goals of efficiency. They argue that generous publicly funded social provisions such as education and even healthcare should be viewed as an investment in human capital that will fuel economic growth in both the short and long term. By redistributing wealth, the government spreads the costs of economic adjustment dictated by globalization among the citizenry, avoiding major political

Table 3.1   Social versus liberal market economies

	Social market economies	Liberal market economies
	Austria Belgium Denmark Finland Germany The Netherlands Norway Switzerland Sweden	Australia Canada Ireland New Zealand United Kingdom United States
Strength of unions	High	Low
Institutionalization of collective bargaining systems	High	Low
Coordination among firms	High	Low
Public provision of social welfare and employment protections	High	Low

Source: adapted from Pontusson, 2005.

disruptions. As shown in Table 3.1, the countries included in Pontusson's SME scheme are Germany, Austria, Switzerland, Belgium, the Netherlands, Denmark, Sweden, Norway, and Finland.

On the other hand, liberal market economies, such as those found in Australia, Canada, Ireland, New Zealand, the United Kingdom, and the United States, are organized around the belief that a trade-off exists between equality and efficiency. Market liberals argue that the redistributive social welfare institutions characteristic of SMEs reduce economic efficiency by hampering growth and, as a result, contribute to unemployment. LMEs are characterized by more robust competitive markets, and firms rely more on market-based coordination mechanisms rather than the collaborative and institutionalized interaction between firms in SMEs (Hall and Soskice, 2001: 27). Unionization is low and government adopts a more *laissez-faire* approach toward the economy. Social welfare provision in LMEs is minimal, and the privatization of many social services is encouraged.

Some scholars have recently argued that more than two categories of capitalism are needed in order to adequately deal with some major states that do not fit into either category, such as France and Japan. We will discuss the particularities of the French economy later in the chapter.

Social Market Economies (SMEs)

How are national governments in social market economies responding to the pressures of globalization? Are we witnessing a 'race to the bottom' as the welfare provisions that characterize these states are slashed? The *welfare convergence thesis* expects that government welfare policy choices will be constrained by the demands of global capital and global competition. Governments will be forced to abandon policies that are not favoured by investors and financial markets, policies such as nationalization of industries, redistribution of income, and spending on social welfare programmes, especially if such spending is seen as inflationary. For example, Geyer predicts:

> Despite varying national contexts and the policies of differing political parties, the welfare states of the advanced industrial countries should become increasingly similar as the forces of globalization squeeze them into a market-oriented welfare-state model. In essence it does not matter whether the national institutional contexts are conservative or social democratic, if the welfare state is conservative, liberal or social democratic, or if a leftist or rightist party is in power, the constraints have become so extreme that only market-conforming welfare-state structures will be allowed. (Geyer, 1998: 77)

While fears about the demise of the welfare state have been prevalent, research from the Varieties of Capitalism literature has marshalled evidence refuting the claim that globalization will spell the end of the generous welfare state (Mosley, 2000; Hall and Soskice, 2001; Adserà and Boix, 2002; Pontusson, 2005; Swank, 2005). Duane Swank argues that Geyer's predictions have not been realized: 'As most scholars of the welfare state readily agree, there is no evidence of systematic dismantling of national systems of social protection, nor is there evidence of significant convergence across welfare regimes' (Swank, 2005: 184).

Rather, many recent studies show that governments in social market economies are solidifying their welfare systems even in the face of stiffer global competition. Swank observes that while income replacement rates have modestly declined in most SMEs, pension benefits have remained stable and social services for the elderly, families with children, and the long-term unemployed have increased on average (Swank, 2005: 184). As market forces have increased inequality in these states, Pontusson finds that governments have countered by increasing income redistribution (Pontusson, 2005: 197). Social policy cuts and reforms do occur, but evidence suggests that they are 'at the margins'. According to Pontusson, 'They are reforms that are not major cost-cutters – shorter working hours, less generous cost-of-living adjustments for welfare benefits, etc. The most expensive programmes – healthcare, pensions – remain intact and enjoy widespread support' (Pontusson, 2005: 183). Swank concludes that after a decade of extensive research on this question by political economists, no evidence exists to show that globalization is directly impacting welfare provision (Swank, 2005).

Institutions in SMEs contribute to the consistently higher levels of public social spending in these countries as compared to their liberal counterparts. Union density is high enough in most of these economies that political parties supported by organized labour tend to do well in national elections. These parties are usually left-leaning and supportive of high government spending on pensions, unemployment benefits, disability benefits, and health coverage. In many SMEs, active labour market policies fund worker training and vocational skills to maintain a skilled workforce. Policy-makers in SMEs face markedly higher levels of political resistance to neoliberal welfare state reforms in the face of globalization pressures than do policy-makers in liberal market economies (Swank, 2005: 189). The strongest resistance may come from a citizenry that is accustomed to broad and generous social benefits, and votes accordingly, but firms in SMEs are also more likely to support high social spending than firms in LMEs because many rely on highly coordinated relations with a stable workforce trained in industry-specific skills (Hall and Soskice, 2001; Thelen, 2001). When employers have to make significant investments in worker training, as is often the case with the production of high-tech goods, it may be in the interest of the employer to maintain a stable and reliable workforce by providing employees with incentives to commit to long-term employment with the firm (Manow, 2001). Where the costs of worker training are high and/or time-intensive, employers will be more likely to accept higher labour costs to avoid frequent worker turnover. Thus, one reason why the SMEs have been able to maintain higher wages and higher levels of social spending than LMEs is that the model of production in these states, based on highly skilled labour and capital-intensive production, favours greater cooperation between employers and labour leaders and higher levels of social protection.

Another reason why social spending in SMEs has not converged downward toward the level of LME states may be that unionization rates have remained higher in SMEs. As shown in Figure 3.1, OECD data indicate that while LMEs have seen a significant decline in the percentage of wage earners that are union members, union membership in SMEs has remained remarkably stable and high, comprising close to 50 per cent of the workforce.

Several cross-national studies have also found a link between government social spending and trade openness that suggests that the domestic institutions of globalizing countries remain distinctive. David Cameron's oft-cited study of 18 advanced capitalist countries found that as national economies become more open to global trade, governments increase their tax revenue as a per-centage of GDP (by raising and adding new taxes) in order to increase their spending (Cameron, 1978). According to his analysis, the states with the most open economies – small European countries such as the Netherlands, Norway, and Denmark – tended to experience the following chain of events. Exposure to trade led the majority of domestic production and employment to become con-centrated in a few large, efficient firms. The relatively homogeneous labour force concentrated in these firms was better able to organize and form strong unions. This unionized workforce soon gained the electoral strength to repeat-edly elect leftist parties that boosted social spending and income supplements, policies long advocated by unions.

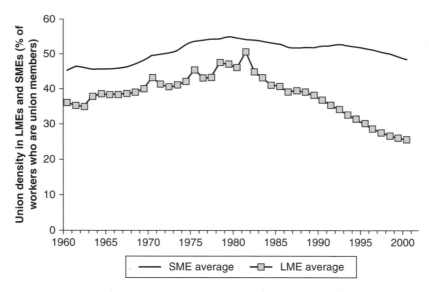

Figure 3.1   Union density rates in LMEs and SMEs, 1960–2001
Source: *OECD Factbook* 2008.

Cameron concluded that there is a causal link between openness to global trade and the size of a country's public sector that explains the expansion of social welfare policies in the highly open national economies of Europe since the 1960s. Similarly, Peter Katzenstein argues that the small, open states of Europe increase taxation and spending on social programmes and income replacement in order to compensate for the ways that globalization threatens certain domestic groups, such as unskilled workers (Katzenstein, 1985).[3] This argument has become known as the *compensation hypothesis*. These findings have been strengthened by several statistical studies based on a large number of countries in recent years that have produced similar results (Garrett, 1995, 1998; Rodrik, 1998). Garrett elaborates the argument:

> [P]erhaps the most important effect of globalization is to increase social dislocations and economic insecurity, as the distribution of incomes and jobs across firms and industries becomes increasingly unstable. The result is that increasing numbers of people have to spend ever more time and money trying to make their future more

---

[3]Torben Iversen disagrees that openness to trade and government spending are causally related. In his 2001 study, he found that the strength of trade openness as an indicator of government spending was significantly weakened when a deindustrialization variable was introduced to the model. He concludes that deindustrialization is the key variable in explaining welfare state expansion. As blue-collar industrial and agricultural jobs are lost, massive labour market displacements have shaped popular preferences for governmental social compensation and risk mediation (Iversen's chapter in Pierson's 2001 book). Critics of this argument object that trade is in fact the cause of deindustrialization.

secure. ... Given this nexus between globalization and economic insecurity, it is not surprising that government policies that cushion market dislocations by redistributing wealth and risk are at least as popular today as they have ever been. (1998: 7)

These findings are justified theoretically in the *embedded liberalism thesis* proposed originally by Karl Polanyi, and extended to the modern global economic system by John Ruggie and others (Polanyi, 1944; Ruggie, 1982; Katzenstein, 1985). The argument is that governments provide their citizens with social services to offset the job and income insecurities posed by economic openness and the global market. In this way, national policy-makers *embed* the market within the broader set of national social and political rules and cultural understandings (Caporaso and Tarrow, 2009). In practice, this means that in the SMEs, policy-makers have sought to pursue free-market strategies while also maintaining the generous welfare states that their citizens have come to expect. According to Swank, 'It may be desirable to maintain systems of ample social insurance and compensation in order to minimize socio-political volatility that can emanate from public anxiety over economic vulnerability and from realized job and income losses' (Swank, 2005: 186–7). By compensating citizens for the risks posed by global competition, national governments may be better able to make the economic reforms and adjustments necessary to be competitive.

While it remains to be seen how increased integration into the global economy will affect the welfare state in the long term, the evidence at this point does not suggest that globalization is eroding the diversity of socio-economic institutions and traditions that distinguish the advanced social market economies of Europe from their more neoliberal counterparts in the Anglo-Saxon states. As shown below in Figures 3.2 and 3.3, data from the OECD indicate that social spending as a percentage of GDP in SME states has remained fairly stable since the 1980s,

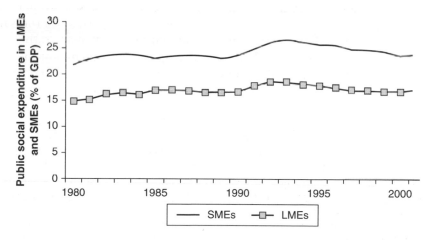

Figure 3.2   Public social expenditure as a percentage of GDP in LMEs and SMEs, 1980–2003

Source: OECD Factbook 2008, Social Expenditure Database.

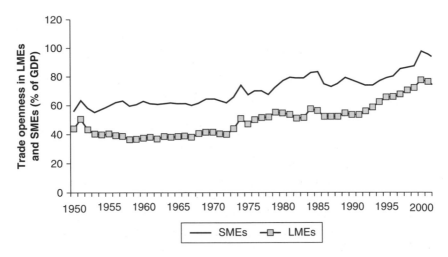

Figure 3.3   Trade openness of LMEs and SMEs, 1950–2004

Source: Penn World Tables 6.2, measured as exports plus imports as a percentage of GDP, expressed in current prices.

with some increases in the last few years, even as these countries have become more open to trade. The institutions that support the welfare state have also remained in place, such as strong unions and systems of collective bargaining.

Liberal Market Economies (LMEs)

How is globalization affecting national institutions in liberal market economies, and what has been the response from policy-makers? Research from the Varieties of Capitalism literature suggests that just as actors in social market economies respond to global economic pressures by seeking to entrench their national institutions, actors in liberal market economies (LMEs) do the same. However, because LMEs are organized around market mechanisms rather than institutionalized coordination between firms, the entrenchment of their national institutions leads to different outcomes than in SMEs. Hall and Soskice describe the dynamics of interaction between business, labour, and the government in liberal market economies:

> In the face of more intense international competition, business interests in LMEs are likely to pressure governments for deregulation, since firms that coordinate their endeavors primarily through the market can improve their competencies by sharpening its edges. The government is likely to be sympathetic because the comparative advantage of the economy as a whole rests on the effectiveness of market mechanisms. Organized labor will put up some resistance, resulting in mild forms of class conflict. But, because international liberalization enhances the exit options of firms in LMEs, as noted above, the balance of power is likely to tilt toward business. The result should be some weakening of organized labor and a substantial amount of deregulation, much as conventional views predict. (Hall and Soskice, 2001: 57)

In responding to competition from abroad and mobile capital markets, policy-makers in LMEs must increasingly deregulate and liberalize the market to reduce the cost of doing business domestically. This is because LMEs are more susceptible to the flight of firms abroad than SMEs are. While firms in SMEs require highly-skilled workers and institutionalized coordination that may not be available elsewhere, firms in LMEs often rely on cheaper labour and unfettered market structures that in some cases developing nations now provide. Hall and Soskice cite evidence that over the past few decades deregulation his indeed been widespread in liberal market economies and much more limited in social market economies (Hall and Soskice, 2001).

Furthermore, levels of unionization have fallen significantly in liberal market economies, but not in social market economies. Trade union density has stayed remarkably stable in SMEs. Union membership has dropped in LMEs as a result of deregulation and pressure by business to reduce labour costs. In the US, only 12 per cent of wage and salary workers were represented by unions in 2007. This is down from 20 per cent in 1983 (Walker, 2008: 29). Thelen (2001) argues that firms in these countries took advantage of the political shifts in the 1980s toward Thatcherism/Reaganism to successfully win more freedoms from constraining labour regulations at the plant level. One reason firms in these countries have successfully persuaded policy-makers to support deregulation strategies is the high risk of firm exit to developing countries with lower labour costs and stronger market mechanisms. This is not such a threat in SME states where specialized production in high-quality, high-tech goods requires a well-trained, stable workforce and highly developed institutions for cooperation among employers. Another reason firms in LMEs have been successful in weakening unions is due to the structure of collective bargaining in LMEs. Thelen argues that the strength of collective bargaining institutions in LMEs relies primarily on the strength of unions, since the type of employer organization that helps to underpin collective bargaining in SMEs is relatively weak in LMEs. Thus, firm efforts to achieve greater freedom and flexibility in plant-level operations bring them directly into conflict with overarching union structures. Policy-makers have been sympathetic to business because of the risk of flight abroad, and unionization levels have dropped as a result.

As shown in Figure 3.2 above, spending on social welfare in the liberal market economies has increased slightly in the past two decades, although it still remains much lower than social spending in social market economies. The rate of spending growth per capita, however, has markedly slowed, in both LMEs and SMEs (Pontusson, 2005). Generous increases in social spending are difficult in a globalized economy because as capital becomes more mobile, governments feel pressure to cut corporate tax rates to reduce the costs to firms of doing business domestically. With the reduction in tax revenues, it is more difficult for governments to sustain generous social policies. The political costs of social policy cutbacks are less acute in LMEs than in SMEs because of the more wide-ranging exit options available to firms. Resistance to cuts in social policy will come from labour and left-leaning political parties, but the government may be more sympathetic to business in LMEs to prevent them from sending jobs offshore. Swank argues that while there is no systematic evidence of trade openness forcing cuts in social welfare provisions in SMEs, as discussed above, there is some evidence of trade openness leading to certain reductions in LMEs, specifically in unemployment benefits and active labour market policies (Swank, 2005).

If there is no conclusive evidence that globalization is causing systematic and wide-ranging social policy cutbacks in LME states, then what explains the strains on the welfare state, deregulation, and de-unionization in these economies in recent decades? Many scholars are now focusing on domestic sources of welfare retrenchment pressures, both in social market and liberal market economies. Paul Pierson argues that four major 'post-industrial' changes in the world's wealthy democracies have put major strains on their welfare states (Pierson, 2001). First, economic growth has slowed in these economies as productivity has slowed with the move away from manufacturing to service-based economies. Second, there also comes a time when large, generous welfare states such as some of those in the SME states simply don't need to grow anymore, or when it becomes politically impossible to raise taxes enough to finance further growth. Third, the populations of the advanced capitalist democracies have been ageing rapidly, as a result of both lower birth rates and people living longer lives. A larger elderly population strains the welfare state through its demands on pension and healthcare spending. Finally, changes in traditional household structures have put pressure on the welfare state. As women have entered the workforce, demands have risen for state-sponsored child care and maternity leave. The number of single-parent households has also risen dramatically, and these households are at a much greater risk of poverty and dependency on social services than the traditional two-parent households.

In sum, social welfare provisions in both social market and liberal market economies have been under pressure, especially in liberal market economies, but the conventional wisdom that blames social policy cutbacks on globalization has not thus far been conclusively proven empirically. There are some advanced capitalist states, however, that don't fit nicely into either the social market or the liberal market categories described above. These states may contain some characteristics of both types of economies, and their strategies for managing globalization pressures may deviate from some of the patterns we have described above. In the next section, we will examine in greater depth the case of one such state: France.

France

France is perhaps the most paradoxical country regarding its position on globalization. On the one hand, France is home to José Bové and his anti-globalization supporters. Bové is famous for attacking a McDonald's in southern France as well as writing *Le Monde N'est Pas une Marchandise* (*The World is Not for Sale*). France is also headquarters for ATTAC (Association pour la Taxation des Transactions financière et l'Aide aux Citoyens), which as Meunier notes, is an organization whose goal is to promote the 'Tobin tax' on international financial transactions (Meunier, 2003: 20). France defends its cultural exception in world trade negotiations, subsidizes domestic film makers and French cinema, and talks often of 'civilizing', 'mastering', or 'humanizing' the market. The market as an institution does not have the same mystique as in the US and UK and the state is recognized as playing an important role in French society. As Meunier puts it, 'criticizing globalization "sells" in France' (Meunier, 2003: 20).

At the same time, France adjusts extremely well to globalization, and successive governments have adopted neoliberal measures such as privatizing firms, decreasing sectoral intervention and price controls, and adopting a monetary policy more closely aligned with monetarism than Keynesianism. While France's image may be one of extensive state control of the economy, France is actually quite open to both imports and foreign direct investment.

The interesting question is how to account for the duality within popular attitudes toward globalization and as well as state policies. One answer is that in France both elites and the populace at large are fundamentally ambivalent, admiring *dirigisme* and a strong French state as well as the benefits of globalization. In short, France is ideologically Ricardian, accepting the market and comparative advantage, as well as Colbertian, admiring a strong state (even a mercantilist one) for its ability to shape the French position in the global economy and to produce public goods where the market fails. As Meunier puts it, 'different cocktails of pro and anti globalization coexist within most French people' (Meunier, 2003: 33). To summarize, an irresistible force (globalization) meets an immovable object (French admiration of their state), and the outcome is similar to that described by Stephen Krasner (1999) in his book *Sovereignty: Organized Hypocrisy*. Krasner argues that the defence of sovereignty is doomed to be hypocritical since it pits two strong forces against one another. States want to be free to exercise exclusive authority within a territory at the same time that they find it convenient to intervene in the affairs of other states when it is in their interests to do so. The result is that states behave in inconsistent ways, and norms that are in one sense widely shared are habitually violated.

A second answer, given by Vivien Schmidt (2007), is that the disconnection between practical policies toward globalization and the anti-globalization rhetoric has to do with the failure of French policy-making elites to develop a viable discourse of globalization. In a sense, French elites are 'rhetorically entrapped' (Schimmelfennig, 2001). They are forced by the logic of globalization to adapt to global economic pressures but are hard put to express what they are doing in neoliberal terms to a sceptical public. Electoral pressures dictate anti-globalization rhetoric, since this places blame on the 'outside world' for job insecurity, fears about retirement, immigration, and cultural identity without endangering the wealth and standard of living aided by ties to the global system. As Vivien Schmidt argues, 'French elites seem trapped in the old discourse, unable to develop new ideas capable of legitimating France in Europe and the world' (Schmidt, 2007: 992).

While France's role in globalization is ambivalent, the French state has nevertheless had to adapt to European and global pressures. Yet, France is among those advanced capitalist economies that do not fit well into either the liberal market or social market economic categories. Prior to the late 1980s and 1990s, France's political economy fit what analysts call the statist model (Katzenstein, 1985; Culpepper, 2006). Statist economies differ from social market and liberal market economies because of the greater involvement of the state in the structure and functioning of the national economy, not only at the macro level but at the sectoral and firm levels as well. Thus, state ownership of firms, price controls, and allocation of credit were all characteristic of state-economy relations until the 1980s. In social market economies, economic actors coordinate around institutionalized systems of collective bargaining among employers, labour, and the government. Liberal market economies are sometimes referred to as uncoordinated market economies (Huber and Stephens, 2001), but in actuality coordination occurs around market transactions. Economic actors in these economies coordinate around market mechanisms rather than through long-term, trust-based relations between employers and workers. Statist economies, in contrast, are characterized by high levels of government influence over corporate governance and finance, industrial relations, and education and skills training. Economic actors look to the state to resolve coordination problems that arise in these areas, such as bargaining over wages and working conditions, providing vocational education for workers, and ensuring firm access to finance and technology.

The French system fitted this statist model of political economy until the mid-1980s. The socialist government of François Mitterrand had failed in its *dirigiste* efforts to relieve France from the economic stagnation it had suffered since the oil crisis of the early 1970s. Under pressure from the European Union to open France to greater market competition, Mitterrand began a process of market-led modernization that began to reduce the state's direct control over the economy (Hall, 2006: 6–7). Since this time, firms and labour have been freer to determine the strategies they will pursue, but they have struggled to coordinate their action either around market mechanisms, as in liberal market economies, or around institutionalized collective bargaining, as in social market economies. The legacy of *dirigisme* in France – the French state's highly interventionist role in directing the national economy – was to create a strong popular distaste for the free market while allowing business and labour organizations to remain relatively weak and disorganized, leaving the French political economy in a category all its own.

In France today, the political economy can be characterized by its lack of an organizing principle around which economic actors can coordinate (Culpepper,

2006: 46). Statism has fallen by the wayside but another coherent system based on the interests of French firms has failed to replace it. This is a gap that is experienced in both institutional and discursive (ideological) terms. First, France cannot be considered a liberal market economy. While finance and corporate governance have been significantly liberalized through broad privatization and firm-led changes to financial markets, the government still wields significant control over firms, as in the passage of a mandatory 35-hour work week for all workers. Furthermore, France continues to maintain a large and expensive welfare state of the type eschewed by liberal market economies, which instead attempt to shift responsibility for social welfare into private hands.

However, it is also inaccurate to describe France as a social market economy. In industrial relations, the weaknesses of French unions under *dirigisme* led to the emergence of uncoordinated firm-level negotiations over wages. Unions remain ill-equipped to assist their members in firm-level employment negotiations. In the areas of education and skills training, French employers' associations and trade unions have failed to provide information about and funding for the specific types of skills development training that they prefer, as the social partners do in Germany. Thus, large firms have assumed a greater role determining the direction of French vocational education, by working with the state to provide the firm-specific vocational training their production needs require (Culpepper, 2006).

What forces are responsible for the decline of the state-led political economy in France? Have the dramatic moves in France toward market liberalization been primarily a result of external or internal forces? While all the advanced capitalist economies have been forced to adjust to a new international climate of greater capital mobility and cross-border trade, it is important to attempt to identify the specific causal mechanisms that have driven change in these countries. While the conventional argument blames globalization for the new condition of 'permanent austerity' that countries face, some analysts question whether the sources of change are actually internal in nature. Hall observes that France has been subject to the same domestic demographic shifts – population ageing, women's entrance into the work force, declining birth rates – that have put fiscal stress on the welfare state in all the other advanced capitalist countries (Hall, 2006). France has also certainly been subject to the same global economic pressures that limit national autonomy over taxation, regulatory practices, and social spending.

The French U-turn from Keynesianism (which implied high domestic spending as well as capital controls) to neoliberalism represents a dramatic policy change. Mitterrand was elected President of France on the Socialist Party platform in 1981 and started to carry out its policies of reflation soon after. However, while capital was not fully mobile in legal terms in 1981, financial markets did not look kindly on the inflationary consequences of high government spending. Despite repeated attempts by Mitterrand to limit the outflow of capital on several occasions in the early 1980s (Abdelal, 2007: 58), capital continued to exit the country. Neither capital controls nor currency devaluations were able to prevent this and by the spring of 1983, Mitterrand and the French socialist government reversed course.[4] Hall argues that this 'Great U-Turn' in France away from socialism and toward market liberalization was a result of a choice by the Mitterrand administration to continue the process of European integration (Hall, 2006). France joined the European Monetary System (EMS) in 1978, which pegged the currencies of the European Community together in the hopes that greater exchange rate stability among these currencies would boost trade and investment in the common market. However, Mitterrand's expansionary policies pulled the French Franc down relative to the German Mark. If France wanted to stay in the EMS, the administration would have to cut its budget significantly and allow further opening of French markets to competition from European companies, and this is exactly what Mitterrand's 'Great U-Turn' accomplished. Thus, France's moves toward more neoliberal economic policies in the 1980s, with their attendant cuts in the social benefits central to the French welfare state, can be interpreted more as an affirmation of the European integration project than of a desire to prepare France for competition in a globalized world. Of course, one could argue that the neoliberal policies promoted by the EU were themselves a result of the desire to compete in the global economy. The demands that European integration imposed on the French government in the 1980s may have been the direct drivers of neoliberal reform in France, while globalization provided the context for the EU's policy goals.

How have French political institutions affected France's ability to adjust to the demands of market liberalization and global competition? Perhaps even more important than party configuration in France has been the refusal of French politicians from any party to convince the public of the ways that full entry into a liberal, globalized economy can be beneficial. Political parties in France have instead sought to demonize globalization, using it as a scapegoat for social policy reforms that are highly unpopular (Smith, 2004: 65; Hall, 2006: 19). Rather than embracing market liberalization as an inherent good, as the Thatcherites did in the UK and the Reaganites did in the US, French politicians have continually portrayed globalization and market liberalization as a force against which the French public must be defended. In a strange reversal of form, Monica Prasad argues that the neoliberal turn in the UK and US was principled (or ideological) while the French embraced neoliberalism pragmatically (Prasad, 2006: 236). Perhaps because neoliberal ideology has often been demonized in French political discourse, it has been more difficult for French politicians to push through much-needed fiscal and social policy reforms in times of austerity than it has been for policy-makers in other European welfare states.

The weakness of collective bargaining in France has also been a key institutional feature affecting the direction of French economic adjustment in the past few decades. Swank argues that where institutions of collective interest

---

[4]For an excellent account of the pressures leading to the turnaround, as well as the turnaround itself, see Rawi Abdelal, *Capital Rules*, 2007. Cambridge, MA: Harvard University Press, ch. 4.

representation are strong, the effects of fiscal stress and international capital mobility should be neutral or even supportive of social policy (Swank, 2001). In France, employers' associations and trade unions are weak, and the demands of global economic competition have indeed placed serious fiscal stress on the French welfare state. While one would expect that in this environment it would be easy for business to successfully lobby for the adoption of social policy reforms and the retrenchment of the welfare state, French political parties have been exceedingly reluctant to acquiesce on this front. If French politicians do not develop a serious centrist reform effort of the expensive welfare state, and if economic actors do not begin to coordinate themselves around clear mechanisms – whether these are market mechanisms or collective bargaining institutions – France may well face a political economic crisis as internal demographic pressures and external economic competition pressures continue to increase.

To conclude this section, the Varieties of Capitalism research programme is useful for helping us understand different national responses to globalization in the advanced capitalist countries. As discussed above, evidence suggests that institutional differences in these countries persist and lead to divergent policies rather than convergence, as often predicted. We saw that in social market economies, strong labour institutions persist in the face of global economic pressures, as do collective action mechanisms among firms as well as government-sponsored social provisions and protections. Governments have strengthened social welfare institutions in these countries as they have opened themselves to trade, and cuts that have been made have tended to be made at the margins. In liberal market economies, by contrast, we have seen some evidence that globalization leads to the kinds of weakening of labour institutions and deregulation that many have feared. Whether this is caused by globalization or by some other process such as demographic changes, is still a matter for debate. In short, there is no clear evidence of convergence of domestic socio-economic institutions across the advanced capitalist countries as they open their markets and borders to global trade.

Responses to Globalization in Developing Countries

How do governments in developing countries respond to globalization? On the whole, does globalization affect institutions in these countries according to the same patterns we have seen in some of the developed countries, or is the situation fundamentally different? First we must justify why we believe developing countries are conceptually different from developed countries and why they merit a separate analysis. One reason we believe they are different is that institutional weaknesses in many developing countries prevent them from successfully managing change in the global economy. Strong and entrenched political and socio-economic institutions in developed countries, such as the free market, the democratic process, labour institutions, political parties, systems of production, worker training and education, and coordination among firms, have all been important factors in the ability of these states to successfully manage global economic pressures while pursuing their unique national goals (of equality, efficiency, or political stability for example) and maintaining their own distinct socio-economic policies. Developing countries are plagued by institutional and economic weaknesses that are visible through low levels of per capita income, low economic growth, widespread poverty, dysfunctional governments, weak social programmes, and outdated technology. These problems severely constrain the ability of governments in developing countries to confront change in the global economy.

Another reason that developing countries are conceptually different from developed countries is that they are heavily dependent on loans from wealthy governments and international financial institutions such as the International Monetary Fund and the World Bank. Indebted governments then find themselves locked in a position where they must devote a significant percentage of already scarce resources to loan repayments. This reduces the amount of funding they can devote to institution building and human capital development, keys to developing stable political and economic systems as well as coping with globalization. In addition, loans from abroad are frequently tied to conditionalities imposed by the lending country or organization. These conditions may include measures such as liberalization of a country's markets to foreign trade, privatization, fiscal austerity, reduced taxation, and stabilization of the currency. Conditions such as these, imposed by foreigners, which limit government autonomy over domestic policies, put developing countries in a weak bargaining position when it comes to their ability to respond to changes in the global economy. The range of possible actions and policies is severely constrained because of the risk of loan default.

Third, the way developing countries are integrated in the global economy may have different implications for government policy compared to the developed world. Many developing countries, such as China and the other East Asian economies, are heavily dependent on exports to the developed world to achieve economic growth, making their economies highly volatile. When spending is down in the developed world – such as during global financial crises – developing economies take a hard hit as well. Because of their heavy reliance on exports, and their dependence on financing from the developed world, developing countries may be in a more precarious position in the competitive global economy (Rudra and Haggard, 2005). In order to protect the tradable sectors, many governments will pursue policies during economic downturns that are quite different from those pursued in the developed world. While wealthy OECD countries increase social spending to stimulate their economies, developing countries often slash it under pressure from actors involved in the tradable sectors, who prefer to keep taxes low (Wibbels, 2006). Furthermore, developing country governments are unlikely to be able to borrow heavily from international markets to finance social spending, as many are already highly indebted, and they are also unlikely to have large stores of surplus capital available. Thus, in times of crises and in times of economic adjustment or income shocks that result from increased integration into global markets, developing countries are unlikely to have the same ability to compensate society through increased social spending, as developed countries can and do.

In the context of weak institutions, compromised autonomy over socio-economic policy decisions, and a high dependence on trade with the developed world, how do developing countries act to maximize the benefits and minimize the costs of globalization on their publics and economies? In the realm of social policy, we saw that in developed countries, government spending on social programmes has tended to increase with globalization, as governments seek to compensate domestic groups for the insecurities posed by mobile capital. In developing countries, however, the situation appears to be quite different. As shown in Figure 3.4, the average share of GDP allocated to social spending in developing countries has fallen over the past thirty years and continues to fall.

Although some studies suggest that the compensation hypothesis holds even in the developing world – citing evidence that government spending increases with trade openness – these studies tend to look at aggregate government spending, rather than social spending specifically (Rodrik, 1998; Garrett, 2001). In contrast, numerous other studies conclude that the 'race to the bottom' effect feared by many of globalization's opponents does in fact characterize social policy in the developing world, if not in the developed world. These studies tend to make distinctions between different types of

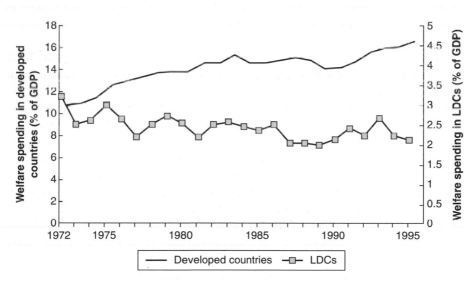

Figure 3.4   Welfare spending trends in developed and developing countries

Source: Rudra, 2002. Data from IMF, International Financial Statistics, and Government Finance Statistics, various years.

economic integration and different types of government spending (Avelino, Brown, and Hunter, 2005). As trade increases, studies suggest that governments in the developing world have cut social spending, especially in the areas of pensions and unemployment benefits (Kaufman and Segura-Ubiergo, 2001; Rudra, 2002). Some conclude that capital openness also has a negative relationship with social spending in the developing world (Quinn, 1997; Rodrik, 1998) though others dispute this finding (Garrett, 2001). Kaufman and Segura-Ubiergo (2001) find that the negative effects of trade on social spending are compounded as capital accounts are liberalized.

In their study of Latin American countries, Kaufman and Segura-Ubiergo (2001) emphasize the importance of distinguishing among types of social spending. Their conclusions suggest that globalization does not constrain all types of spending equally, perhaps because different types of social spending are guided by different political logics. They found a strong negative relationship between trade openness and social security transfer spending. This may be because social security transfers are often financed through payroll taxes, which directly affect the cost of labour. Thus, business groups are likely to lobby hard against this type of spending. However, they did not find strong evidence that globalization leads to cuts in spending on healthcare and education. In fact, capital liberalization was associated with increases in health and education spending. This may be because it would be much more politically costly for governments to cut programmes that reach a much larger swath of the public than do social security transfers such as pensions. Business may also view health and education programmes as important human capital investments that don't directly drive up the costs of labour. Additionally, these findings may support the argument made by others about the importance of strong labour institutions. Without strong institutions for collective action and negotiation with government and firms, like those that exist in developed economies, workers in emerging economies may find that governments have fewer incentives for maintaining generous pension funds than funding for education and healthcare.

Why do we observe different responses to globalization in developed and developing countries, at least in terms of social spending trends? Many analyses point to the importance of domestic institutions. As discussed above, scholars have found labour institutions to be an important factor in the maintenance and growth of the welfare state in the advanced capitalist economies, whether they are of the social market or liberal market variety. Rudra (2002) argues that workers in developing countries are less capable of organizing to defend social programmes than their counterparts in developed countries for several reasons. First, the high numbers of low-skilled workers face significant collective action problems because many people remain unemployed and ready to work. This puts workers in a weak bargaining position with employers. Second, there are generally not strong national labour institutions in developing countries that can negotiate with governments and firms on behalf of workers.

Furthermore, most developing countries lack the democratic institutions through which workers in developed countries can gain representation in government. Several studies suggest that in the developing world, democracy is strongly associated with social spending (Adserà and Boix, 2002; Avelino, Brown, and Hunter, 2005; Rudra and Haggard, 2005). These studies find that democracies spend more than autocracies, perhaps because democratically elected leaders have greater incentives to respond to calls for social programmes that can protect workers from economic instability. Adserà and Boix argue that when political participation is restricted, powerful economic actors in the tradable sectors will benefit from openness while those most hurt by it will not have the political clout to lobby for compensation. Thus, more autocratic governments should be able to reap the benefits of increased trade without paying for compensation of groups that lose out. Adserà and Boix show that in free-trading authoritarian regimes in East Asia, the public sector is smaller than in democratic countries, with similar levels of economic integration.

While labour institutions are generally weak in the developing world, how have they been affected by globalization? Has openness further weakened the power of unions and collective bargaining mechanisms? In the developed world, most research suggests that globalization has weakened the power of left-labour movements, though Garrett (1998) is a notable dissenter, arguing that in many of these countries, labour's power has increased with openness. Given the need of most developing countries to attract international capital, one might predict that market reforms in these countries would weaken the power of organized labour and left-leaning political parties. This has largely been the case. Capital is much more mobile than workers, and factory owners can close up shop and move production elsewhere if labour costs increase (Kaufman and Segura-Ubiergo, 2001). Wibbels and Arce (2003) describe the process in Latin America whereby the move from import substitution-based economies to market economies led to high levels of unemployment which in turn weakened unions. At the same time, these market reforms strengthened collective action mechanisms within the business community, which has enjoyed a stronger bargaining position with government. In developing countries where labour institutions are weak in the first place, low-skilled workers are unlikely ever to unionize if they want to keep their jobs in a competitive global market (Rudra, 2002). Although labour institutions have survived in the developed economies through support from domestic political coalitions, the need for developing-country governments to send pro-market signals to their foreign lenders and to foreign firms renders it far more difficult for organized labour to maintain the political support it needs to remain strong and effective. Finally, the way developing countries integrate into the global economy may have different implications for labour institutions. Mosley and Uno (2007) show that foreign direct investment tends to generate a 'race to the top' for collective labour rights in developing countries as good labour practices are transferred from developed-country corporations to their factories in the developing world. On the other hand, trade appears to contribute to the expected 'race to the bottom' scenario, as local owners of capital in developing countries seek to continually reduce labour costs in order to compete in global markets.

In addition to social spending, taxation is another policy area where government choice may be constrained by globalization pressures. As capital becomes mobile, governments feel pressure to reduce corporate taxation in order to prevent firms from relocating to other countries with lower tax rates. When corporate tax rates are cut the taxation burden must be shifted onto labour. Recent research suggests that in developed countries taxes on capital have indeed declined sharply, while taxes on labour have increased (Rodrik, 1997a; Garrett, 1998). Is fiscal policy in the developing world converging with fiscal policy in the developed world, and is globalization the cause of this process? Wibbels and Arce conclude from their study of Latin American countries that the evidence is mixed that globalization is constraining government tax policy in developing countries. The most significant indicator of globalization, trade, did not have a significant impact on the ratio of corporate to labour tax. Rather, they argue, 'Political leaders still retain a degree of autonomy to respond to these forces – albeit less autonomy than their counterparts in advanced industrial countries' (Wibbels and Arce, 2003: 130). While the dependence of developing countries on international financial institutions does require them to keep their policy decisions in line with the tenets of neoliberal economics and to generally keep corporate tax levels low, Wibbels and Arce argue that governments nevertheless retain a good degree of freedom to develop their own distinctive tax systems.

Another subject of much scholarly debate is the effect that globalization has on democracy in the developing world. The conventional wisdom of the day, also known as the 'Washington Consensus', maintains that as countries liberalize their economies, democratization is likely to follow. This may happen because governments must improve transparency and rule of law to attract international investors (Maxfield, 2000). Economic integration may also spur democratization as economic changes cause conflict among the ruling elites and the formation of new economic and political interests (Haggard and Kaufman, 1992; Keohane and Milner, 1996). There is also an argument to be made that globalization allows democratic ideas to diffuse to the developing world, enhancing political competition. Indonesia appears to be a case where integration with the global economy (and the Asian financial crisis) paved the way for a successful popular challenge to Suharto's rule and the institutionalization of democratic reforms. On the other hand, in China the economic liberalization of the past decades and booming economic growth have yet to weaken the powerful grip of the authoritarian Communist Party. Many scholars see the Chinese case and many others as evidence that the story is not so simple, and that the effects of globalization on democracy in the developing world are contingent upon the type of economic liberalization a country experiences as well as domestic conditions. Rudra argues that when elites provide a 'social safety net' to their publics, to cushion them from instability and insecurity as the economy liberalizes, they are more likely to retain political power and as a result, they are more likely to make some democratic concessions (Rudra, 2005). In other words, elites can use social spending as a way to gain favour with the masses who are then more likely to support them in a democratic election. Przeworski's work on democratization suggests another qualifier: globalization may strengthen democratization only if countries have achieved a certain level of economic development. In countries with per capita incomes of less than $6,500, democracy is likely to be fragile and unstable no matter what other variables (such as globalization) are at play (Przeworski et al., 2000). Eichengreen and Leblang (2008) find that globalization has a positive relationship with democracy, running in both directions. Globalization is found to strengthen democracy, but democracy is also found to increase the likelihood that governments will make liberalizing economic reforms. The work on the relationship between globalization and democracy illustrates the need to consider that a host of variables – both international and domestic – are responsible for the policy changes we observe as developing countries join the global economy.

Conclusion

This chapter has considered the ways that globalization affects domestic political economies, with reference to one of the major debates in the literature concerning globalization: whether we are witnessing a 'race to the bottom' of domestic policy-making across countries. This debate about how countries respond to the seemingly homogenizing impulses of the global economy remains a fruitful avenue for research, as more and more data become available for the countries beyond just the wealthy industrialized economies of the global North. In these advanced capitalist economies, it is worthwhile to restate our argument here that national capitalist institutions remain quite distinct even in the face of pressures to be competitive in the global economy. Firms and institutions are not the same across all countries, even within close-knit regions such as Western Europe, and they do not react the same way to similar challenges. Instead of converging to a single 'best practice' economic model, scholars find that national capitalist economies are strengthening their institutions in ways that serve their unique national comparative economic and institutional advantages. In the coordinated, social market economies of Europe, this means that firms will be more supportive of social policies such as health, social security, education and labour protections because of their reliance on a highly skilled, stable workforce. In liberal market economies such as those of North America and Oceania, governments often face greater pressure from business interests for deregulation, since this strengthens the market mechanisms around which firms in LMEs are organized. Without this deregulation, firms in LMEs are more likely to relocate abroad than are firms in SMEs, because they face competition from developing countries that also offer largely deregulated markets and cheaper labour. While social spending is much less generous in the liberal market economies than in social market economies, at this stage in the game it appears that the compensation hypothesis holds across the developed world. In the developing world, however, we see more evidence that a 'race to the bottom' is taking place in some policy areas. Policy decisions in these countries are generally constrained by debt institutional weaknesses, and reliance on the advanced industrialized world for much-needed financial assistance.

Developed countries have been successful in managing global economic change while also protecting their distinctive domestic institutions, but developing countries have not been able to enjoy such levels of autonomy. Social spending as a percentage of GDP continues to fall across the developing world as globalization has increased, especially in the areas of social security transfers. Globalization also appears to impede the development of the types of strong unions and other labour institutions that have been so central to the maintenance of social and labour protections in the developed world, at the same time that trade has been linked to worsening labour rights. But the news isn't all bad. Recent work suggests that developing-country governments may be making more investments in human capital through education and health spending, investments that may raise productivity without directly driving up labour costs. Certain forms of global production, such as foreign direct investment, may actually strengthen labour rights and policies in the global South. And contrary to what many experts have expected, recent work on fiscal policy shows no evidence that increased trade and capital openness are shifting the burden of taxation from capital to workers in the developing world. Finally, a large body of work suggests that globalization has positive consequences for democracy. It is important to remember, however, that domestic politics matters as well. The political economic changes we observe in both the developed and developing worlds are not only the result of integration with the global economy; they also stem from the domestic political institutions and histories in these countries. The political parties that govern make a difference in the types of policies that governments adopt, as do the strength of democratic institutions and workers' rights institutions. It is often the interaction of globalization pressures and domestic political realities that determines the ways that governments respond to the competitive global environment.

4 GLOBALIZATION AND GOVERNANCE

In this chapter, we focus on the regulation and governance of global economic, social, and cultural processes. Consistent with our overall approach, we see globalization as constituted by political decisions in the first place. Free trade, open capital borders, migration, and the internationalization of the entertainment industry, where they exist, all resulted from explicit political decisions. In short, globalization is not the result of blind and uncontrolled technological forces; quite the opposite – globalization is endogenous to politics. Second, once in place, globalization is not a self-regulating process. Markets at the global level can become imbalanced just as they can at the national level. They can suffer from insufficient demand, under- or over-investment, trade imbalances, excessive debt, currency speculation, fraud, tax dodging, and many other problems that may need political regulation. There is nothing qualitatively different between national and global operation of markets. Both require politics as a precondition for their existence and continued operation.

As globalization generates interdependence among countries and people that once had little contact with each other, the question arises: who (if anyone) is in charge of the process? Who coordinates relationships among states and non-state actors? The market economy is a coordinating device but even at the local level it is not self-regulating. Who solves problems that affect multiple countries, perhaps on multiple continents? Who regulates global commerce and manages interstate conflicts? The globalization of economies, military threats, transnational migration, and environmental problems requires governance. Yet, in an international system that remains largely anarchic, in the sense that it lacks centralized political institutions, national governments agree neither upon the extent to which, nor the means by which, governance of international processes should develop.

The present global system presents itself as one in which an 'irresistible force' (globalization) meets an 'immovable object' (the state system). Something has to give but it isn't clear what the outcome will be. The nation-state has been around for a long time, since 1648 and the Peace of Westphalia. While characteristics of the Westphalian state (territorial control, exclusive domestic authority, sovereignty) have often been exaggerated, this form of political organization has dominated the landscape of the world for the last three-and-a-half centuries. Will nation-state governments retain their positions of primacy in international affairs and will Westphalian state forms transform and migrate to the regional and global levels? Could other actors or institutions more efficiently perform some of the functions currently performed by national governments? Will the nation-state start to cede sovereignty to regional and global organizations, and in doing so, will we see not only a shift to a new locus of authority, but also a qualitative transformation of sovereignty?

Scholars and policy-makers alike have proposed numerous possibilities over the years. Some ideas have become reality: Woodrow Wilson's brainchild, the League of Nations, was the first comprehensive attempt to institutionalize relations between states through the creation of a global organization aimed at preventing international aggression. Though the League failed in its mission and dissolved with the onset of World War II, many other institutional arrangements have been created at the global and regional levels to govern relations between states and prevent conflicts, whether military or economic. The United Nations, the World Trade Organization, the North Atlantic Treaty Organization, and regional economic organizations such as the European Union, NAFTA, MERCOSUR, and ASEAN are all attempts at coordinating relations among states, in very different ways and with varying degrees of success. At the same time, non-state transnational actors have also organized around distinct issue areas such as trade and the environment to better coordinate relations at the global level. For example, private commercial actors have developed an efficient system of private rules and regulations known as the *Lex Mercatoria* to overcome cooperation and commitment problems at the transnational level, reduce the transaction costs of commerce at long-distances, and design a standardized system of rules to govern this cross-border activity. International advocacy organizations such as the World Wide Fund for Nature, Greenpeace, and Human Rights Watch seek to influence national and international laws governing specific social issues, and they have sometimes been very successful in impacting global environmental and human rights norms in areas such as women's rights, the antislavery movement, and environmental conservation.

To anticipate the rest of the chapter, we summarize our argument about the likelihood and forms of global government. Global government has often been treated as a normative issue, as a necessary (and desirable) phase in human social evolution (from tribe, to city-state, to Empire, to nation-state, to global state), and ultimately as a practical realization of an ethical community at the global level.[1] Global government has also been thought of as the inevitable

---

[1] By 'ethical community' we mean a community of shared aims, including the sharing of resources, wealth, and common burdens.

result of the playing-out of functional pressures, the rise of interdependence, and the growth of interconnections among people across borders, etc. Additionally, we should bear in mind that international and transnational government, both regional and global, can be created as an expression of force. One set of countries, or classes, or religious groups may become ascendant and impose its will on the others.

We believe that all three forces – values, interests, and power – contribute to pressures for global government. It is a mistake to choose only one of these three factors, not only because they are all important in their own right, but also because they interact with one another in synergistic ways, so that the whole is more than the sum of its parts. Values and ideas have economic underpinnings; interests are shallow if not tethered to important values, and adding power to any constellation of interests and values can alter outcomes in dramatic ways.

Finally, we argue that it is important to keep an open mind about the forms of global governance. In particular, we warn against looking exclusively for forms of global governance that mirror the political institutions surrounding the rise of the nation-state, e.g. centralized, hierarchical, exclusive authority structures. There are other candidates for global political organization, such as firm-to-firm politics, sector-to-sector arrangements (e.g. rules for automobiles, pharmaceuticals, etc.), hierarchical regional and global organizations, and highly decentralized, almost voluntary arrangements among actors at many different levels.

The Case for Global Governance

The history of international relations may provide the strongest argument for global governance. Humans have resorted to violence to deal with conflicts since the dawn of time. Tribes and ethnic groups fought each other over land and resources, ancient peoples formed armies for the same reasons, and even today, nearly every state in the world relies on a national military to feel secure. While violence between states still persists, economic interdependence gives states another mechanism through which to coerce other states: economic threats and promises. States can alter trade with other countries in ways that prove devastating to domestic industries and citizens in those countries, or states can reward other states for desired behaviour by conferring privileged trading status upon them.

The modern system of states is organized around the principle of national sovereignty. States are the foremost units of political authority in this system, and relations among them are largely anarchic in that there is no overarching governmental authority regulating their interactions with enforceable rules. In this anarchic international system, states are free to do as they wish to advance their domestic interests subject to the constraints that are posed by the existence of others. That is, it is important to remember that 'freedom under anarchy' means legal freedom to act according to the processes (and laws) of each state concerned. Each country's freedom to do as it wants is limited by the ways its actions affect others and the way in which others respond. Country A is free to raise its tariffs toward the goods of country B but B may respond with a retaliatory tariff. If states were completely isolated from each other, there would be no need for global governance. Each state would essentially be an island: it would go about its domestic business without any contact – either positive or negative – with the outside world. Some countries have experimented with radical forms of national self-sufficiency (the People's Republic of China, Burma, and Albania), but these experiments have eventually been abandoned because of the huge costs of autarchy. Obviously, a world of isolated states could not be further from reality in this day and age. Countries today are so interdependent that a recession in one can set off recessions in others all over the globe. Disturbances within the financial system of one country can quickly spread to others, as we know only too well because of the current financial crisis. Pollution from one state can travel via air or water to degrade the environment of its neighbours. Domestic unrest and poor governance can trigger flows of refugees to other countries.

In addition to isolation, there is another situation in which global governance would not be necessary, and that is if states could coexist in perfect harmony. Robert Keohane argues that one of three outcomes will result from transnational processes: harmony, cooperation, or discord (1984: 51). He defines harmony in this context as a situation in which one state's policies automatically advance another state's goals; they are mutually beneficial. He cites the invisible hand as the classic example of harmony: in the free market, as each economic actor pursues her own self-interest, the interests of all others are advanced as well. Discord is a situation in which a state's pursuit of its self-interest detracts from the interest of another state, such as when a state's lax regulations on industry create water pollution that travels downstream to degrade water quality in a neighbouring country. As one state gains, the other state loses. At best, discord can inspire cooperative behaviour (such as reduction of trade barriers or negotiations to avoid war), and at worst, it can lead to conflict (such as trade wars or violence). Cooperation is not required in instances of harmony since states are already benefitting from their contact. However, in instances of potential discord cooperation may be required to make outcomes acceptable to the parties concerned. Cooperation, according to Keohane, occurs when actors 'adjust their behaviour to the actual or anticipated preferences of others, through a process of policy coordination' (1984: 51). Policy coordination can happen through negotiation between national governments but it can also take place among other agents such as firms, NGOs, and labour unions.

If states existed in perfect isolation from each other, or if all interaction were perfectly harmonious, there would be no discord. There would also be no need for cooperation, and hence, no need for rules and structures to facilitate cooperation and govern relations between states. Our world is highly interdependent, however, and liberals argue that the key to achieving cooperation rather than discord between national governments lies in the creation of international institutions (Keohane and Nye, 1977; Keohane, 2001). Proponents of international institutions argue that they increase the potential for gains from cooperation by reducing the negative externalities that one country's policies can have in other countries. They can help self-interested national governments overcome the massive collective action problem that inhibits effective cooperation at the international level. However, many argue that the institutions currently in place are outdated and inadequate (Slaughter, 2004: 8). They were created in the 1940s when the world looked very different and faced very different challenges than it does today. To manage contemporary problems, many scholars, policy-makers, and citizens alike believe it is time to re-vamp or recreate institutions of governance.

At the same time, liberals such as Robert Keohane, Anne-Marie Slaughter, and Judith Shklar have warned about what Keohane terms the governance dilemma. institutions can foster peace and prosperity, but they can also foster exploitation and oppression (Keohane, 2001: 1). Shklar reminds us that 'no liberal ever forgets that governments are coercive' (1984: 244). How could a world state ever represent all the peoples of this diverse world? Slaughter calls this the globalization paradox. She writes, 'We need more government on a global and a regional scale, but we don't want the centralization of decision-making power and coercive authority so far from the people actually to be governed' (2004: 8). Before we discuss the possibilities of global governance, let us turn to the developments that necessitate its existence in the first place.

Global Issues and Global Solutions

The possibility for international conflict or international cooperation arises from the globalization of a wide variety of issue areas that create positive or negative externalities across borders. States have goals and interests that may be affected positively or negatively by the interests and actions of other states. At the same time, cooperation may also arise not because there is a potential conflict, but simply because there is a possibility for actors to increase gains and efficiency through a new institutional structure. For example, the EU found that the patchwork of different national pension systems in its member states was preventing workers from moving freely throughout the EU in search of work. In order to enhance labour mobility, which would increase economic efficiency, EU member states have had to coordinate elements of their national social policies such as pension schemes and eligibility for unemployment so that workers don't lose out on social benefits as a result of a move to another member state. This example shows that rules can be enabling as well as restrictive and regulative. Rules, such as property rights, may foster exchange where none existed before. A law against piracy will doubtless encourage ships to sail in waters that would have been avoided, and a law specifying food labelling requirements might encourage people from different countries to buy and sell food items that would have been looked at with distrust absent the rule. International trade is another example of an issue area where cooperation happens not because of any externalities, but because there are strong economic incentives for states to harmonize their regulatory policies in order to facilitate commerce.

Our point here is that international cooperation, as well as the institutions necessary to foster this cooperation, may be required for efficiency as well as distributive reasons. Efficiency politics has to do with achieving joint gains where none existed previously, while distributive politics has to do with who gains and who loses. Often these two processes are present within the same issue area. International trade, for example, can be seen as a process which first creates some additional value for trade partners (the gains from trade). But this very same act of exchanging goods across borders also entails a secondary activity of dividing up the gains. Both the gains from trade and the division of those gains are part of the same concrete activity of international trade.

When we define globalization broadly as 'networks of interdependence at multi-continental distances' (Keohane and Nye, 2000: 2), we are including issue areas in our analysis that expand beyond trade and economic issues that are often viewed as the central aspects of globalization. A more expansive definition of globalization encompasses cross-border movements as wide-ranging as germs, terrorism, pollution, and capital, to name just a few. As we elaborated in the introductory chapter, there are a multitude of issues that have become global in scope and may require some form of global governance and/or the creation of formal international institutions for better management. There are significant barriers to cross-border economic exchange, and national governments that want to reap the benefits of free global markets must commit themselves to the reduction of these barriers, a process that is often arduous and politically difficult. As economies of scale take the world's biggest corporations beyond the national market into international markets, regulation becomes more problematic. Furthermore, the economic specialization that can greatly increase a country's economic efficiency also creates webs of interdependence among states that could prove devastating if severed or if some countries threatened to manipulate these interdependencies for political or economic gain. To be successful and sustainable, economic specialization depends on international cooperation. Beyond the economic realm, advances in military technology have removed most geographic barriers to the use of force, and globalized transportation networks mean that non-state actors also now have greater potential to traffic weaponry across borders and execute international or transnational crimes. The mobility of labour is another important dimension of globalization. Labour mobility is important for the optimal functioning of markets, but immigration remains a highly contentious and political issue in many developed countries. Environmental problems such as climate change, the movement of pollution and disease pathogens across borders, the introduction of invasive species to non-native ecosystems, and the depletion of the ozone layer do not recognize political borders and are becoming increasingly global in scope. Terrorists and organized criminals have operated across borders for centuries, but the same advances in communication and transportation that have revolutionized global commerce have also revolutionized the ability of terrorist and criminal networks to operate across borders, threatening far-reaching points on the globe. This is just a snapshot of the types of issues governments must confront in a globalized world.

Cooperation or Conflict?

The cross-border movements described above represent varying dimensions of globalization, though they are far from an exhaustive list. What is important to understand about these movements is that they render states and peoples highly interdependent and have the opportunity to create either conflict or cooperation. Globalization in all its dimensions creates the possibility for conflict in two major ways. First, the movement of goods, capital, firms, military capabilities, pollution, people (et al.) across borders creates externalities that are massive in scale and may be highly threatening to health, safety, economic success, or national security in countries that had nothing to do with the actions and choices that created the externalities. People are stakeholders but they have no representation. Second, globalization locates important activities in a transnational sphere (e.g. the transnational market) over which national governments, acting individually, exert little to no control. Similarly, governments may lose the ability to carry out certain policies because of constraints placed upon them by the demands of global competition.

Both these processes, the growth of transnational externalities and the shift of activities to a transnational sphere over which national governments have little control, create interdependence between countries. Countries become dependent upon each other economically as trade flows increase; they depend on each other to respect each other's sovereignty and refrain from the use of military force against each other; they depend on each other to minimize environmental degradation that has a transnational impact; and they depend on each other to control national borders and prevent the free movement of international criminals and terrorists to other countries. Unfortunately, states routinely fail to live up to the standards of international responsibility. Keohane argues that this is to be expected: interdependence between states will produce discord since the actions of national governments and private actors alike are self-serving and are not designed to meet the needs and preferences of other states or actors (Keohane, 2001: 1). Discord is expected in an interdependent world. It is no more avoidable in the international system than in domestic politics. The responses to discord are what vary so much: violence, trade wars, bargaining, building common institutions, *ad-hoc* problem-solving, etc.

How can the conflicts of interest created by interdependence be resolved? This is a critical task not just in order to prevent the worst side effects of inter-dependence, which include war, but to seize the potential gains from coopera-tion that liberals have long argued are possible. One way to prevent conflict would be for states to isolate themselves from each other. In pure isolation, there are no externalities that move from one state to another. However, the potential gains from cooperation cannot be realized through isolationism. Not only would states and other actors have to deny themselves the gains from specialization and exchange, but they would also have to avoid policies that have consequences for people on the other side of the border (e.g. production which causes trans-boundary pollution). This is all but inconceivable in today's world. Proclaiming a policy of isolation is easy but how does a country make itself immune from the missiles, pollutants, or global warming effects that originate in other countries? A successful policy of isolation requires more than disengagement. It requires positive action to prevent activities in other coun-tries from affecting one's homeland.

Another solution would be for states to cede sovereignty to a supranational government that would regulate interdependence. This could spell the end of the Westphalian system of sovereign states through the creation of an authoritative world government. Alternatively, states could maintain their sovereignty while creating a system of political and economic union with both intergovernmental and supranational elements, not unlike the European Union. In this type of global governance system, national states would remain the primary building blocks but they would delegate problem-solving authority to agents at the international level. What forms might a system of global governance to manage interdependence take? And more importantly, how would we ensure that institutions of governance secure peace, prosperity, and freedom, rather than exploitation or oppression?

Forms of Global Governance

Scholars have proposed many different ideas aimed at resolving this governance dilemma. In this section we will examine several competing visions for the future of governance in a highly interdependent and conflict-prone world. Our aim is to explore the alternatives regardless of how prevalent each form is in the contempo-rary world. This will allow us not only to describe forms of governance that have existed so far but also to explore other hypothetical forms of global governance.

A Global State

In *One World* (2002), the philosopher Peter Singer's major thesis is that the world constitutes a single unit in economic, social, and environmental terms.

Increasingly one can talk about 'world society' and 'world culture' despite rather significant cleavages in social and cultural terms. It follows that this kind of world (i.e. a unified one) would also create pressures for a centralized political system. An extreme version of such a system would be a world government, a centralized state which in its most democratic version would represent all the peoples of the world. Ideally, such a world government would be able to overcome the wasteful competition that springs from the struggle for survival in an anarchic international system. Alexander Wendt argues that the Westphalian system of sovereign states encourages self-interested, conflict-inducing national behaviour by virtue of its structure, but that this structure could be transformed in order to create more 'internationalized' states, or even a single 'international state' that could transcend territorial boundaries (Wendt, 1994). Wendt argues that state egoism is not exogenously given but is created by the sovereign state system in the following ways. First, the sovereign state system creates in-group/out-group tension as people develop identities based on their national citizenships, rather than on a wider global citizenship. This intergroup tension suggests that 'states are cognitively pre-disposed to be self-interested when they come into contact' (Wendt, 1994: 387). Second, because national governments depend on the support of their citizenries for survival (and re-election, in democracies), they tend to value the needs and preferences of their citizens over the needs and preferences of others in the international system. This self-regarding aspect of modern states is to be expected. State leaders are elected with the understanding that their mandate is to further the interest of their own citizens. The rise and consolidation of states can be seen as a competitive process in which various constituents trade political support to leaders in return for favourable policies. It needs hardly to be said that a leader who ran for public office on the platform of putting the needs of 'others' first would not get very far. Third, anarchy at the international level forces states to think and act self-interestedly since there is no rule of law or global governance regime to ensure their security vis-à-vis more powerful states.

Wendt argues that these determinants of self-interested state behaviour are not inevitable. He believes that they could be overcome through efforts at creating a collective identity that extends beyond national boundaries. To be successful, this may require a transcendence of the nation-state as we now know it, as its existence is a structural impediment to transnational collective identity formation. Only through the formation of a collective identity that extends beyond national borders could cooperation be truly institutionalized, as it is in stable nation-states. Wendt's arguments about how this collective identity among states may be formed depart from rationalist ideas about the relationship between structure and identity. Wendt argues that rising interdependence among states creates a powerful incentive to identify with others and find cooperative solutions to problems. While rationalists such as Keohane argue that states may create institutions to successfully manage discord and achieve cooperation, Wendt's argument is that cooperation will actually change state identities to be less exclusive and more inclusive of other states' interests.

Through rising interdependence, interests may become more collective, and states may seek the creation of 'transnational structures of political authority' that serve and protect their common interests (Wendt, 1994: 392). These authority structures could be conceived of as an 'international state', but could at the same time be decentralized and divorced from territorial boundaries. Wendt writes:

> In the Westphalian system, state agents and authority structures did coincide spatially, which leads to the familiar billiard ball imagery of 'states' (actors, under which authority structures are subsumed) interacting under anarchy. But the two concepts need not correspond in this way: political authority could in principle be international *and* decentralized. (1994: 392)

Wendt cites the proliferation of international institutions in the past few decades as evidence that this shift in political authority is beginning to take place. However, for any system of international authority to be truly effective, it must be legitimate and binding, and this is where today's global institutions often fall short. Legitimacy implies the consent of those that a governance institution purports to govern. In the international system, states and their citizens must accept the authority of a global institution over national policy choices if it is to assume any power. Additionally, global governance institutions must have the capability to enforce their policies through negative sanctions, such as fines, imprisonment, threats of exclusion, and shaming techniques. This is a characteristic that many of today's international institutions lack. The World Trade Organization has complex enforcement procedures that often work well, though far from perfectly, but other organizations such as the United Nations are notoriously unable to coerce states to abide by their prescriptions in any meaningful way. Coercive capability does not necessarily mean that a governance body has the military capability to exert physical force as an enforcement mechanism. In fact, this has very rarely been the case. Coercive capability is best thought of as enforcement powers, which can include the capacity to impose economic sanctions to punish states, levy financial penalties, threaten exclusion, or withhold financial aid or other material benefits to states that defect.

While the concept of the 'international state' evokes a geographic entity with a centralized power structure, similar to today's nation-states, Wendt's contribution to thinking about global governance in these terms is to disentangle the notion of the 'state' from geography and centralized political power. Rather, an international 'state' may develop when interdependence between nation-states causes national interests and identities to change in ways that begin to align with the identities of other nation-states. This 'identity realignment' is already taking place in Europe, where it is common for citizens to think of themselves as both European and French, Italian, Spanish, or German. If interests and identities become more collective through interdependence and continued cooperation, states may seek decentralized political authority that coordinates their activities in mutually beneficial ways. Through decentralization, there would be no need to dismantle states as we know them. In this way, Wendt argues, the international state can preserve 'the forms if not the substance of sovereignty' (1994: 393).

While Wendt's analysis is interesting and provocative, there are two areas where it is problematic. First, the issue is not so much whether or not states are self-interested as how inclusively the boundaries of the self (the we-group) are drawn. A city state will have boundaries that are narrow compared to a national state which in turn will have boundaries that are less inclusive than a regional or world state. There is little in his approach that leads us to believe that the growth of larger political organizations will lead to the decline of self-interest. Rather, what he seems to be saying is that small units of identification and interest, such as the nation-state, may be replaced by larger units which calculate costs and benefits in terms of more encompassing political units. This is an important claim. The number of political units may decline as some assimilate and join forces with others or the number may increase as secession and fragmentation increase. While these trends are important in many different ways, it is clear that the existence of self-interest is not at stake.

Second, Wendt's implicit analysis of identity seems to rest on a transaction-based account whereby the more that states interact with one another, the higher the level of transactions, and the greater the opportunity for identities to correspond to the scope of these transactions.[2] It may be the case that identities form this way but it may also be that the boundaries of community have a darker side and that identities may form around groups which have shared difficult experiences and collective suffering. Wars have played an important role in defining lines of community in many parts of the world. It is difficult to imagine American nationalism without taking into account the War for Independence, the Civil War, World War I, and World War II, episodes which forged both common identities as well as divisions that exist until today. The same can be said for the relevance of wars in the emergence and development of China, India, Pakistan, Belgium, France, Germany, and Great Britain. All of this is not to dismiss the importance of transactions in the formation of state boundaries and identities. It is simply to caution that our understandings of community should be alive to a variety of influences and that we should not rule out communities of fate and suffering on *a priori* grounds.

Regional Governance

An alternative to governance at the global level, regional trading organizations have proliferated across the globe in recent decades as a way to create an open

---

[2]In a later article (2003), Wendt invokes the politics of recognition as an explanation for shifts in identity.

economic space among states in a particular geographic region. Regions have often been advocated as practical compromises that provide 'half a loaf' in the face of the difficulties presented by integration on a global scale. If it is impossible to solve problems of global pollution and trade, at least these problems might be managed on a regional scale. In a more dynamic sense, regions are advocated as half-way houses on the way toward more comprehensive integration schemes. As the EU demonstrates, the size of a regional organization need not be fixed. The EU has increased from a small organization of 6 original member states in 1957 to 27 members today. The European Free Trade Association (EFTA) has experienced the reverse process, going from a membership of 7 countries in 1959 to 4 today.

For all the talk about globalization as a worldwide phenomenon, most of the economic and even non-economic contacts among peoples and countries occur within regions. This is true if we think of trade, foreign direct investment, tourism, exports of books and movies, emails, and many other patterns of diffusion. This raises a puzzle for those who argue that efficiency is the guiding hand behind globalization. As Bhagwati (1992) has pointed out, from a global standpoint, regional trade institutions are clearly sub-optimal and may even pose obstacles to further integration (i.e. they may not be half-way houses at all). Clearly, there will be missed opportunities for trade among partners from different regions, economically inefficient trade diversion from one region to another, and the usual welfare losses that go along with protectionism among regions. In addition, spatial concentration of economic activity may have costs in security terms, making trade partners highly vulnerable to disruptions intended or not. As argued in a different context (Choi and Caporaso, 2002: 480), 'both neoclassical economics and realism would seem to hesitate about regional organization. Yet economic and political activities increasingly cluster in regional patterns.'

In the last few decades, several international organizations have developed among geographically proximate countries. The 1980s witnessed the creation of the Canada–US Free Trade Agreement (CUSFTA) which was expanded into the North American Free Trade Agreement (NAFTA) in 1992, as well as the passage of the Single European Act in 1986, which laid out plans for completing a single market within the European Community by 1993. The subsequent 1992 treaty signed at Maastricht created the European Union and set out the timetable for achieving economic and monetary union by 1999. The Asia-Pacific Economic Cooperation (APEC) was established in 1989 with the goal of becoming a free trade area, and in 1992 several South American countries signed an agreement to establish a customs union (MERCOSUR).

What are some explanations for the willingness for states to enter into regional organizations? State actors may believe they will gain economically from the creation of regional organizations both as a result of the removal of trade barriers among members, as well as a result of the tariffs that they may erect against non-members. Thus, they create a set of institutions at the regional level to govern the process of trade liberalization and economic standardization among member states (Mitrany, 1943; Deutsch et al., 1957; Haas, 1958, 1964). Economic regionalization strengthens firms within regional borders by providing economies of scale in production, enlarging the free trade area, and denying these advantages to firms from outside the region (Gilpin, 2000: 337). Regional governance institutions can also help disseminate information to national actors, reduce transaction costs, and create stronger incentives for states to cooperate economically and politically in the future (Keohane, 1984). In contrast, some scholars argue that states create regional organizations primarily for security purposes. These arguments posit that states have an incentive to liberalize trade with allies, because the gains from trade will strengthen their alliance, and at the same time, they have an incentive to limit trade with adversaries to prevent those adversaries from becoming stronger (Mansfield and Bronson, 1997: 188).

How deeply integrated are the member states of regional organizations? The depth of integration these organizations can achieve depends upon their members' willingness to accept some limits on their autonomy in certain policy areas. At one end of the spectrum, some organizations seek no more integration than the construction of a preferential trading agreement within their borders (EFTA), and at the other end of the spectrum, the EU has created a political and economic union wherein members cede sovereignty to a supranational governance body in a wide range of domestic issues. Regional organizations are innovative for the way their member states create supranational or intergovernmental institutions to achieve joint policy goals, and this is also why the study of these organizations is important for understanding how international governance at the global level may somehow develop.

Scholars have characterized regional integration as a continuum stretching between two ideal-type modes of governance: intergovernmental and supranational (Sandholtz and Stone Sweet, 1998: 8). These two approaches differ in terms of who they view as the central actors, the role of preferences, the nature of central integration processes, and integration outcomes. Andrew Moravcsik (1998) describes intergovernmentalism as a form of governance in which national governments retain their authority and control over the integration process and over the organization's decisions. States are the central actors, and the roles of social actors and international institutions are secondary. The processes that are central to integration have to do with hard bargaining over distributive gains and losses once the collective-gains frontier has been established. National governments define their objectives, bargain to reach cooperative agreements, and then select the appropriate institutional arrangement to implement the agreement. Intergovernmentalists take the preferences of state leaders not as given but as produced through a process in which economic concerns (productive and commercial) are paramount. In making policy decisions, Moravcsik writes that 'bargaining outcomes are decisively shaped by the relative power of nation-states' (Moravcsik 1998: 5–7). Thus, if one knows the interests and power of the major actors, one can accurately predict outcomes of the integration process. The outcomes of integration reproduce the state, perhaps even reinforcing state power and interests.

The movement of the European Community toward Economic and Monetary Union (EMU) in the late 1980s and 1990s provides an example of intergovernmental decision making. EMU is formally part of the Treaty of European Union which came into effect in 1993, but the groundwork for EMU was laid in the 1980s. EMU is considered one of the great Franco-German compromises that pushed European integration forward when it could have otherwise floundered (Hendriks and Morgan 2001: 65). François Mitterrand, who was elected President of France in 1981, sought to use both the European Monetary System (EMS) and EMU as a way to solve France's domestic and foreign policy problems. Mitterrand wanted to deal with problems of inflation caused by domestic spending as well as to find a way to counteract Germany's emergence as Europe's economic powerhouse at a time when France's relative economic importance was on the decline. The member states of the EU wanted to create a common economic space in order to compete with the US in the global economy. However, tighter economic integration in Europe, which France accepted as a fact of life by 1983, presented a dilemma for France. If France continued with its policy of austerity within EMS, it effectively meant that it would have to shadow 'German monetary policy ever more closely' (Abdelal 2007: 74). The costs of hewing to the EMS line with no further currency devaluations were considerable and undoubtedly asymmetric, with France absorbing more of the costs than Germany. Yet the market left France little choice. If Mitterrand continued to spend, inflation was sure to result and if inflation occurred, it would be tempting to devalue. However, this is precisely what was ruled out by the French policy of austerity that resulted from the turnaround of 1983. The difficulties faced by France with regard to its competition with the Deutschmark made it receptive to – indeed actively in favour of – a political solution.

To protect French national interests on an international as well as European stage, France moved quickly to establish the preconditions for EMS. It is important to remember that the Single European Act by itself did little to liberalize capital markets (Abdelal, 2007: 67). Capital markets were not liberalized until the adoption of the capital movements directive in June of 1988. Given France's coolness toward capital liberalization before the spring of 1983, it may seem surprising that France took a leading role in adopting the capital movement directive. Yet the French, led by Jacques Delors as President of the European Commission, effectively spearheaded movement toward capital liberalization from 1986 to 1988, unveiling their two-stage plan in May of 1986 (Abdelal, 2007: 67) However, France needed German support in order to succeed, and this support was by no means forthcoming without opposition. Germany had much to lose by adoption of a single currency. After all, the Deutschmark was effectively calling the shots in Europe, and Germany had extracted a measure of monetary discipline from France as a result of the French turnaround in 1983.

Since France believed it had lost policy autonomy in monetary affairs in the early 1980s, it made sense for France to seek a form of monetary union in which its political weight and skills would be fully represented. A seat at the table was better than simply fighting it out within the context of international financial markets. However, it is more difficult to explain German cooperation. Why did they agree to become a member of an economic union where they were called upon to trade their market clout for political-diplomatic power? It is a good question and it may have been the case that Germany would not have gone along except for events starting with the fall of the Berlin wall in November 1989.[3] With that, it was all but certain that Germany would re-unify and become the Gross Deutschland that historically was much feared.

One way that Germany could credibly signal its commitment to Europe, rather than a desire to return to a looser balance of power type of an international system with a looser balance of power, would be to bind itself more closely to Europe. Chancellor Kohl wanted to re-unify Germany without serious opposition from other European countries so he repeatedly drove home the point that with re-unification, there would be a European Germany rather than a German Europe. Thus, Kohl chose to assert German commitment to integration by agreeing to move more quickly on EMU than he would have otherwise liked. In return, France recognized that the German economy would dictate the direction of monetary union, given the strength of the Deutschmark and the German economy. In short, France accepted the European Central Bank modelled along lines of the German Bundesbank. Through rational bargaining founded on firm national preferences, France and Germany were able to provide the necessary leadership to design a plan for EMU that was acceptable to each other and, for lack of a better option once EMU was decided, to the rest of the countries that joined.

At the other end of the governance continuum, some regional organizations have designed supranational institutions to govern certain policy areas. The member states of the EU have created several institutions of supranational governance, including the European Court of Justice, the European Commission, and the European Parliament. Sandholtz and Stone Sweet define a supranational mode of governance as one in which 'centralized governmental structures (those organizations constituted at the supranational level) possess jurisdiction over specific policy domains within the territory comprised by the member-states. In exercising that jurisdiction, supranational organizations are capable of constraining the behaviour of all actors, including the member-states, within those domains' (Sandholtz and Stone Sweet, 1998: 8). These constraints are authoritative in nature. They bind states legally, and running against these rules is running afoul of the law. Thus, these constraints are different from

---

[3]We do not argue that Germany would not have joined EMU without the fall of the Berlin Wall and the end of the Cold War. Indeed, there is evidence that Germany was taking this option seriously, well before the events triggered by the fall of the Wall in November 1989. However, these events made EMU much more likely and speeded up the pace of negotiations

those that might be imposed because of economic dependencies or power relations. Supranational governing bodies are partially autonomous bodies to which national governments have delegated responsibility for policy-making. Once responsibility is delegated, it is no longer clear who is in control. On one reading, national authorities are still in control, but in situations where agents have most of the information, contacts, and resources, they will also have most of the discretion to act, and to act is to make policies. National actors may delegate decision-making in this way when it becomes too costly to maintain separate national rules and intergovernmental decision-making processes over an issue of transnational significance.

The supranational model could not be more different from the intergovernmental model. To start, supranational integration scholars do not simply focus on political actors, as intergovernmentalists do. International governance has a social and economic base, these scholars argue, and in line with traditional functionalist practices, they attribute great importance to private social actors, such as interest groups, trade unions, gender equality groups, business organizations, and environmental groups. Without this social base, integration would lack any popular appeal. Just as it is difficult and uninteresting to analyse domestic politics without interest groups, lobbying, and voting constituencies, it is also unproductive to approach international governance by focusing exclusively on political elites. If politics at the global level were cut off from society, it could scarcely be democratic. This is a concern we come to later in this chapter.

Second, the preferences of the various groups that have a stake in the trajectory of integration are not given, nor are societal and economic interests easily aggregated into a homogeneous preference function on the part of political leaders. Preferences of groups remain disaggregated – those of farmers, gender groups, environmentalists, and factory workers have to be dealt with, often, separately from one another. Occasionally they do conflict, as when claims for equality on the part of female workers conflict with concerns for cost-cutting on the part of employers. But it is in precisely cases such as this that the ECJ plays an important role. Judicial dispute resolution, legislation, and bureaucratic decision-making take the place of interstate bargaining as the key processes, and the outcomes, far from reproducing the state, bring about significant transformation of the state and the emergence of supranational government.

In *European Integration and Supranational Governance* (1998), Sandholtz and Stone Sweet develop a full model of supranational integration in which domestic, transnational, and supranational actors participate in the development of supranationalism. Their central question has to do with the conditions under which political institutions emerge at the supranational level. They rely heavily on the demands made by private social and economic actors, environmental actors for environmental politics, farmers for agricultural politics, business and labour groups, as well as consumers for trade politics and so on. Demands emerge when individuals and groups want access to the markets of other countries, fairness in cross-country regulations, protections for the externalities caused by others, and so on. Landmark cases such as Costa v. ENEL (1964) and Defrenne v. Sabena (1976) involve mundane matters such as Italian legislation regarding the status of an electricity company in Italy and the firing of a flight attendant by Sabena Airlines.[4] Since these demands are likely to be aimed at the regulatory or economic practices of firms in different countries, we have many situations of what we previously described as discord. How will these conflicts be resolved, if they are resolved at all? Sandholtz and Stone Sweet argue strongly that an independent institution is needed to resolve the conflicts – a third-party dispute resolution mechanism. The European Court of Justice (ECJ) is the institution on which they focus most centrally.

At the present time, the intergovernmental/supranational debate has not travelled well beyond Europe, probably for the most part because integration has not advanced beyond government-to-government cooperation elsewhere around the globe. But the basic template for the two approaches describes the main lines of theoretical debate in Europe and it can in principle serve as a set of guidelines for other areas of the world. Regardless of where global integration takes place, it will involve state actors as well as private actors. To the extent that integration is advanced, it will involve disputes that are difficult to solve on an *ad-hoc* state-to-state basis. Some level of delegation and discretion will be necessary, and thus we have in place the elements for the rivalry among state actors, private actors, and international institutions.

Disaggregated States

Another form of global governance may be the creation of functionally specific international regimes that govern certain transnational issue areas. States will delegate responsibility when they anticipate receiving efficiency gains from creation of these regimes. In contrast to regional organizations, as described above, these regimes would be led by the world's foremost technical experts in each issue area, rather than by politicians. David Mitrany argued that the problems created by new and complex processes of globalization may require highly technical solutions that national politicians are unable to provide. Instead, cooperative solutions to transnational problems would be best achieved if the specifics were left up to the world's top experts on those issues, who would work collaboratively with the best interest of the global community in mind, rather than for any one nation-state. Technical experts should lead the way toward solutions to complex transnational problems because the majority of these issues are apolitical: they are complex economic, environmental, or social problems that require sophisticated solutions untainted by politics, ideology, or national interest. Mitrany argued that nationalism and cultural and ideological differences get in the way of problem-solving at the global level, so new

---

[4]By 'mundane' we do not mean unimportant.

transnational institutions unaffiliated with any particular nation-state must be created. He argued that this should be done at a decentralized global level, focusing on function instead of territory, rather than at a regional level, to ensure the most efficient allocation of resources worldwide (Mitrany 1943).

One of the earliest examples of a single-issue international regime created to enhance efficiency is the Universal Postal Union. This organization is non-political and exists to coordinate the postal policies of member states so that international mail exchange is as efficient as possible. Another good example of a functional international regime is the International Criminal Police Organization, also known as Interpol. Interpol was established as an apolitical organization to improve international police cooperation. Interpol maintains a large database of major unsolved crimes to aid national police in apprehending criminals who may have travelled across borders or belong to transnational crime networks. The International Energy Agency (IEA) was created in the wake of the 1973 oil crisis to prevent further crises in the supply of oil. The IEA now provides member states with technical advice on climate change policies and the development of clean energy sources.

The decentralized international regimes of technical experts that Mitrany described in the first half of the twentieth century are not unlike the 'islands of transnational governance' that Alec Stone Sweet argues have been created by transnational commercial actors over the past few decades. Stone Sweet describes governance institutions that the commercial trading community has created for itself as a way to reduce the costs of navigating a myriad of national legal systems. He writes:

> The trading community now commonly sees national legal systems as constituting an obstacle to doing business, which it seeks to avoid. With the help of lawyers and academics, this community is now engaged in the effort to 'unify' or standardize contract law; and various standardized, anational model contracts are in fact being intensively used. A system of private, competing transnational arbitration houses has emerged, providing traders with a range of alternatives to litigating their disputes in state courts. (Stone Sweet, 2002: 334)

Stone Sweet argues that the consequence of this system of governance created by non-state actors is that national governments have lost much of their authority in regulating contracts and arbitration in transnational commerce (2002: 334). State courts have gradually ceded their regulatory power over transnational commercial disputes to the new institutions created by the trading community, allowing them to function much more autonomously.

Recognizing the ways that non-state actors like the transnational trading community have developed complex networks and have outgrown national regulatory systems in many ways, Anne-Marie Slaughter calls for the creation of disaggregated 'governance networks' of national governmental officials. She argues that these networks of officials such as regulators and judges are the most effective way for governments to respond to the types of private networks that Stone Sweet describes. While Mitrany's regimes run by 'global technocrats' put power in the hands of non-state actors such as the trading community, Slaughter's concept of governance networks puts national governments back in control of global processes, but in a disaggregated, decentralized way. These networks are organized around issue areas of transnational import, such as environmental problems and criminal justice, as well as the sharing of best practices on domestic issues. Slaughter writes that the 'disaggregated state'

> is simply the rising need for and capacity of domestic governance institutions to engage in activities beyond their borders, often with their foreign counterparts. It is regulators pursuing the subjects of their regulations across borders; judges negotiating mini-treaties with their foreign brethren to resolve complex transnational cases; and legislators consulting on the best ways to frame and pass legislation affecting human rights or the environment. (Slaughter, 2004: 12)

Governance networks can expand the capacity of national governments to govern globally in several ways. First, they can enhance their regulatory powers by sharing information about transnational corporations or criminals. Second, they can build trust with each other and form incentives to communicate and keep up a good reputation internationally. Third, they can share information and best practices. Fourth, they can offer technical assistance to less developed nations. According to Slaughter, 'they can provide all the functions of world government – legislation, administration, and adjudication – without the form' (2004: 4).

Slaughter envisions these networks as the key actors in a 'disaggregated system of states' in which state forms do not change, but their interactions with each other do. State agencies network horizontally with their counterparts in other countries, and they also network vertically with their counterparts in supranational organizations such as the European Court of Justice or other regional tribunals. The network format allows government actors to respond quickly and flexibly to problems; it allows them to share information and harmonize their policies; it gives control of global processes to governments rather than private actors; but perhaps its most important contribution is that it keeps global governance in the hands of actors with national constituencies to hold them accountable for their actions. Inasmuch as national actors are democratically elected and held accountable domestically, global governance will remain democratic to the same degree.

Multilateral Governance

States may also govern the global economy multilaterally, working cooperatively to tackle global problems while adhering to normative principles and maintaining control over the globalization process. Ruggie defines multilateralism as 'an institutional form that coordinates relations among three or more states on the basis of generalized principles of conduct: that is, principles which specify appropriate conduct for a class of actions, without regard to the particularistic interests of the parties or the strategic exigencies that may exist in any specific occurrence' (Ruggie, 1993: 11). Multilateralism differs from regional govern- ance because geography is not necessarily a determining factor in membership in a multilateral organization. Unlike regional organizations, states from all over the globe can join a multilateral organization, depending on the issue. Collective security organizations are examples of multilateralism: states that join the organization agree to defend each other in the face of aggression.

Multilateralism entails universal beliefs among parties to the arrangement both about *what* should be done, and about *how* those things should be done. It presumes that three or more states will be participating, and it presumes that these participants will be committed to cooperation beyond purely self-interested behaviour. Multilateralism can take the form of overarching, 'multipurpose' institutions such as the United Nations, or it can exist in agree- ments governing specific tasks and issues. Multilateral governance is different from the idea of a global state because multilateral organizations often are con- cerned with only one issue, rather than many different issues, as a state would be. Multipurpose organizations such as the UN are much less common than single-issue 'regimes', such as the International Atomic Energy Agency. Ruggie notes that there was a proliferation of formal multilateral institutions during the twentieth century, such as the League of Nations and the postwar Bretton Woods regime governing money and trade issues. States expect 'diffuse reci- procity' from multilateral institutions, meaning that in the long run, each party to the regime will receive relatively equal benefits from membership, or at least that they will be treated equally in a procedural sense, although they may not receive equal benefits from every issue that arises. As a result, multilateralism creates an incentive for long-term cooperation. Mark Zacher argues that certain issue areas are more amenable than others to multilateral governance. States may not want to hand over authority to multilateral organizations in some policy areas, but in other policy areas, notably the governance of common inter- national spaces such as the sea and the air, states have successfully instituted cooperation and control through multilateralism (Zacher, 1993: 428).

What role does multilateralism play in governing globalization? Ethan Kapstein argues that states have created an effective and functioning framework for gov- erning global financial markets that is applicable to other issue-areas, such as pollution and telecommunications. This framework is a 'two-level structure, with international cooperation at the upper level and home country control below' (Kapstein, 1994: 177–8). International cooperation refers to the countless agree- ments states have reached among themselves in order to regulate the financial sector, and home country control refers to the way that states have maintained authority over their national institutions so that 'every international bank is ulti- mately accountable to a single, national regulator' (1994: 2). Cooperative inter- national agreements have produced regulatory policy convergence across states, and these agreements are supplemented by domestic supervision by national governments of the firms located within their borders. According to Kapstein, and contrary to many other analyses, states remain in control of globalization of the financial sector. While this form of cooperation may not be as effective as supranational governance, it has allowed states to reap the benefits of inter-dependence while safeguarding their roles as the primary actors in the global economy (1994: 180).

Global Governance and Democracy: The Question of a Global *Demos*

The dilemma posed by globalization is that economic actors are pushing for more integrated transnational markets through the removal of barriers to international exchange, yet effective and democratic international institutions to manage this process have not yet been developed. This chapter has argued that the transnational nature of global processes necessitates cooperation through institutions at the international level, though this cooperation may take a variety of forms. Governments today are trying to enhance the competitiveness of their economies through the reduction of national laws and regulations that inhibit the free flow of trade and capital, but they must also answer to citizens who demand that national protections for vulnerable groups of the population remain in place. Many policies that governments have traditionally used to regulate business and provide social safety nets for citizens – such as taxation, labour protections, and public expenditure on social services – are more diffi-cult to institute in an economy where firms can pick up and move to countries where it is less expensive to do business. We may not be seeing a 'race to the bottom' that many have predicted, but economic globalization is certainly con-straining the policies available to governments to achieve domestic goals such as equality or the public provision of certain social services. In this way, does globalization erode democracy? If the constraining pressures of globalization erode democracy at the domestic level, is there a way to achieve democracy at the global level?

If democracy is rule by the people, we must ask 'who are the people?' at the global level. When this question is asked in context of the development of our modern nation-states, the aspirant peoples are recognized as relatively small groups centered in places that today we would think of as provinces, cantons, or states (in the US). In Germany, the states of Hesse, North Rhine-Westphalia, and Bavaria played a key role in the formation of what is now modern Germany, while in Italy it was the Piedmont, Emiglia-Romagna, the Veneto, and the region around Rome. France emerged from the expansion of the Ile-de-France and Paris into the surrounding countryside. In the global context, the scale is much larger and includes both national and sub-national units. Can people from all over the world, varied and remote as they are, be considered as one people? Simply posing the question leads to a resounding 'no'. While global democracy may simply be impossible globally, vigorous discussions of regional democracy continue to take place within the European Union (Hix, 2008; Weiler, 1995). Yet, most scholars reject an ethnic identification of Europeans in favour of a civic identity in which Europeans self-identify around a set of symbols standing for the political institutions and policies of Europe as a whole. Indeed, as Thomas Risse has effectively argued, the European identity that forms the basis for the European demos can and usually does vary by country. What we find is a set of 'Europeanized national identities' rather than a uniform and free-standing European identity (Risse, 2010: 5). Each national identity inter-acts with European institutions and policies thus giving a distinctive shape to the European experience within each country. Each country is affected by Europe but not necessarily in the same way. Risse generalizes that European identities tend to be stronger in the original members of the European Union (France, Germany, Italy, Belgium, the Netherlands, and Luxembourg) and the Southern European states (Spain and Portugal) but weaker in Scandinavia and Great Britain (Risse, 2010: 5).

The obstacles to a global *demos* are particularly compelling if we define 'the people' in primordial terms. Primordial connections imply that there is some strong, affective bond that is based on kinship, race, ethnicity, religion, or cul-ture and that the visible sharing of these traits holds people together and pro-vides a common identity. In this model of peoplehood, the sharing of affective bonds provides the foundations for the institutions under which people live, rather than the other way around. Italy, Germany, and Japan are often given as examples of ethnic nations that pre-existed their states and eventually gave rise to states. While this approach has relevance in smaller national settings, it seems hopelessly ill-equipped to handle problems of loyalty and identity at the global level. The problem is also not mitigated if we see nations as constructed entities, which they certainly were. Not only were past nations 'imagined com-munities' in Benedict Anderson's (1991) terms, but they were also created through a historical process that involved war, taxation, and the formation of modern welfare states, in which citizen loyalty was exchanged in return for specific material benefits such as pensions, medical insurance, and unemploy-ment insurance.

So where does this leave us? If global democracy is not possible and if globalization already exists, does this imply that globalization means either authoritarianism or privatization? To some, the latter would be a happy out-come, since it would involve escape from cumbersome national political regu-lations and political control. To others, an alteration of the boundary between state and market of this magnitude would be anathema and would undermine the historic achievements of national politics over the last several centuries. As Ferrera (2005) has argued, the modern state-building project was based on selective closure of boundaries so as to discourage easy exit from the emerging states. This partial closure of borders made it possible to identify a core population for both extraction (taxes) and the conferring of benefits.

From this perspective, it is not surprising that the loosening of borders comes along with the overall decline of 'voice' and the increase of 'exit' strategies (Hirschman, 1970).

We argue that globalization as privatization is not likely to endure. Markets have consequences, not just for the participants directly involved, but also for outsiders. There is no clearer example of this than the current financial crisis, where millions of people who did not directly participate in creating the crisis are nevertheless feeling the consequences. Globalization implies some form of global governance, whether democratic or not. But if there is no single global demos, and such is not likely to come into being anytime soon, how is global democracy possible?

We offer two answers to the question. The first relies on a form of indirect democracy which takes the extant democratic states and the peoples of each country as the foundation. Neither the institutions of democratic governance nor the social bases of peoplehood are reconstituted at the global level. Instead, governance takes place through international governmental organizations, which themselves are products of international treaties to which states are the parties. The democracy that exists in these organizations is due to the relationship between the multiple *demoi* in the individual states, their elected officials, and the responsible relationship between the behaviour of these officials within international organizations and their domestic constituencies. This is the delegation model of democratic governance. The people of each country are the primary democratic constituencies. The chain of control and responsibility runs from the people in each state, through their national representatives, to the behaviour of these representatives at the global level. This approach makes sense in that it takes the existing governments of the constituent states of the international system as the starting point. It also accepts the societies that underpin these states and does not try to transform national societies into one global society. The problem of diversity is then 'solved' as quickly as one can say 'principal–agent' since each government is responsible for its own people. There is no need to forge loyalties and identities at the global level. It is highly likely, however, that agents at the global or regional level will acquire some autonomy and freedom of manoeuvre as they acquire expertise in the local setting, thus creating problems from the standpoint of democratic accountability. Centralization is also likely to occur as attention shifts from national capitals to global governance arenas such as Brussels, Paris, Beijing, and Davos. The shift to regional and global centres is likely to involve a shift from reliance on domestic to foreign policy elites.

A second way to identify 'the people' does not focus on attitudes and subjective perceptions so much as the common predicaments in which people find themselves in the global structure (Held, 1995; Cabrera, 2004). Almost all people are affected (though in different ways) by global warming, ozone depletion, water scarcities worldwide, trade, and by the work of people in countless locations. To be affected by globalization means to have a stake in it. We can say that 'it matters to us' that multinational corporations do business around the globe, that vertical chains of production tie together the manufacture and sale of goods worldwide, that money sloshes with various degrees of freedom across the globe, and that the Amazon forests are being depleted. However, to be affected by something, to have a stake in globalization is by itself not politically significant. To make the transition to politics, people with a common stake must become aware of their collective predicament and must mobilize to alter their situations through bargaining, protest, or public policies.

It is not so difficult to imagine that a people, or rather various peoples, already exist worldwide if we use the second definition. It is an observable fact, widely perceived, that we are affected by what happens beyond our borders. And it is a short step from here to acknowledge that some of these effects are not as welcome as others, and that groups of people furthering their self-interest may organize and bring pressure to bear on national, transnational, and international institutions to do something about it. This second definition of people(s) as those having a stake in globalization outcomes identifies people in places where the primordial approach would not. The focus would no doubt be regional rather than global. People of Europe recognize European institutions as a focus of identification in the European Union (EU), the European Convention for Human Rights (ECHR), and the North Atlantic Treaty Organization (NATO) just as people in South America recognize the Common Market of the South (MERCOSUR) and people of Asia the Association of South-east Asian Nations (ASEAN).

The Dark Side of Global Governance

Our assumption throughout this chapter has been that if globalization is a given, then some form of global governance is inevitable. We can already see governance in the rules regulating contractual relationships among firms, in the bilateral investment treaties (BITs) among scores of countries, in the institutions of the IMF, World Bank, G-8 and G-20, and in the 'islands of transnational governance' created by firms, legal actors, and arbitration houses (Stone Sweet, 2002: 323). It is hard to imagine the alternative to global governance. We already expressed our reservations about an ungoverned globalization based on private forces. Would banks, multinational corporations, tourists, trade organizations, and global civil society actors be completely self-regulating? And the alternative of eliminating globalization by returning to the autarchy of the interwar years seems unthinkable given the magnitude of cross-border exchanges that take place.

In the previous section we considered the possibilities of the development of 'global democracy' alongside globalization. Here we assess the dark side of global governance, again as a set of potentials. We see three major areas of concern: the distance between 'the people' and global governance institutions; the possibility for oppression and tyranny; and the ways in which cosmopolitan ideologies may suppress distinctive national ambitions and identities.

Distance, Globalization, and Supranational Authority

Democracy and the territorial development of the nation-state have proceeded in lock-step with one another. This is a proposition that many would subscribe to, including those writing in the Stein Rokkan (1999) tradition of state-building but also political theorists such as Seyla Benhabib (2005). The struggle for political and social rights has gone through several stages: from civil rights to rights of participation to social and economic rights. The extension of social and economic rights in particular involved selective closure of borders, so as to prevent opt-in and opt-out actions on the part of citizens. It also allowed the state to identify and tax its citizens, to cut down on tax evasion, to conscript people into the armed services, and to target individuals as beneficiaries of welfare programmes.

The attempt to create the same institutional relationships between people and institutions at the regional and global levels runs into some obstacles. Global institutions are far removed, not only in a physical sense but also in terms of control and accountability. There are many new links in the chain of delegation that now is supposed to run from citizens of all countries, through their nationally elected officials, up to and through the representatives in the relevant international institutions. Even assuming a democratic model, the possibility for slippage, agency drift, and loss of information along the way is likely to be severe. As a result, international institutions are likely to lose touch with the sentiments of their original constituents even if intentions are good. And need we emphasize that intentions may not be good? Elites may have their own ideas about desirable courses of action. Even in the EU, among the most democratic international institutions in existence, many of its most important actions, starting with the Rome Treaty establishing the European Economic Community (EEC), have been the result of elite cartels. That the EU has delivered policies favoured by mass publics is not a defence of democracy. Democracy requires active participation and representation – not just the benevolent engineering of policies that are favoured *post hoc*. Institutions, especially democratic institutions, work in part through the provision of good information. As with markets, so too do political institutions require accurate and reliable information about the wants of constituents, the costs and benefits of alternative policies, and the consequences of their (the institution's) public actions. There is both a supply and a demand side to democracy. Institutions must be capable of delivering desirable goods (supply), but desires about political goods must also have established channels of communication to policy-makers.

Oppression and Tyranny

In 'The Liberalism of Fear', (1989) Judith Shklar makes a simple point well known to those who fear even the most necessary governmental institutions. Political institutions, or any institutions for that matter, are not intrinsically good things. Their capacity for overcoming collective action problems and delivering public goods, topics that are extensively written about in liberal theory, is rivalled by their capacity for corruption, predation, bureaucratic ineptitude and tyranny. As Shklar argues, there are many social sources of oppression but none has the 'unique resources of physical might and persuasion at their disposal' the way the state does. (Shklar, 1989: 21). She champions liberalism, not because it has a substantive *summum bonum*[5] but because it strives to avoid a *summum malum*, namely the cruelty and fear that a tyrannical state can inspire (Shklar, 1989: 29). Since liberalism insists on setting up walls between the state and various spheres of society – walls that protect religious expression, market exchange, and private life in general – it provides the best defence against tyrannical government.

However, the dangers of an oppressive state are real and the conditions that allow this oppression are present in extreme form at the global level. Global institutions are removed and distant from the concerns of people; they face more extreme problems of aggregation of preferences given the diversity and dispersion of preferences. They are likely to lack the checks of civil society that characterize the domestic and local levels of politics. Interestingly, the EU recognizes the importance of civil society and spends resources to constitute civil society networks. Finally, the international system has high levels of inequality both across and within countries. As democratic theorists have shown (Dahl, 1985; Lindblom, 1988), institutions rooted in high levels of inequality have difficulty producing democratic outcomes. If those who are powerful create the institutions, why wouldn't we expect those same institutions to work to the advantage of those who are most well off?

The possibility of global tyranny merits another caution. Tyranny at the national level may face opposition from within the country and also from outside. The international system may provide pressure by way of economic competition, human rights organizations, pro-democracy groups such as election monitoring organizations, and so on. The Soviet Union was brought down by a combination of think tanks, pressure groups, religious organizations, and by economic competition with the United States, all of which forced tough trade-offs within the Soviet Union among those who backed military expenditures and those who supported investment in industrial capital and consumption (Risse-Kappen, 1995: 187–91). Similar 'external' checks do not exist when the institutions in question are not national but global. Here, all the checks must come from 'inside', so to speak, from the constituent states. There is no external environment of competition to act as a brake on a tyrannical global state.

Dynamics of Inclusion/Exclusion, Cosmopolitanism, and Solidarity

The development of the modern nation-state involved the progressive consolidation of territory, citizenship, and identity. These three great historical

---

[5]That is to say, liberalism advances no one substantive conception of the good life.

forces, for all their distinctiveness, tended to move together in broad historical terms. The idea of citizenship took on meanings associated with membership in a particular state, i.e. to be French was associated with learning the principles of French Republicanism, French history, and French political institutions. In this light, the idea of transnational citizenship would appear to be an oxymoron, and supranational citizenship would be incoherent without a supranational state. In historical terms, nationalism became a major force shaping the loyalties and identities of those within a political community. Today, there is a limited unbundling of territory, nationalism, and citizenship. Increasingly, people exercise rights across borders. An economic national from one country may exercise limited rights in another. In the EU countries, individuals have local voting rights, can run in local elections, enjoy legal standing, and have the right to search for work and to be treated without discrimination once a part of the workplace. This emerging cosmopolitanism is generally thought to be a good thing: people can cross borders easily, can look for work in foreign countries, and have the right to be treated equally in the workplace.

However, there is a dark side to cosmopolitanism. Those who advance an open global system often present their views innocently, as if it's all about expanded choice, freedoms that only bring benefits, all controlled by openness, transparency, accountability, and good governance. But behind this cosmopolitanism as the neutral engine of expanded choice lies a value system: commercial civilization, consumption, and even personal freedom are the often unstated values of the cosmopolitan position. What could be wrong (or lacking) with these values?

One concern is that global cosmopolitanism will uproot traditional values and undermine the thick identities that have been built up over centuries. The concern is that giving free play to globalization harms communitarian values: stability, fixity of place, identities that rest on long-term commitments and loyalties, etc. Identities are of course always being built up, torn down, and transformed. However, the scale of identities has usually been small and the proliferation of states – often driven by affective forces smaller than the larger states – suggests that the geographic scope of identities is devolving to smaller units. Globalization is a force which is contrary to this in some ways. The scale of economic and environmental interdependence is larger, and presumably the governance structures have to keep pace. Externalities of a given size must be governed by political institutions with the same scope. Yet, identities stubbornly resist. The economic forces that constitute interdependence over a large area do not necessarily bring their own culture with them. Cosmopolitanism may weaken smaller-scale identities that bind people to places with which they can identify: villages, cities, regions, even countries. A cosmopolitanism that makes us all citizens of the world may be too thin a gruel to sustain the loyalties and identities of peoples.

Conclusion

The globalization of a variety of issues has been met with rising calls for governments to develop new tools to manage complex processes. In this chapter we have attempted to provide a framework for thinking about the diverse nature of the cross-border movements that have the potential to create conflict or spur cooperation between states. We have also sought to highlight the different forms that global governance may take, urging creativity in our ideas about what governance can look like. Better governance at the global level may not look anything like the domestic governance structures to which we are accustomed. It most likely will not be territorially based; it may not be centralized; it may be issue-specific; states may be the central actors, but other actors with expertise in certain issues may assume central roles; supranational institutions may develop as they have to an extent regionally; or states may just develop more effective ways to negotiate intergovernmentally. Whatever course it takes, global governance institutions must strive to meet democratic standards. The spread of democracy has characterized recent world history. Democratic states must work to ensure that new institutions at the global level adhere to this same ideal.

INTERNATIONAL INSTITUTIONS AND THE GLOBAL ECONOMY

Introduction

At the end of World War II the world's developed countries designed a number of international institutions whose purpose would be to govern currency relations, international monetary relations, and trade relations among states. Known as the Bretton Woods system, these institutions were designed by policy-makers who were eager to devise a multilateral system that could prevent future breakdowns of the international financial system such as the one that devastated economies all over the world during the 1930s. As states adopted 'beggar thy neighbour' economic policies during the 1930s, world trade declined, foreign investment dried up, and economics shrank. Policy-makers in the world's wealthy countries agreed that a multilateral system of governance was needed to regulate the international economy, maintain economic stability, and facilitate the liberalization of trade and capital. Though these institutions have changed over the decades and have met with varying degrees of success, their legacies thrive today in the form of powerful organizations such as the International Monetary Fund, the World Bank, and the World Trade Organization.

As we have emphasized throughout this book, economic globalization has enormous wealth-creating power, but it also generates highly complex issues and processes that require sustained cooperation among governments. The regulation of a complex international economy requires serious coordination among governments, and this often requires the creation of international institutions. The term 'institutions' is typically used by scholars to mean persistent sets of rules and norms that constrain human behaviour. North (1989: 1321) defines institutions as 'rules, enforcement characteristics of rules, and norms of behaviour that structure repeated human interaction'. These rules must be durable enough to predictably influence actor behaviour and shape expectations. Institutions can be both formal and informal, written or unwritten.

Institutions can also be formal organizations, or they can be regimes, which Keohane (1988: 384) defines as 'complexes of rules and organizations'. In this chapter, we will primarily use the term institution to refer to formal organizations operating at the international level to regulate or govern issues of international concern.

Globalization requires cooperation and coordination among national governments, but governments will vary in their willingness to cooperate on different issue areas and in their preferences about what cooperation will entail. States create international institutions when they believe that their interests will be best achieved through cooperation with other states in a structured, institutionalized framework with clear members, rules, goals, procedures, and norms of behaviour. Institutions of global governance, then, may be expected to be rational-functional, in that they are created by rational, interest-driven state actors in anticipation of the effects they will achieve (Keohane, 1984). States do not create international institutions just for the fun of it; they create them because they believe the institutions will help them attain certain goals. Once created, institutions reinforce themselves as actors adapt their behaviour according to institutional norms. For example, the US and UK sought authorization from the UN Security Council for the invasion of Iraq in 2003 before going to war. Though the refusal of the Security Council to support the use of force did not stop these states from invading Iraq anyway, these states nevertheless chose to move through UN procedural channels and to attempt to justify their actions as legal from a UN perspective. True, if the UN were a more effective institution, the US and UK may not have gone to war without the support of the Security Council, but the fact that these two states attempted to pull the UN on board at all – and tried to persuade the international community that the war was legal based on prior UN resolutions concerning the situation in Iraq – is evidence of the ways that state actors have adapted their behaviour because of institutional norms.

We have discussed different types of global governance in depth in Chapter 4. In this chapter, we will consider the roles that existing international institutions play in the global economy. First, we will analyse the types of problems that arise in international politics which often lend themselves to institutional solutions. Second, we will briefly describe some of the key international organizations that structure the global economy. Third, we will discuss the ways that leading theoretical approaches – neorealism, neoliberal institutionalism, functionalism, and constructivism – expect institutions to influence state behaviour. Fourth, we will analyse two potential problems caused by international institutions, delegation dilemmas and democratic deficits, and we argue that these are two issues that should be of great concern to states and their citizens. Finally, we will undertake an analysis of the International Monetary Fund, which is perhaps the most important international institution in today's global economy. We will use insights from IR theory and principal–agent analysis to argue that the IMF wields a considerable degree of autonomy and acts as a reliable agent of only a small handful of wealthy states.

Why Create International Institutions?

As globalization increases interactions among states and requires cooperation on a host of policy issues, the demand for institutions to regulate and coordinate these interactions also increases. There are different types of problems, however, that will likely require different institutional solutions. Understanding the different reasons why states often fail to cooperate, even when it is in their interest to do so, will help us identify more precisely *how* institutions can affect state behaviour. Focusing on the different ways that institutions may matter in international politics moves us beyond the tired debate in the international relations literature about *whether* institutions matter. We accept that institutions do matter and undertake the more interesting challenge to understand precisely how and to what extent they matter. In this section we will distinguish between two different types of collective action problems that institutions can help overcome: collaboration problems and coordination problems. Analysing collective action problems theoretically allows scholars to generate expectations about institutional effects that can then be tested empirically.

Collaboration Problems

One type of problem that states may face is the collaboration problem. Krasner (1991) characterizes collaboration problems as those involving market failure. Cooperation would result in the most efficient outcome, while the failure to cooperate leaves everyone worse off, yet cooperation remains very difficult to achieve. Collaboration problems are modelled game-theoretically in the classic Prisoner's Dilemma metaphor. In the Prisoner's Dilemma, two players could benefit from cooperating with each other, but they are unable to communicate, and fears about the other player's commitment to cooperating create individual incentives to defect. Defection becomes the best strategy, because if Player A cooperates and Player B defects, Player A becomes a 'sucker', the worst possible outcome. It is better not to cooperate at all, forgoing the potential gains from cooperation, than to be left a sucker. Without mechanisms in place to overcome the strong incentives to defect, cooperation will never occur.

We can conceptualize trade relations between two countries as a type of Prisoner's Dilemma, especially when viewed from the standpoint of the producer.[1] Even though free trade is a superior outcome, when viewed from the standpoint of the consumer and overall national income, national governments

---

[1]From the standpoint of the consumer, free trade is the best solution. From the consumer side, a good argument can be made that it is better to lower one's tariffs even if a trade partner keeps its tariffs in place. Lower tariffs result in the availability of more goods at lower prices. However, from the producer standpoint, jobs will be lost with free trade, and job loss will be severe if tariffs are asymmetrically lowered. Thus, the question of the optimal policy is more difficult. There are actually three separate sets of incentives when considering trade policy: those of the producer, those of the consumer, and those of the political actors.

have a strong incentive to use tariffs to protect export industries. Tariffs allow governments to protect key industries (who are also likely to be key political constituencies) from foreign competition. However, protection harms other domestic groups, such as consumers who will have to pay higher prices, and it harms foreign producers whose goods are less competitive in protected markets. While the most economically efficient solution would be for all countries to eliminate tariffs, governments are unlikely to unilaterally do so. They have no way to be certain that their trade partners will reciprocate, and they have no way to prevent trade partners from 'cheating' by distorting trade another way, such as through export subsidies. The US, for example, would be unwilling to cut tariffs, if only for political reasons, if it was not convinced that the EU would embrace the same reforms. This continued protection is a suboptimal outcome, both for American and European consumers as well as for exporters elsewhere in the world.

What is the way out of this dilemma? What are the conditions under which cooperation will emerge? Axelrod contributed an important insight in his seminal work, *The Evolution of Cooperation* (1984). He showed that defection is no longer the best solution to the Prisoner's Dilemma when the game is played repeatedly. As he puts it, 'What makes it possible for cooperation to emerge is the fact that the players might meet again' (1984: 12). Through repeated interaction, players can punish each other for defection and reciprocate when the other cooperates. Mutual reciprocity and the shadow of the future allow cooperation to become possible. Although this does not require a central authority, in the real world, institutions can create the condition Axelrod found necessary for cooperation: repeated interaction. Policy-makers from states that are members of the same international organization may have to interact regularly at summits and policy negotiations. The knowledge that they will deal with each other repeatedly over a range of issues is likely to encourage mutual reciprocity and cooperative behaviour. In addition to ensuring that states have to deal with each other regularly, institutions also play crucial policing roles: they can serve as independent third parties to monitor state behaviour, enforce policy commitments, and provide information to states about policy decisions in other countries. In this way, institutions increase the information available to states, strengthening the possibility that any state that defects from cooperation will be punished by other states. Thus, institutions can help states to overcome fear and distrust to reach cooperative outcomes that they would not have been able to achieve otherwise.

To return to our trade policy example, one way out of the dilemma in which countries have incentives to maintain trade barriers, despite the benefits they would both gain from free trade, is through the creation of an organization tasked with monitoring the liberalization of trade. Many scholars argue that the General Agreement on Tariffs and Trade (GATT) and later the World Trade Organization (WTO) have played just such a role. From 1947 until the WTO was created in 1995, thousands of tariff barriers were eliminated in the context of negotiations within the GATT framework, liberalizing billions of dollars' worth of trade. The GATT was a set of rules that sought to liberalize trade in goods primarily through the reduction of tariffs, but as trade expanded to contentious areas such as trade in services and intellectual property, and as states began using more non-tariff barriers to protect their industries, GATT members decided that an organizational body should be created that could supervise trade. The WTO was thus born and it was granted the power to settle trade disputes between countries and review governments' trade policies. Trade liberalization in sensitive areas such as agricultural products has certainly not been easy, and many WTO trade rounds have been stymied by disputes between wealthy and poorer countries, but this institution has played an important role facilitating repeated interaction between states concerning trade issues, monitoring trade and enforcing agreements.

Coordination Problems

A second type of collective action problem that scholars have identified is the coordination problem. In these types of conflicts, states agree that cooperation is always preferable to defection, but there are several cooperative solutions. 'The problem states face in this situation,' write Martin and Simmons, 'is not to avoid temptations to defect, but to choose among these equilibria' (1998: 104). Coordination problems that do not involve distributional conflicts are relatively easy to resolve. An example of this type of problem is the decision about which side of the road drivers should use. Before any rules have been established, it doesn't matter if drivers drive on the left or the right side of the road. What matters is simply that they all choose the same side and abide by that rule. Coordination problems are more complicated when actors have different preferences about which solution should be adopted. This type of problem is modelled game theoretically by the Battle of the Sexes game. This game entails a hypothetical conflict between spouses. It is assumed that both spouses want to cooperate with each other, but they have different preferences about what that will look like. One wants to take a beach vacation, while the other wants to vacation in the mountains. Neither spouse wants to vacation separately, so the goal of cooperation is to decide *where* to go, not *whether* to go. The problem lies in the fact that one spouse is going to have to compromise, receiving a lower pay-off than the other one. Thus, there is a distributional conflict. This coordination problem is different from the collaboration problems described above, because here no one has any interest in defecting from the solution. While a state is easily tempted by defecting from free trade rules and protecting its export industries, no one is tempted to defect from the rules of the road and suddenly start driving through traffic on the wrong side. No one has any interest in defecting from the rule, and no one has an interest in not creating the rule in the first place. What is necessary to resolve these types of problems is a mechanism to help the two parties coordinate and decide on a rule.

Taking an example from international politics, Krasner (1991) cites international telecommunications as a classic coordination problem. All states have an interest in maintaining telecommunications links among their countries. This requires considerable coordination of disparate national systems, however, to ensure compatibility both technologically and economically, and it became necessary to create an international regime, consisting of the International Telegraph Union (the name was changed to the International Telecommunications Union in 1932 and its portfolio was expanded to include radio and telephone transmissions), and INTELSAT (global communications satellites) to ensure that global communications could flow smoothly. Another example of a coordination problem in international politics is the setting of global industrial and commercial standards. When the technical and safety standards of goods differ across countries, this presents a considerable barrier to trade. The International Organization for Standardization is a non-governmental organization composed of representatives of national standardization authorities. These representatives work within the ISO to set product standards that the member countries then often adopt as national law, facilitating product compatibility and, as a result, international trade. Film, for example, is always marked with a number that identifies its speed – ISO 200, ISO 400, etc. – and these numbers refer to ISO standards on film photosensitivity that have now become industry standards.

Matters get complicated when states have divergent interests in the solutions that are chosen to resolve coordination problems. Krasner (1991) argues that state power plays a major role in the decisions that are chosen by international regimes tasked with resolving coordination problems. In the telecommunications industry, for example, states like the US, whose firms led the way in developing new technologies, pressed hard for a market-based international regime that would allow their firms to sell their products worldwide, while other countries with less competitive firms had a greater interest in maintaining national monopolies. Power and politics can be expected to play a significant role in resolving coordination problems, especially when the gains from cooperation will not be distributed evenly.

The Institutional Framework of the Global Political Economy

The international financial architecture of today's global economy was for the most part designed by the developed countries of the West in the aftermath of World War II. During the late nineteenth century, industrialization, imperialism, and British hegemony fuelled the 'first wave' of globalization, with substantial international trade and investment occurring between the European powers, their colonial territories, and the United States. World War I severely disrupted patterns of international trade, ended British hegemony, and broke down the financial regimes that Britain had helped maintain before the war. The inter-war period was disastrous for the global economy. Both the US and the European states responded to difficult economic times (culminating in the Great Depression) by erecting trade barriers, and world trade plunged from $35 billion in 1929 to $12 billion in 1933 (Cohn, 2005: 27). After World War II, the US emerged as the new global hegemon, willing and able to provide leadership to revive the global economy and create an institutional framework that could prevent another devastating globalization collapse.

Led by the US and Great Britain, the planners at the Bretton Woods conference in 1944 designed a framework for a new international economic architecture that would ensure multilateral economic cooperation, international financial stability, and the liberalization of trade and capital. In this section we will briefly review the roles of the three major international organizations that emerged from Bretton Woods – the International Monetary Fund, the World Bank, and GATT (now the World Trade Organization) – as well as another important institution that emerged at roughly the same time, the OECD (formerly the OEEC).

International Monetary Fund

The IMF was tasked with managing the international monetary system – the system of exchange rates and balance of payment. The IMF would facilitate international trade by stabilizing exchange rates through a fixed exchange rate system. The goal of this system was to prevent competitive devaluation of currencies and resulting trade wars. The IMF also provides short-term loans to countries with balance-of-payments deficits and helps to maintain the fixed exchange rate system that encourages international trade. The IMF has grown from 29 to 187 members, and it has also expanded its mission. It now works extensively with developing countries to help them achieve economic growth, maintain macro-economic stability, and reduce poverty. It provides loans to aid countries with economic restructuring, and in return these countries are expected to adopt the IMF's policy prescriptions. These prescriptions are known as the 'Washington Consensus' and they contain a host of neoliberal economic reforms designed to strengthen market mechanisms to achieve growth and economic development. The Fund is led by a managing director, traditionally a European, elected to renewable five-year terms. The Fund's decisions are voted on by its member states, according to a 'one dollar, one vote' principle whereby the countries that contribute more money to the Fund have greater voting power.

World Bank

The World Bank's mission is to alleviate global poverty. After World War II, it provided long-term loans to aid countries with post-war reconstruction; today it uses its loans and economic development expertise to promote development in the world's poorest countries. The World Bank is staffed with development experts and it is recognized as the world's foremost source of knowledge on poverty reduction. Its assistance to developing countries is to be used to create an environment that is conducive to productive economic activity, job creation, and investment. Its loans help countries improve physical infrastructure, invest in human capital through health and education programmes, reform institutions to strengthen government capacity, fight corruption, and develop financial systems. The World Bank's funds come from donations by its 187 member countries, and it is traditionally headed by an American managing director. Voting rights are similar to those in the IMF, allocated according to the 'one dollar, one vote' principle.

GATT/World Trade Organization

The General Agreement on Tariffs and Trade (GATT) was established in 1949 to liberalize global trade and gradually reduce member states' tariffs and other trade barriers. The GATT was a set of rules, not an organization. It was successful in liberalizing billions of dollars' worth of trade over the course of eight negotiation rounds, but it was weak on enforcement, dispute resolution, and the regulation of many new areas of trade, such as trade in service and intellectual property rights. In 1995, GATT members agreed to create the World Trade Organization, a full-fledged international organization that has an expanded capacity to resolve trade disputes among members, negotiate trade liberalization, and enforce compliance with liberalization agreements. The WTO has 153 members and it is governed formally according to consensus decision-making rules. In theory, all 153 members must agree on the outcomes of negotiations. Scholars argue that in practice, however, bargaining in trade rounds is highly power-based, and the outcomes of negotiations typically favour the interests of powerful states (Steinberg, 2002).

Organization for Economic Cooperation and Development

The Organization for Economic Cooperation and Development (OECD), created in 1961, is the successor to the Organization for European Economic Cooperation (OEEC), which was created in 1948 to administer the Marshall Plan for the recovery of Europe. It changed its name when it opened its membership to non-European states. The OECD is an organization composed of 32 wealthy countries, and these members articulate a commitment to democracy and market-based economics. Its member states produce about two-thirds of the world's goods and services. The OECD is committed to trade and investment liberalization and it provides a forum in which its members can coordinate their economic policies, review each other's compliance with liberalization, resolve common problems, and share best practices. The OECD does not create binding treaties; it uses non-binding instruments of persuasion, allowing members to pressure other members to maintain liberal policy commitments. Abdelal (2007) argues that despite the OECD's possession of only 'soft power', it has exerted considerable influence on member states to change certain economic policies. He maintains that the OECD played an important role in creating the international consensus on the value of capital liberalization during the 1990s. The OECD also collects and publishes extensive economic data from its member states, enabling analysis of the domestic and international effects of a wide array of economic policies.

Institutions and International Relations Theory

A major focus of IR theory is on the potential for institutions to help states cooperate in the anarchic global system. The different theoretical approaches come to radically different conclusions about the degree to which international institutions constrain state behaviour and enable interstate cooperation. In this section, we will examine the arguments of neorealist, neoliberal institutionalist, functionalist, and constructivist approaches about the influence that international institutions can have over state behaviour.

Neorealism

Neorealist analyses of international relations begin with the assumption that the international system is anarchic, and under anarchy there is no authority to prevent states from acting aggressively or violently against each other (see Waltz, 1959, 1979). States are constantly threatened by the existence of other states in the absence of a governing authority. Driven by the need to survive, states will concern themselves with power and the development of capabilities to defend themselves against aggression from other states. Power becomes the most important way for states to achieve security, and as such, states will seek power and they will try to prevent other states from becoming more powerful. They will be motivated by relative gains, by increasing their power capabilities relative to other states, and they will act to prevent other states from making relative gains in capabilities. Power capabilities can be both military and economic. Military power is immediately threatening, but wealth and economic prosperity also enable states to wield power and influence that can threaten the survival and interests of other states. The constant threat posed by anarchy and the distribution of power mean that interactions between states are characterized by fear and distrust (Grieco, 1988: 498).

For all these reasons, neorealism is pessimistic about the ability of international institutions to constrain state behaviour and enable cooperation (see Mearsheimer, 1994/5). Neorealists argue that the anarchy of the international system generates conflict and competition among states that don't often share common interests. Even when states do share common interests, they will often fail to cooperate because of fears that others will gain more than they will from cooperation. This concern with relative gains will impede cooperation even when cooperation could create positive outcomes for all involved. Thus, the fear that cooperation will be more beneficial to others will prevent cooperation among states, and it will render international institutions incapable of effecting long-term cooperation. If a state signs an international agreement and then feels that others are gaining relatively more from that agreement, neorealists expect the state to exit the agreement or fail to comply.

A notable example of relative-gains concerns impeding cooperation is the United States' objections to the Kyoto Protocol. The US has refused to join the Kyoto Protocol seeking to limit greenhouse gas production because the agreement requires only industrialized nations to reduce their emissions. The parties to the agreement argue that the developed world has been the source of the vast majority of the world's greenhouse gas emissions and they should bear the responsibility of reducing emissions. They also argued that developing countries should be allowed to work toward achieving social and economic development goals before being required to invest in expensive new production technologies. The objections from some developed countries, such as the US, to the argument that some states should make cuts while others do not, indicates a concern with relative gains.

Realists would not be surprised that international institutions such as the Kyoto Protocol fail to constrain the behaviour of powerful states such as the US. International institutions, in the realist view, do not have an independent effect of their own – they merely reflect the distribution of state power (Mearsheimer, 1994/5: 7). If the world's most powerful state doesn't want to join an agreement such as the Kyoto Protocol, it won't, and realists would predict that this institution will have little effect. (Indeed, in designing a successor agreement to the Kyoto agreement, the G-8 leaders have recently embraced a US-favoured cap-and-trade plan called the 'Washington Declaration' which is non-binding, and which would apply to both developed and developing countries.) For realists, international institutions reflect the strategic interests of the world's powerful countries. They are tools that the powerful countries design and use in order to maintain or increase their power and influence. They serve the interests of those who control them, and as such they are unlikely to constrain or change state behaviour.

Krasner (1991) applies realist arguments about power and relative-gains concerns to coordination problems in which there is a distributional conflict. In situations such as global telecommunications, when all states want to cooperate but some will reap greater gains than others depending on what type of regime is chosen, Krasner argues that power will play the determining role in deciding the outcome. As a result, international regimes are often merely the offspring of power politics. They will reflect the interests of those with the capabilities to win at the bargaining table.

Neoliberal Institutionalism

Neoliberal institutionalist theories emerged largely in response to the neorealist theories that dominated the field of international relations during the Cold War. While accepting the same assumptions as neorealists about self-interested state behaviour and the difficulties of cooperation under anarchy, neoliberals argue that realists are nevertheless too pessimistic about the prospects for cooperation (see Keohane, 1984). The neoliberal institutionalist research programme has sought to specify the conditions under which cooperation is more and less likely. Along with neorealists, neoliberals argue that there are significant impediments to cooperation among states, namely distrust of other states' motives, fears about cheating, and fears that other states will have greater relative gains from cooperation. As demonstrated in the Prisoner's Dilemma, when there are short-term gains to be had from cheating and reneging on agreements, states will fear entering the agreement in the first place, sacrificing the long-term gains they could achieve from cooperation. The fear of being a 'sucker' – of cooperating when the other state cheats – will prevent a number of mutually beneficial cooperative agreements from being made.

Unlike realists, however, neoliberals assert that institutions can serve as a mechanism to alleviate these fears and facilitate cooperation when states have shared interests. A major reason for this, in the neoliberal view, is that states are often more concerned with absolute gains than with relative gains. An actor concerned with absolute gains will ask, 'What will benefit me the most?', rather than asking how much a competitor will benefit. In the neorealist framework, states are deterred from cooperating when they feel that another state may benefit relatively more from cooperation. Neoliberals acknowledge that relative-gains concerns matter under some conditions, but they argue that institutions can actually alleviate these concerns by providing information about gains and settling disputes over the distribution of benefits (Keohane and Martin, 1995). This argument reflects the neoliberal position that international politics is not always just a zero-sum game: in many situations, several states can benefit from cooperation and they often are secure enough not to be overly preoccupied with relative gains.

Neoliberals argue that institutions provide several important functions that make cooperation between states more likely. First, institutions can enhance the 'shadow of the future', providing a forum in which states are likely to meet repeatedly over time, decreasing the possibility that they will defect from agreements and cheat each other (Axelrod and Keohane, 1985). Second, institutions can serve as 'focal points' around which actors' expectations can converge, simplifying negotiations that can at first seem dizzyingly complex, with a myriad of possible solutions (Garrett and Weingast, 1993). Institutions can 'select' certain paths toward cooperation, reducing ambiguity and allowing actors to coordinate around a much smaller set of possible solutions. Third, institutions can link different issues that are important to states, raising the negotiation stakes, because if Country A doesn't cooperate on an issue that is important to Country B, then Country B is unlikely to cooperate on issues important to Country A (Davis, 2004). Fourth, institutions provide information to reduce uncertainty about the outcomes of cooperation (Keohane, 1984). By providing states with the information they need to feel confident entering into an agreement, institutions make it less costly for states to join the agreement. Fifth, institutions perform valuable policing roles by monitoring state compliance with agreements and publicizing non-compliance. These are functions that the state would otherwise have to perform, and that may be too costly or impossible. Most broadly, neoliberal institutionalists argue that institutions reduce the transaction costs associated with reaching international agreements. High transaction costs reduce economic efficiency by preventing transactions from taking place; institutions can lower these costs and allow states to reap the long-term gains from cooperation.

Garrett and Weingast (1993) argue that the institutions of the European Community (EC) created the focal points necessary for European countries, with a variety of diverging interests, to successfully agree upon the form that the EC's internal market would take. Although the EC members recognized the mutual economic gains to be had from the creation of a liberalized EC-wide market, there were many competing visions for the way the market would be constructed and the rules that would govern it. Garrett and Weingast claim that the European Court of Justice (ECJ) provided a solution for implementing the internal market that it could also credibly enforce. In its landmark *Cassis de Dijon* decision in 1979, the ECJ declared that the internal market should be organized around the principle of 'mutual recognition': goods and services sold legally in one country should be able to be sold in all other countries. With its power as the legal branch of the European Community, the ECJ would be able to legally enforce this principle, relieving the member states of the costs of monitoring compliance. The ECJ did not force the EC member states to accept this principle, but they nevertheless did, suggesting the power of the court's decision to coordinate member states' expectations around a cooperative solution that could be enforced by a non-state institution.

Another example highlights the role that institutions can play in linking unrelated issues in international negotiations in order to strengthen the possibility that negotiations will be successful. Davis (2004) conducted an empirical analysis of agricultural trade liberalization and found support for her hypothesis that trade negotiations linking multiple trade sectors in a single negotiation were more likely to lead to successful reforms. She found that in earlier GATT trade negotiations that did not link multiple trade sectors, liberalization of the agricultural sector was less likely to occur. In the Uruguay Round, however, GATT negotiators created formal, credible links among trade issues so that states were forced to make progress on all the issues on the table. The result of this round of trade talks was significant liberalization of the agricultural sectors in both Japan and the EU, two polities with hugely powerful farm lobbies.

Functionalism/Neofunctionalism

Functionalist theories of international relations seem to be particularly well-suited to an analysis of global economic institutions. David Mitrany argued over half a century ago that increasing economic integration among states would create a demand for institutions to manage economic activity at the international level. National governments would be ill-equipped to manage complex, cross-border economic activities, and this would necessitate the creation of international institutions to resolve the technical and technological difficulties that could hamper economic activity. Cooperation would occur not on ideological grounds but on technical grounds: cooperation would be a functional response to the new challenges posed by increasing economic interdependence, and international organizations created along functional or technical lines would be better suited than national governments to manage international economic interactions. Mitrany (1965) argued that the new 'post-national' institutions would be of varied form and composition; they would be designed with function in mind and their design and capabilities would therefore differ across issue areas. Perhaps some institutions would be non-governmental bodies composed of technocratic experts, such as scientists, and others would be intergovernmental organizations composed of national policy-makers. Mitrany (1948) also introduced the concept of 'spillover' into the study of international cooperation. He argued that successful cooperation among states was likely to spill over into other areas of activity, creating the need for more cooperation and, likely, more institutionalization at the international level. For example, in order for goods to flow freely through the EU's internal market, EU member states have had to cooperate on all sorts of non-trade-related issues. An EU-level police organization, Europol, was created to better fight crime in the context of open borders among the EU member states. The European Commission also gained significant competencies in creating EU level health, safety, and labour regulations that were necessary to ensure the free movement of goods and people across EU member states.

   Ernst Haas (1958) would later build on Mitrany's theories to develop what is now known as neofunctionalism. Haas theorized that the primary push for economic integration would come from domestic interest groups. Haas expected societal groups to understand the ways they could benefit from economic integration and to lobby national governments to integrate further. He wrote, 'Political integration is the process whereby actors shift their loyalties, expectations, and political activities toward a new center, whose institutions possess or demand jurisdiction over preexisting national states' (1958: 10). In this way, domestic demand (from firms, consumer groups, or other interests groups) for economic integration will push for deeper cooperation and institutionalization at the international level.

Another key difference between Mitrany's functionalism and Haas's neofunctionalist approach was that while Mitrany theorized that the new 'post-national institutions' would take various forms, depending on their functions, Haas expected these institutions to take on a specifically regional, supranational, and political character. He argued that political leadership would be required to manage economic interdependence among states and that this in turn would lead to the creation of supranational institutions, such as those of the European Union. States would delegate responsibility over an increasing number of economic – and political – issue areas to international institutions. Whereas functionalists expected economics and politics to remain largely separate, neofunctionalists argued that political cooperation would be an unintended consequence of economic or technical cooperation. Political leadership could not be expected to come from national governments with myopic national interests; rather, it must come from supranational institutions whose interests are by definition transnational and pro-integration. Supranational institutions would be best equipped to make economic policy with a transnational scope.

Functionalist and neofunctionalist approaches have often been applied to the study of regional integration, especially in Europe, but they are fundamentally approaches to studying international relations more broadly. We can identify two key insights forwarded by functionalist approaches. First, these approaches emphasize the role that societal groups sometimes play in the creation of international institutions to facilitate international economic cooperation. Second, functionalist approaches show how supranational institutions are the likely institutional form to result from deeper economic integration. However, functionalism and neofunctionalism are often critiqued for being unable to account for the trajectory of European integration, which was the empirical case to which Haas most rigorously applied his theory. Neofunctionalist expectations about the development of supranational institutions have also failed to materialize for the most part outside the EU context.

Constructivism

The constructivist turn in international relations theory has sought above all to question some of the primary assumptions of rationalist approaches concerning anarchy and state behaviour. Wendt's famous phrase, 'anarchy is what states make of it', critiques the dominant conception of anarchy in the international system as an ontological given. Constructivist IR scholars inject social context into the study of state behaviour, arguing that many features of international relations that we take for granted – such as anarchy and self-interested state behaviour – are not 'given' and unchangeable, but socially constructed. Constructivist theories of international politics, then, proceed from two assumptions (Wendt, 1995). First, the structure of the international system is social as well as material. Therefore, social relationships affect state perceptions of security, not just the distribution of material power. Five hundred British nuclear weapons are less threatening to the US than five North Korean nuclear weapons. Power and material realities matter but only in the context of social relationships and shared understandings between states. There is a shared understanding that the US and Great Britain are allies and that their material capabilities are not threatening to each other.

The second assumption is that the international structure shapes and defines actors' interests and identities, not just their behaviour. Constructivists argue that state interests and identities are shaped by their interactions and their environment. Pre-existing interests don't dictate how actors will interact with each other; rather, institutions and actors are mutually constituted. Institutions shape actors and their interests in the same way that actors and interests shape institutions. Institutions shape interests and identities by conferring standards of what is appropriate behaviour in the given situation. Constructivists argue that actors will ask, 'What kind of a situation is this?' and 'What should I do now?' to decide how to act in a given setting (Checkel, 1998: 326). This is a very different logic of action than that proposed by rationalists. Rationalists argue that actors generally behave according to the logic of consequences, acting strategically and efficiently to achieve a goal that will maximize their self-interest. Their interests and identities do not change through participation in a political community. Constructivists, on the other hand, argue that actors will behave according to the logic of appropriateness when they internalize norms through socialization in a political community. These norms not only constrain the range of appropriate behaviour, they also begin to constitute actors' identities (March and Olson, 1989). In this way, norms and ideas embodied in different institutional settings or political communities can shape and alter state conceptions of their identities and their self-interests.

Some constructivists argue that EU enlargement is a good example of the power of institutional norms to constrain state behaviour. The EU has cast enlargement as a normative project to export democracy and as a moral obligation to re-unite a divided continent. Prior to the 2004 enlargement, the EU had long assured the states of Central and Eastern Europe that it was willing to extend membership provided they met certain liberal democratic criteria, and when it was clear they had reached these criteria the EU kept its promise, despite significant concerns about the economic and political ramifications. Schimmelfennig, whose overall approach combines rational choice and constructivism (2001), proposes the strategic use of the concept of 'rhetorical entrapment' to show that this long-standing normative commitment is necessary to explain the continued support of enlargement from states who expected material losses from it. Member states like Greece, Spain, and Portugal that expected short- to medium-term net economic losses from the 2004 enlargement nevertheless acted according to a 'logic of appropriateness' and were supportive. European integration had long been legitimized by a pan-European ideology, a 'single Europe' with no barriers between East and West, and as a force opposed to Cold War divisions. It would have been very difficult to exclude the newly liberated countries from Central and Eastern Europe from membership in the European Union after decades of preaching that they were part of a broader Europe whole and free. Constructivists argue that this support is evidence of the ways that EU membership has strengthened the commitment of its member states to EU norms, transforming their individual interests and identities in the process.

With these two assumptions as their starting point, constructivists come to very different conclusions about international institutions than neorealists or neoliberals. First, constructivists argue that international institutions and organizations are able to disseminate norms that may eventually change state conceptions of their self-interest. Finnemore (1996) argues that the World Bank was able to persuade states around the world of the value of poverty alleviation as an economic development goal. She argues that the bank's influence and highly regarded expertise gave it the credibility to convince states that reducing poverty and distributing the gains of economic growth more equitably was in their national interest. Finnemore and Sikkink argue that international organizations contribute to worldwide norm cascades by 'pressuring targeted actors to adopt new policies and laws and to ratify treaties and by monitoring compliance with international standards' (1998: 902). Abdelal argues that the international consensus that developed in the 1990s about the desirability of capital liberalization was the result of the efforts by a few international financial organizations – the EU, the IMF, and the OECD – to codify capital mobility as a norm. He describes these international organizations as 'teachers of their norms and rules' that were able to successfully convince national policy-makers that capital liberalization was in their economic interest (2007: 18).

Constructivists also argue that international organizations play a role that goes far beyond the neoliberal claim that institutions merely reduce transaction costs to facilitate cooperation between states. Barnett and Finnemore (1999) argue that international organizations exercise autonomous power over states in ways that states could not have anticipated when these organizations were created. International organizations become powerful when they have established themselves as expert authorities on an issue, much in the same way that domestic bureaucracies exert power over public policy. Bureaucratic international organizations, staffed by experts in their respective fields, develop a 'rational-legal authority' that in turn confers on them legitimacy and power (Barnett and Finnemore, 1999: 700). In addition, constructivist approaches also expect international organizations to have goals, interests, and cultures of their own, giving them a much greater role as autonomous actors than neoliberal or neorealist approaches allow. Many analysts have noted the way the IMF's influence has greatly expanded over the years to affect areas of domestic economic and social policies that go far beyond the bounds of its original mandate to monitor exchange rates and help states resolve balance-of-payment crises.

Problems Arising from Institutions

International relations theory suggests that states create international institutions and organizations in order to resolve cooperation problems and manage complex transnational issues. In this chapter, we have examined some of the theoretical expectations about why and when states create international institutions, and we have cited many examples of institutions that are successfully performing these functions. But in reality, the picture is not quite so rosy. Institutions do not merely resolve international-level problems, they also create new ones. Some institutions seem to be ineffective, while others have at times betrayed state interests and even worsened the problems they were charged with solving. Coglianese (2000) distinguishes between two types of institutional effectiveness. He argues that institutions may suffer from policy ineffectiveness when they are unable to solve the problems they are expected to solve, or they may suffer from political ineffectiveness when they lack political legitimacy and support from national governments and domestic publics. As we might expect, many problematic or ineffective institutions have ceased to exist, but in some cases, they persist, providing a puzzle for theoretical approaches that expect states to withdraw support from institutions that do not further their interests or perform their delegated tasks. In this section we will analyse two serious institutional problems related to political ineffectiveness. The first problem is the delegation dilemma: how do states maintain authority over agents to whom they have delegated important tasks? The second problem is more normative: how do states ensure that international institutions are democratic?

Delegation Dilemmas

What happens when states delegate complex and extensive tasks to large and powerful international organizations? Are states really able to control these organizations to ensure that their policy preferences are implemented? An example concerning the environmental effects of World Bank projects is illustrative.[2] In the 1980s a World Bank highway construction project in Brazil, designed to ease urban population pressures and promote rural development by encouraging migration to remote Amazon regions, resulted in a series of social and environmental disasters. Waves of settlers took advantage of the new highway infrastructure and poured into rural Amazon villages. They suffered from widespread malaria outbreaks, brought with them diseases that decimated indigenous populations, and burned down extensive swaths of rainforest to develop the land for agriculture. Environmentalists grew increasingly alarmed by the massive deforestation that accompanied this World Bank project and similar rural development projects in Indonesia and Malaysia.

---

[2] See Nielson and Tierney (2003) for a detailed study of this case.

International environmental NGOs mounted high-profile campaigns to lobby the World Bank to reform its environmental assessment procedures, with little success. Soon governments began demanding reforms at the World Bank, led by major donors such as the United States. In the mid-1980s the US Congress threatened to withhold funding, other governments in Europe and Japan began applying pressure, and the Bank finally implemented a round of reforms in 1987. Environmentalists monitoring the case, however, argued that little had actually changed in the Bank's procedures for conducting environmental assessments during the loan approval process. It wasn't until 1994, when the United States government followed through on its threats and withheld $1 billion from the World Bank, that the Bank committed itself to meaningful reforms to better assess the expected environmental effects of projects early in the project development phase. The Bank's board of directors, consisting of officials appointed by member governments and answering to these governments, closely monitored the reform process. Reforms greatly increased transparency and granted Bank board members – as well as the public – access to planning documents and environmental assessments. At the board's request, the Bank also overhauled its hiring, adding many more environmental scientists and engineers to its staff than it had ever previously employed. This case is puzzling for IR scholars for several reasons. First, how did the World Bank gain such autonomy from member state governments throughout the 1970s and 1980s? Second, why did it take nearly ten years for member state governments to successfully force change in an organization they supposedly control?

Organizational behaviour that deviates from member state preferences is a challenge for both neorealist and neoliberal theories. Neorealists expect organizations to perfectly reflect the interests of the powerful states. Neoliberals expect organizations to facilitate cooperation between states by reducing transaction costs and providing states with important information, but they lack a theory of independent organizational behaviour. Principal–agent theory, however, can provide a useful framework for understanding how and why international organizations are able to act autonomously from the states that created them, as well as how and why they are able to be constrained.

The principal–agent framework, derived from microeconomic theory, conceptualizes states as 'principals' and international organizations as their 'agents'. States as principals may delegate authority over certain issues to international institutions when they believe they will benefit from this transfer. Essentially, they hire these agents to perform tasks for them when they expect that the costs of performing these tasks themselves are higher than the cost of delegating them. States expect their agents to represent their interests, further their goals, adhere to their policy preferences, while also remaining accountable to states. The agency delegated to international institutions can range from merely analysing transnational problems and making policy recommendations, to creating and enforcing policy, to settling policy disputes between states. For example, when a state joins the WTO, that state delegates responsibility to the WTO for supervising global markets and implementing trade agreements. The state benefits from letting another organization with expertise in a certain policy area do this work.

Delegation implies that the state has granted authority to an international institution to carry out certain tasks but that, ultimately, the state retains the ability to reclaim that authority for itself. The United States initially delegated authority over the settlement of legal disputes among states to the International Court of Justice (ICJ) upon the Court's creation in 1946. However, when the Court ruled against the US in a case between the US and Nicaragua in 1988, the US withdrew its automatic acceptance of the Court's rulings. It now accepts ICJ rulings on a case-by-case basis, presumably, whenever the Court's rulings are in favour of US interests. It is not always so easy for states to reclaim authority that they have delegated. It is difficult to imagine how a member state of the Eurozone would reclaim control over its monetary policy from the European Central Bank (ECB), given that national currencies no longer exist. The ECB enjoys independence from political interference, giving it great credibility both nationally and internationally, but this independence also means that it is difficult for member states to influence its policies. While delegation of the management of certain issues to international or regional organizations can create efficiency gains for states, a problem arises from the fact that the agent is an actor in its own right. The question is: what if the agent wants something different from the principal? And how does a state ensure that international or regional organizations, to which it has delegated responsibility over certain issues, act in line with its interests and policy preferences?

Analysts using the principal–agent framework have identified several problems that principals may face when trying to ensure that their agents implement their preferences (Nielson and Tierney, 2003). First, there is an information asymmetry problem. Specialized agencies tend to have more information about a specific issue than a more multipurpose organization will, such as a state. Second, the principal faces monitoring problems. It can't observe everything that the agent does. Third, the agent's preferences and interests may differ from those of the principal, creating what is known as 'agency slippage'. While each actor is constrained by rules and is accountable to other actors along the chain, longer chains of delegation run greater risk of slippage (Hawkins et al., 2006: 8). A fourth problem frequently encountered with multilateral international organizations is the problem of multiple principals. As the number of principals increases, collective action problems surface as well as conflicts over diverging interests. Nielson and Tierney note, 'agency slippage has a tendency to increase with the number of actors doing the delegating' (2003: 248). The World Bank and the IMF each have 187 member states, which means they each have 187 principals, who must somehow coordinate their preferences if these organizations are to further all of their interests. In the World Bank case described above, the US was unable to force meaningful change at the Bank until other powerful principals jumped on board, creating a winning coalition strong enough to reform Bank practices.

Institutional design can help prevent some of the dilemmas associated with delegation. First, principals can maintain a greater degree of control over their agents under rule-based delegation than under discretion-based delegation, although writing and enforcing rules is costly (Hawkins et al., 2006). As discussed above, the World Bank had acquired a considerable degree of autonomy in its operations since the 1970s, for the most part using its own discretion to make lending decisions. That changed substantially after the 1980s when the US failed in getting the Bank to adopt stronger environmental protection practices. In the 1990s, after a coalition of principals had been established and the US had followed through on threats to withhold Bank funding, the Bank underwent significant reforms to meet its principals' demands. At this time the principals rewrote the rules to put greater constraints on the World Bank's loan approval procedures. Second, principals can design strong monitoring mechanisms, such as transparency requirements. Third, principals can use hiring as a way to staff agencies with officials who are likely to carry out their demands. The World Bank member states did just this when they required the Bank to greatly increase the number of environmental scientists on its staff. Finally, and most straightforwardly, principals can design budgeting procedures such that they are able to sanction a deviant organization by withholding its funding. As Nielson and Tierney argued, the US Congress's decision in 1994 to renew World Bank funding at $1 billion less than was typical was a big wake-up call for the Bank. Its serious reform efforts came shortly after these sanctions.

The time and resources that states must put into regaining control over international organizations that do not adhere to their interests can be very costly. Good institutional design that incorporates strong monitoring mechanisms, effective rules, hiring oversight, and other institutional checks and balances can reduce the risks that international organizations will act counter to their interests and lose their political legitimacy.

International Institutions and Democracy

We have argued in this chapter that the complexity of international cooperation on economic issues often makes it attractive for states to delegate certain activities to international institutions. We have also argued that the global nature of the new economic sphere requires global governance of some sort, and we have considered the different forms that may take. But we have yet to ask the more normative question. If globalization requires governance, to what standards should we hold international institutions? Should international institutions meet the same criteria we set for domestic institutions? Our answer to this question is that governance institutions on the global level must above all else be democratic. As scholars such as Keohane and Shklar have warned, there is nothing inherently good about institutions: institutions can be dangerous, oppressive, and coercive, and they can disproportionately benefit certain members of society over others (Keohane 2001; Shklar 1989). For decades the community of democracies has dedicated substantial resources to aiding other countries in democratization efforts; the advanced democracies that wield global power should be equally committed to maintaining these ideals at a global level, even if that means sharing power with weaker states.

How can global governance institutions enhance international order and cooperation, without serving the interests of only the rich and powerful? Can they represent equally the interests of the billions of people on this planet? Could these institutions be truly democratic? Robert Dahl, a leading democracy theorist, argues that they cannot (Dahl, 1999: 19). Others (e.g. Grimm, 1995) argue that the idea of global democracy is all but incoherent because there is no demos beyond the nation state. Even in Europe, which shares a common civilization, there is no single demos but rather a variety of national demoi representing the cultures and preferences of different peoples. Contrary to Grimm's views, there are many ways of defining a demos. We can think of a people not only in terms of common culture but also in terms of shared stakes in certain outcomes. People around the globe are affected by trade, capital mobility, MNCs, financial transactions, and migration. Certainly, those who are affected would want to exercise some control over their fates.

To sort out the issues regarding global institutions, we must consider what we mean by democratic. Several concepts are commonly put forth: participation, accountability, responsiveness to citizen preferences, representation, openness, rights, legitimacy, political competition, and separation of powers (Caporaso, 2003: 365). Dahl judges international institutions according to their ability to maintain popular control over governments' policies and decisions, through representation and accountability, as well as their ability to provide an extensive body of rights (1999: 20). Keohane argues that there are three democratic criteria that global institutions should satisfy: accountability, participation, and persuasion (2001: 9). Caporaso has argued for a focus on accountability and rights (2003: 365). Following these theorists, we will examine participation, accountability, representation, and rights, considering whether global governance institutions can meet these criteria of democracy.

Participation

In a healthy democracy, individuals will participate in the governance process. This may be through voting or through their ability to make their views known to policy-makers. The town meeting style of participation between citizens and policy-makers has often been heralded as the ideal. This level of participation can of course only happen locally; how would participation look at a global level, with thousands of miles of distance between policy-makers and constituents, as well as between constituents themselves? Today, global communications can happen instantaneously, but this depends on electronic technology.

Even if this technology were available worldwide (which it is not), would cyber-participation be as meaningful as participation in a polity whose officials are relatively accessible in real life? And how would citizens in isolated, undeveloped regions participate in global governance?

Perhaps a more serious problem than inaccessibility of global institutions is the sheer size of the world's population. There are fewer opportunities for participation in government as the size of a polity increases. At the local level, citizens in many democracies can attend town-hall meetings and public information sessions, with the ability to voice their opinions on issues and get issues on the agenda. At the state or provincial level, these opportunities still may be available. At the national level in a big country like the United States, however, it is difficult to know how to participate other than casting a vote every few years in a national election and sending letters off in the mail to the assistants of far-away representatives. In the EU, rates of voter turnout for European Parliament elections are much lower than they are for national-level elections. At the global level, it is difficult to imagine effective participation at all in governance. One could monitor the websites of international institutions to stay informed, and join advocacy groups that lobby on global issues, but it is hard to imagine what more meaningful participation would look like.

Keohane argues that global democratic participation will certainly have to take place within smaller units, but these do not have to be geographic units. He argues that people will first participate in global governance through the members of their communities who are now dispersed around the globe (2001: 10). People will communicate with their community members who may be in a better position geographically to participate in global institutions, and these connections will give a voice to those who would be otherwise disconnected from the political process. This sounds rather optimistic, and it seems to stretch the idea of 'meaningful' participation. Without more certain and institutionalized access to means of participation, such as voting and access to national-level policy-makers, the vast majority of the world's population will remain disconnected from and unaware of global decision-making processes.

Accountability

Governments are accountable when they must take responsibility for a state of affairs (Caporaso, 2003: 366). If a person says 'I am accountable to no one here', this implies that the person cannot be called to account for his or her actions; he or she is not responsible to any person or institution. Citizens must also have the ability to use the democratic process to punish or reward a government for outcomes. Accountability implies transparency, because citizens must be able to access the information necessary to decide whether a government is indeed responsible for a given policy outcome. If governments are secretive and hide information about their decision-making procedures, or if the public does not have the ability to punish officials (through removal from office) for failing to uphold their promises, governments are not accountable. How would global governance institutions be held accountable to the global public?

Domestically, foreign policy may be the policy area in which governments are held least accountable by their publics. Matters of national security and foreign intelligence are kept tightly confidential, and citizens tend to accept this. In addition, most citizens lack the ability and information to assess complex and remote international relations. Without the relevant international experience or knowledge of foreign affairs necessary to form strong public preferences on complicated international matters, the opinions of elites tend to prevail in foreign policy matters (Dahl, 1999: 28). The average citizen knows even less about contentious issues in global-level institutions such as the World Trade Organization or the United Nations, preferring to trust national government officials to oversee issues in the global arena. National envoys to international organizations are not elected officials, so they are not accountable to a voting public.

Another reason it is difficult to hold international institutions accountable is that chains of delegation from the public to its agents at the international level are so long. There is usually a long line of bureaucrats separating the public and its representatives in international organizations, increasing the risk of agency slippage. People who have spent their careers working in international organizations and developing specialized expertise over a certain policy area may have strong policy preferences that do not align with the preferences of the public they represent.

While these realities make it hard to imagine democratic accountability at the global level, Keohane and Nye suggest broadening our conception of accountability to include non-majoritarian forms of accountability. National governments can hold international governance regimes accountable by withdrawing from membership or withholding dues payments; international courts could hold states responsible for breaking treaties and international contracts through legal accountability; the media can hold states to reputational accountability through publicizing transgressions; finally, consumers can use the market to hold firms accountable to certain operating standards, through the use of boycotts, for example (Keohane and Nye, 2003: 390–1). Perhaps the most famous example of this is the Nestlé infant formula boycotts. Launched in the United States in 1977 but spreading quickly around the world, consumers protested Nestlé's aggressive marketing of infant formula to mothers in less developed countries, where bottle-feeding is attributed to higher infant mortality because of the unsanitary conditions and dirty water in which the formula is often prepared. In addition, poor mothers often dilute the formula to make it last longer, inadvertently leaving their children malnourished. The World Health Organization (WHO) responded to the protesters' campaign with the issuance of an International Code of Marketing of Breast-Milk Substitutes. The Code attempts to ensure that mothers are not discouraged from breastfeeding by, among other things, forbidding the advertising of infant formula to the general public and banning the distribution of free formula samples in hospitals. Nestlé now claims to comply with the WHO Code.

Though these dimensions of accountability can be very effective, they are not democratic, in that citizens cannot use these mechanisms to hold governments accountable to them. One way to increase domestic accountability at the global level may be through creating stronger links between these global institutions and domestic governments. Keohane (2001) argues that this can be done by emphasizing the chains of delegation between a national government and the activities of those it has appointed to global institutions. In the EU, for example, citizens often hold national political parties responsible for their positions on matters of European integration. Citizens may need to demand more domestic debate about elected officials' positions on global issues. During the most recent presidential campaign in the US, the candidates' opinions about NAFTA featured prominently in the public discourse. More domestic-level discussion of global issues may be the first step in bringing accountability to issues of global governance.

Representation

In representative democracies, citizens delegate governing responsibility to government officials they elect to represent their interests. This is an essential feature of democracy in all but the tiniest communities where people could ostensibly represent themselves. Elected officials serve as agents for the public. Dahl (1999: 21) observes that in modern, large, complex states, the extent of delegation is so enormous – moving from elected officials to high-ranking executives to any number of bureaucrats – that it is impossible to say to what degree final policy outcomes are actually representative of constituent preferences. The European Union is famously said to suffer from a 'democratic deficit' (Follesdal and Hix, 2006; Hix, 2008). If this regional organization is viewed by many as being too far removed from the European public to accurately represent public preferences, how could global governance structures ever be representative of the diversity of preferences and interests the world over?

At the global level, Dahl writes that 'to speak in this case of "delegating authority" would simply be a misleading fiction useful only to the rulers' (1999: 22). Organizations like the United Nations that purport to be democratic because every country has a representative and decisions are taken on a 'one country, one vote' basis do not have a strong track record for effectively enhancing global cooperation. The world's wealthy and powerful countries often prefer to negotiate in more exclusive clubs such as the UN Security Council, NATO, or the IMF, whose voting system is based on the amount of dues a country pays. It is unlikely that a global parliament, composed of representatives from every country, would ever assume any meaningful power over national governments. The European Parliament has certainly had problems in this regard. Furthermore, many states are host to a variety of diverse sub-national regions and ethnic groups with different levels of autonomy from each other: would these groups be represented at the global level? If not, how would citizenries decide who would represent their country at the global level?

Rights

A final defining characteristic of democracy is the guarantee of certain rights to every citizen of a polis. Rights are meant to be fundamental individual-level protections that even changes in the distribution of political power cannot reverse. They are based in law, and if the separation of powers in a democracy is respected, they will survive any legislative or executive attempts to withdraw them. Thus, in order to exist, rights require a state. The state defines, legalizes, and protects the rights of all its citizens. Is it possible to conceptualize rights at a level above the state? Caporaso argues that at the global level, the protection of rights would require a stable political authority structure that is insulated from changes in the power and interests of states; unfortunately, this does not exist (2003: 379). At present, there exists no global authority that can enforce universal human rights from oppressive national governments.

However, the EU has made an unprecedented step in extending individual rights upward from the national level to the regional level. The EU has 'constitutionalized' its treaties by allowing individuals to have standing under EU law (Stone Sweet and Caporaso, 1998: 102). Whereas national governments in the EU were once the exclusive guarantors of rights to their citizenries, EU citizens now have a higher authority to which they can appeal if they feel their rights have not been protected by their state or have been violated by a domestic actor, public or private. Cases at this level are decided by the European Court of Justice (ECJ), and EU member states have accepted the supremacy of EU law over national law, where the EU Treaty contains provisions relevant to the case at hand. Rights in the EU have thus become regionalized; could this process happen in a similar way at the global level?

While states have resisted the creation of a supranational legal authority to enforce international law and punish transgressors, it could be argued that national governments – at least democratic ones – should be more willing to accept an international court that adjudicates cases between states and individual, rather than between two states. Today, international courts such as the International Court of Justice (ICJ) and the International Criminal Court (ICC) adjudicate cases among sovereign states. Individuals have not traditionally had standing to challenge international law violations in international courts, although this may be changing, as some human rights laws and trade laws (NAFTA, Chapter 11) are being applied to individuals and firms. Concerned with infractions of their sovereignty, states have by and large resisted being subject to any supranational legal authority, and subjection to the jurisdiction of the ICJ and the ICC remains voluntary. However, a case between a state and one of its citizens is not international in nature, so would a ruling against the state in a global court pose a threat to its sovereignty in the international system? In a democracy, the state's willingness to subject itself to the jurisdiction of a global or transnational body in cases of alleged civil rights infringements would not affect its place in the international system, but it would send a strong signal about its commitment to civil rights. Despite the development of supranational rights protections in the EU, there is little indication this trend will take hold anywhere else on the globe in the foreseeable future.

In the next section we will examine the relationship between states and the International Monetary Fund to gain a better understanding of the degree to which the IMF can be considered an autonomous actor, as well as the extent to which it can be considered democratic.

The International Monetary Fund

In recent years, the International Monetary Fund has been vilified as the embodiment of injustice in the global economy – a tool of the rich and powerful and a master of the developing world. The IMF has been characterized at different times as pathological, self-serving, inept, ideological, and patronizing. Leading economists and financiers have likened the IMF to 'medieval doctors who insisted on bleeding their patients' (Krugman, 2002), an 'emperor [with] no clothes' (Soros, 2002), and a 'colonial ruler' (Stiglitz, 2002). Much of this criticism centres on the accusation that the IMF's lending programmes have not achieved their goals of promoting stability and economic growth in the developing world. Stiglitz (2002) charges that the IMF's mistaken policy advice was largely to blame for the East Asian financial crisis of the 1990s. Some view the IMF's experience in Africa as a total failure, as many African countries had higher GDPs per capita in 1980 than in 2000, after spending nearly half of that time period receiving IMF loans and policy assistance (Stone, 2004). On the other hand, the Fund has had some success stories, notably in countries that already had functioning political and economic institutions, such as India, Indonesia, South Korea, and Thailand in the 1970s and 1980s (Kapur, 1998). Why aren't IMF loan programmes more successful? Some blame the IMF itself. Stiglitz accuses the Fund of serving financial and commercial interests from the developed world at the expense of the developing countries that receive its assistance. Others, including the IMF, blame the governments of countries that receive IMF assistance, charging them with poor or incomplete implementation of its policy prescriptions.

A spate of scholarly analysis in the last several years has been concerned with how the IMF can and should be reformed, while many other works from both the scholarly and popular literature have focused on whether its policies in the developing world should be deemed successes or failures. Our goal in this section is not to analyse the effectiveness of the IMF's policies, nor to make normative claims about its role in the developing world. Rather, we seek to develop a theoretically informed understanding of the IMF as an actor in the international economy by applying insights from the IR theories we have examined in this chapter. First, we will examine the way the IMF's activities have evolved over the decades, with an eye to understanding the sources of these changes. Second, we will analyse the extent to which the IMF can be considered an autonomous international actor, or whether it is best characterized as an agent hewing to the policies preferred by its principals. Finally, we will consider whether the IMF is a democratic and accountable actor in the global economy, arguing that the IMF's voting and governance structure contribute to a significant democratic deficit, and leave it susceptible to capture by powerful states.

Mission Creep and the Changing Role of the IMF

The policy-makers at Bretton Woods conceived of the International Monetary Fund as an international body tasked with managing financial relations between states. The IMF would supervise a system of fixed exchange rates in order to encourage international trade. Economists at the time believed that pegging currencies to the US dollar was the best way to maintain the exchange rate stability that would facilitate trade. The IMF's other major responsibility was to aid states threatened by balance-of-payments problems by providing them with short-term loans. These loans would help states stimulate demand to prevent economic downturns that could spread to other states, leading to global economic downturns such as the worldwide depression of the 1930s. In the wake of the oil crisis in the early 1970s, when the US decided to go off the gold standard, the system of fixed exchange rates collapsed and states moved to a floating exchange rate system. Since maintaining the fixed system had been the IMF's primary objective, the Fund now needed to find a new *raison d'être* or risk becoming obsolete (Feldstein, 1998; Dreher, 2004). It was during this time that the IMF stepped up its role as a provider of loans to countries facing long-term liquidity crises. These states typically were the poor developing states with little access to international credit (Kapur, 1998). The IMF also began to realize at this time that simply providing liquidity was often not enough to alleviate the chronic economic difficulties facing the world's poorest countries. Structural problems in these countries' economic systems needed to be resolved in order to achieve lasting economic growth, so the IMF began adding reform conditions to its loans. These conditions typically entailed budget cuts, tax hikes, liberalization of trade, and reduction in the supply of domestic credit, among other measures designed to improve export performance and resolve payment problems. Through these conditionality requirements attached to its loans, the IMF began to be deeply involved in states' domestic economic policies in ways not intended or envisioned by its architects at Bretton Woods.

What was the source of these changes in the IMF's role over the years? Some scholars argue that 'mission creep' is an inevitable by-product of bureaucratization. In any large, technocratic organization, there is an incentive to adapt and expand the mission to adjust to changing circumstances and challenges (Barnett and Finnemore, 2004; Stiglitz, 2002). If it was to remain an important global actor, the IMF needed to expand its mission when the fixed exchange rate regime collapsed. When it became clear that many of the world's struggling economies suffered from more chronic problems than just short-term liquidity crises, the IMF had an incentive to apply its expertise to become involved in these countries. The IMF's loan programme in Uruguay in 1990 is a good example of mission creep. This was a programme that was not designed to resolve the problem the IMF was charged to address: balance-of-payments problems. Uruguay's economy had problems, but a shortage of currency was not one of them. It had high reserves and a balance-of-payment surplus. The IMF's stated objectives in Uruguay were to strengthen public finances and tighten credit policy, and key elements of its programme there were reducing the size of the public sector, adjusting public sector wages, deregulation, privatization, and reforming social security (Vreeland, 2003). While this may have been sound economic advice, it was beyond the IMF's stated mission – and the mission agreed upon by its member states. States contributed money to the Fund for the purpose of resolving short-term liquidity crises, but the IMF loaned money to Uruguay and became deeply involved in restructuring its economy even though it was not suffering from a liquidity crisis.

In one sense, the IMF's much-discussed failures to prevent financial crises or promote sustainable economic development in many of its client states gave it justifications to reinvent itself, adjust its mission and expand into ever more issue areas (Barnett and Finnemore, 2004). When a loan programme fails, the IMF can argue that it needs greater authority to apply more expansive conditionality requirements. The IMF's responses to the various global financial crises over the years have been telling. As the organization charged with preventing these crises, it would be reasonable to expect crises to cause the IMF to reconsider the limits of its capacities. Rather, the IMF has tended to respond by asking its shareholders to expand its resources and its role in domestic economic affairs. After the Latin American debt crisis in 1982, the IMF argued that it needed to enlarge its mandate to include prescriptions for institutional and structural reforms, rather than just liquidity provision in exchange for fiscal and monetary reforms. The Fund began giving loan recipients increasingly detailed policy advice, expanding its reach into domestic economic issues it had previously left alone, such as suggesting whether states should cut spending by slashing military expenditures or social programmes. At the end of the 1980s, the Fund added two more goals to its agenda: poverty alleviation and good governance reforms (Kapur, 1998). After the Mexican debt crisis of 1994, the IMF concluded that less developed countries suffered from a common problem that the Fund was at that point ill-equipped to deal with: a lack of transparency. It asked its shareholders to increase the resources available to the IMF to ramp up its policing powers and correct this problem.

The IMF was perhaps most criticized for its response to the East Asian financial crisis. Several of these countries had been dubbed 'economic miracles' because they had achieved remarkable levels of growth and development since the 1970s. Furthermore, they had achieved this growth without following the Washington Consensus policies advocated by the IMF (Stiglitz, 2002). When Thailand's currency collapsed in 1997 and the East Asian countries began fearing a regional crisis, the IMF stepped in offering loan and stability programmes, but this assistance was tied to a host of conditionalities, one of which was maintaining capital market openness, even as capital fled the crisis countries. The IMF bailout strategy propped up exchange rates, which only further encouraged currency speculators to sell off the East Asian currencies. Economists now largely agree that this policy prescription resulted in a severe worsening in the crisis countries that accepted the IMF bailout packages, and the IMF has also admitted as much (Kapur, 1998; Feldstein, 1998). Malaysia and China, two countries that dared to reject IMF bailout packages, averted deeper crises and recovered much more quickly than their neighbours who perfectly followed the IMF's prescriptions. South Korea also ignored much of the IMF's advice, with the government taking a more active role in economic restructuring than the Fund advised, and its economy recovered quickly.

If the IMF so often misses the mark, sometimes even making crises worse, why does it still exist? Even more puzzling, why has the IMF seemed to become more powerful and more involved in domestic economies in the face of deep and persistent questions about its effectiveness? Rationalist IR theory suggests that international organizations that do not fulfil their mandates and accomplish the goals that states have given them will either cease to exist, or will cease to wield any influence or power. In other words, states will stop investing in them. The IMF's continued influence seems to fly in the face of many IR theories until we consider who the IMF's main stakeholders are, and who bears the costs of its failures. The world's powerful countries, the developed economies that hold the purse-strings and the microphone within the IMF, are not the ones that directly suffer from failed IMF programmes. Rather, the world's developing countries and their impoverished citizens and nascent industries take the greatest risks when accepting loans and conditionality programmes from the IMF. When these programmes backfire, as during the Asian financial crisis, locals lose out as banks shut down, home-grown firms lose access to capital, production slows, and jobs are lost. In 2002, incomes in the East Asian crisis countries were 20 per cent less than they could have been if the growth of the previous decade had not been interrupted (Stiglitz, 2002: 121). When we consider the way power is distributed in the global economy, and the fact that the countries that lose out from IMF mistakes tend to be the least powerful, the IMF's continued influence becomes less surprising. Furthermore, many argue that the IMF bailout policies are in essence bailouts of Western financial institutions (Stiglitz, 2002; Gould, 2003). Thus, even if an IMF programme fails to promote development in the poor countries, its loans may serve developed country interests by buffering their banks in times of crisis. Policies that seem like failures from the perspective of the developing world may actually be quite successful in terms of developed-country interests. In sum, the IMF's persistent 'mission creep' over the years may be tolerated if it furthers the interests of the world's most powerful states.

Autonomous Actor or States' Agent?

Earlier in this chapter we argued that the principal–agent approach can be a valuable analytical tool for understanding the relationship between states and international organizations. We can use insights from the P–A approach to evaluate some of the ways the IMF has interacted with states and affected the trajectory of the global economy over the past several decades. First, let's consider who the Fund's principals are. The Fund has multiple principals, some of which are collective principals. In theory, the Fund has 187 principals – each of its member states. In practice, however, only the five largest stakeholders (the US, Japan, Germany, France, and the UK), each of whom enjoys their own executive director, have the power and influence to act as true principals. The other states share executive directors, and these directors that represent groups of countries are treated by P–A theory as collective principals. P–A theory expects agency slippage to be more likely in situations when there are multiple principals, and also when there are collective principals (Nielson and Tierney, 2003). As the number of principals increases, they find it difficult to coordinate their preferences, as they may have divergent interests. In this situation, it becomes difficult for the principals to control the agent. The agent gains autonomy and has more room to pursue its own interests, as it is aware of difficulties among the principals in agreeing upon policy and coordinating their activities. In the IMF, however, the five largest stakeholders control 40 per cent of the vote share, so they are the only principals whose preferences truly matter. If they can coordinate their preferences, they should, in theory, be able to constrain the actions of the IMF as their agent. Rationalist IR theory, with its state-centric ontology, would lead us to expect that the IMF would act as the agent of the five most powerful stakeholders, and if they can coordinate their preferences to speak with a unified voice they should be able to direct the IMF to further their interests.

Constructivist approaches would focus more than rationalist approaches on the IMF itself as an actor, with its own preferences and interests. What is in the IMF's interest? The IMF's interest is to increase its capacity as an actor and ensure that it stays in business. To do this, the IMF needs to keep lending money, increasing its clientele, and in turn, convincing its donors that it needs an expanded budget. With more resources at their fingertips, IMF staffers have an opportunity to increase their prestige and influence (Vaubel, 1991; Dreher, 2004).

To what extent does the IMF actually operate as an autonomous actor, serving its own interests, and to what extent does it adhere to its role as an agent of states? Barnett and Finnemore (2004) argue that the IMF's primary source of autonomy is its technical knowledge and expertise. Because government officials trust the expertise of IMF economists, they are likely to defer to IMF judgments and be receptive to IMF policy prescriptions. Woods argues that member-state policy preferences provide an 'outer structural constraint' within which the IMF operates with considerable autonomy and discretion (2006: 2). An example of this autonomy is the way the IMF was able to convince governments to reverse their long-standing aversion to capital market liberalization during the 1980s and 1990s. Chwieroth (2007, 2008) and Abdelal (2007) argue that an internal ideational shift took place within the Fund during this time, and the IMF acted as 'an agent of persuasion and disseminator of ideas' (Chwieroth, 2007: 7) that successfully influenced member states' preferences about capital liberalization. Far from merely implementing its member states' desired policies, Chwieroth argues that IMF staff adopted capital liberalization as a new informal norm before the Fund's formal rules had changed. This was able to happen as a result of significant 'slippage' between the Fund's formal rules – approved by member states – and its staff's own ideas (Chwieroth, 2008: 32). Contrary to what state-centric IR theories would expect, the IMF appears to have disseminated new ideas about capital account liberalization that changed the policy preferences of its member states. One way this was able to happen was through the Fund's hiring practices. Through 'screening and selecting' new recruits, principals can use hiring as a tool to ensure that their agents will adhere to their preferred policies. Kahler (1992) finds, however, that IMF member states typically grant the organization's management 'wide discretion' over staff hiring. This would allow the Fund to fill its ranks with staff members that shared its internal economic views but not necessarily those of its member states. Chwieroth's analysis (2008) of IMF administrative recruitment confirms that it hired and promoted a new crop of economists who viewed capital liberalization as desirable well before member states had also adopted this view.

Despite the emphasis many scholars place on the IMF's autonomy as an actor, some highlight the ways that states are still able to use the IMF as a tool to serve their own interests, much as the state-centric IR theories expect. Vreeland (2003) argues that governments sometimes use the IMF as a scapegoat to push through unpopular economic reforms. As mentioned earlier, Uruguay sought out IMF assistance in 1990 despite the fact that it was in no need of a loan. With high reserves and a balance-of-payment surplus, Uruguay drew on less than 10 per cent of its IMF loan. The question becomes, why accept an IMF loan and its accompanying conditionalities if the funds aren't needed? It is possible that signing an IMF agreement sends a credible commitment to potential investors because non-compliance with an IMF agreement is costly. These agreements are costly because they entail unpopular compromises of national sovereignty as well as the risk of punishment by the IMF for failure to comply. This can reassure investors that the government is serious about reform and will not bow to domestic opponents of reform. Vreeland argues that this is precisely what happened in Uruguay when a reform-oriented government sought to make unpopular changes to jumpstart the economy, but feared voter backlash. In the face of widespread popular opposition, Uruguay's President Lacalle was able to push significant reform measures through the legislature using the IMF agreement as leverage. This was an accomplishment that had proved politically impossible before concluding the agreement with the IMF. The same logic may have been at work in Tanzania, whose socialist governments had rejected IMF conditionality agreements for years despite severe balance-of-payments problems. When the reformist Mwinyi was elected president in 1985, he brought in the IMF to help him push through unpopular austerity measures that his political party was unwilling to support. Vreeland's analysis suggests that the IMF is useful to governments not just when they need a loan. The IMF's controversial and much maligned conditionality requirements are sometimes used strategically by domestic political actors in order to achieve their policy preferences. Likewise, states often reject IMF agreements when these agreements don't serve their interests.

Simmons (2000) analyses the legalization of monetary policy under the Bretton Woods agreements to argue that committing themselves to IMF rules helps governments make credible commitments to market actors. The Bretton Woods architects designed 'hard' legal commitments about monetary policy after the 'soft' standards of the interwar years had proved useless. The IMF's Articles initially contained rules to maintain a fixed exchange rate system, and countries pegged their currencies to the US dollar, which was in turn pegged to the gold standard. However, compliance was far from perfect. Several important economies such as Canada, Germany, and the Netherlands floated their currencies when market forces demanded it, and when the US went off the gold standard in 1971 during the oil crisis, the entire system collapsed. During this time most governments continued to comply with the IMF's rules on keeping current accounts free from restrictions and maintaining unified exchange rates. This compliance seems theoretically puzzling because of the fact that the IMF cannot directly enforce compliance with these rules, and countries face incentives to deviate depending on economic conditions. Nevertheless, Simmons argues that states derive utility from adhering to IMF rules because this sends a powerful signal to market actors that they will refrain from interference in free exchange. This does not ensure compliance, but governments with reputations for respecting the rule of law will suffer costs if they break these obligations. Thus, the mechanism behind compliance is the desire to avoid reputational costs by reneging on reforms.

However, Simmons argues that the decision to commit to IMF rules is influenced by other countries' decisions to commit. Any given state does not want to be left a 'sucker' by being one of the few to comply, while others deviate when it serves their interests. In this way, the IMF membership framework serves an important problem-solving role for states and provides a way to make cooperation more likely. By legalizing monetary policy, the IMF provided states with a way to credibly commit to liberalization and openness. As non-compliance would hurt a state's reputation with market actors, states could gain more assurance that their peers would cooperate with the rules. The IMF's ability to monitor deviations from rules and publicize non-compliance further enhances its ability to reduce the transaction costs associated with compliance and facilitate cooperation among states. The utility that states gain from the legalization of monetary rules is an outcome that is predicted by neoliberal institutionalist models of cooperation.

Stone (2004) makes an argument that the IMF's principals should actually allow the organization greater autonomy in its programmes. He argues that the IMF's powerful principals intervene to prevent consistent enforcement of conditionality requirements in countries where they have a political interest. The IMF's loans in Pakistan were suspended when Pakistan conducted nuclear weapons tests, over objections by the international community, and the loans were reinstated in 2001 when Pakistan agreed to aid the US in the war in Afghanistan. Nothing changed with regards to Pakistan's economic performance during this time: it demonstrated a consistent need for IMF assistance. Similarly, Stone argues that the failures of IMF programmes in Africa cannot be blamed solely on corrupt, dysfunctional domestic political and economic systems. Rather, he demonstrates that French, British, and US interests in African countries affect the likelihood that these countries will face punishments or loan suspensions from the IMF. While the Fund's principals have a long-term interest in the enforcement of the Fund's conditionalities, sometimes they have a short-term political interest in allowing lax enforcement. Stone argues that if the IMF were allowed greater autonomy from its principals to enforce its policies, its programmes would be more effective in promoting growth and stability in the developing world.

When analysing the IMF's role in the global economy, IR theorists are often interested in the degree to which this organization acts as a reliable agent of its member states, or whether it wields enough independence to further its own goals that may deviate from those of the states it was designed to represent. We have examined some of the ways that IMF conditionality programmes can at times prove very useful to developing states in furthering domestic economic goals, especially when these include unpopular reforms. At the same time, these states wield little influence as principals guiding the direction of IMF policy. The IMF's governance structure explicitly grants much more power to the five wealthiest member states, which retain considerable control over IMF decision-making. While the IMF has at times persuaded even these states to adopt new economic policies, such as capital liberalization, we argue that the IMF enjoys a considerable degree of autonomy and discretion, remaining a reliable agent only for the wealthiest few states.

Democracy and Accountability

The IMF is a public institution. Its budget is funded by contributions from its member states, which in turn are funded by taxpayers. But is the IMF a democratic

institution? Earlier in this chapter we discussed the ways that international institutions may strengthen their democratic legitimacy and accountability. We
emphasized several dimensions of democracy: participation, accountability, representation, and rights. In this section we will consider how these dimensions of
democracy hold up in the IMF. We can dispense with two of these dimensions up
front: participation and rights. According to Grant and Keohane (2005), there are
two distinct models of accountability – the participation model and the delegation model. In the participation model, political authorities answer to the public,
and it is therefore incumbent upon the public to participate in holding these
authorities accountable. In the delegation model, by contrast, authorities are held
accountable to the actors that entrusted them with power. Since states delegated
powers to the IMF, this model of accountability holds that the IMF should be
accountable to states, not necessarily to individual citizens. Thus, participation by
the citizenry is not the primary way to hold the IMF accountable. Other mechanisms are necessary, stemming from the relationship between the IMF as an
agent and the state as its principal. In reality, citizens participate very little in the
workings of the IMF or the appointment of its management. Rights are the other
dimension of democracy that have little relevance when discussing democracy in
the IMF. The IMF is a technocratic organization with a limited mandate and as
such it does not have the authority to grant or uphold individual rights.

Let us now turn to representation. Does the IMF represent its member states
in a democratic way? The IMF was designed to answer to its member states, but
it does not represent them all equally. Each of the Fund's 187 member states
appoints a delegate to represent that state at the Fund's major meetings in
Washington. On a daily basis, however, the Fund is managed by a smaller board
of executive directors. This board consists of 24 directors, 5 of whom represent
each of the 5 largest IMF donor states: the US, Japan, Germany, France, and the
United Kingdom. China, Russia, and Saudi Arabia also appoint their own directors. The other 16 directors represent the other 179 member states: each director represents a group of countries. The member states vote on the Fund's major
policy decisions, but the votes are weighted according to the 'one dollar, one
vote' principle, whereby the states that contribute the most money to the Fund's
operating budget have the most voting power. With nearly 17 per cent of the
voting power, the US is the only country with an effective veto, but the US and
the next four largest donors (those named above) together hold nearly 40 per
cent of the votes. An important feature of this voting system is that a state cannot
decide to contribute more funding in order to increase its vote share; the entire
executive board must approve each state's contribution – and hence – voting levels
(Barnett and Finnemore, 2004: 49). An advantage of this governance structure
is that the Board is small, flexible, and efficient, but this efficiency comes at the
expense of democracy (Woods and Lombardi, 2006). Since the smaller states do
not enjoy the privilege of appointing their own executive directors, the IMF's
governance structure is explicitly designed to best reflect the interests of its
most powerful principals. The smaller states represented collectively by

shared directors may face considerable collective-action problems coordinating their interests in order to be represented effectively by their directors.

The IMF may not represent its members democratically, but are there strong accountability mechanisms available to its member states? An organization can be undemocratic but capable of being held accountable. At the formal level, there are varying levels of accountability mechanisms built into the IMF's rules to hold executive directors accountable to the states they represent. While states that appoint their own executive director can terminate his or her employment at will, the groups of states represented by a collective director have no such recourse. These directors are held accountable primarily through informal mechanisms such as peer pressure and moral suasion by other IMF directors (Woods and Lombardi, 2006). Accountability is in this way skewed to favour the wealthiest states that enjoy their own executive directors. Another way that states can hold international organizations accountable is by withholding annual dues, or threatening to do so. This mechanism is not available to the IMF member states, because they make a one-time contribution upon joining the organization. This enhances the IMF's autonomy since it is not dependent on raising funds from donors year after year. Its financing comes from its pot of reserves, interest that it earns from lending, and its own investments. A third way states hold their agents accountable is by maintaining a short chain of delegation. This can prevent 'slippage' of preferences from one end of the chain to the other. If the executive board is the link between states and the IMF, the fact that 179 member states share 16 directors presents a considerable problem for holding the IMF accountable to these states. Going one step further, Woods argues that the executive board's oversight of the staff responsible for key day-to-day policy decisions is too weak to be considered 'an exercise of vertical accountability' (2001: 84).

The IMF's governance rules make it less than democratic, and these same rules also mean states are not equally able to hold it accountable. The wealthy states with their own executive directors can dismiss these directors at will, while the majority of states share directors and do not have the unilateral ability to dismiss them. The IMF's programmes have the greatest effect on developing countries, yet these are the states that are disadvantaged in their ability to hold the IMF accountable.

Conclusion

This chapter has sought to illuminate some of the reasons why international institutions exist and how they are involved in globalization processes. Focusing on the institutions that manage the global economy, we have shown that states sometimes face considerable collective action problems that institutions can help resolve. Cooperation over complex economic issues is exceedingly difficult in a world full of different types of economies and states at different levels of development. When economic interests diverge, international institutions can play an important role in bringing states to the table to coordinate their policies and reduce the transaction costs of cooperating, so that all are able to reap economic gains. At the same time, institutions bring with them a whole new set of problems. We have focused in this chapter on two of the most important problems institutions can create for states, from both a practical and a normative standpoint. International organizations develop agency and authority of their own, which increases the potential that their policies and activities will deviate from the preferences of the states that created them and delegated them with power. This is a major problem for states from a policy-making standpoint, but it is also a normative problem when these organizations suffer from a democratic deficit. In an increasingly globalized world, the community of democracies must find ways to ensure that global governance also is democratic. The powerful international institutions that wield such influence not only over transnational issues but over domestic economic policy as well must be designed in ways such that their member states can hold them accountable. Organizations such as the IMF are often criticized for representing the interests of only the world's wealthiest states, and these criticisms are often valid. If globalization continues to enhance the role that international institutions play in governing the transnational economy, and if these institutions are to be sustainable, it is incumbent upon states to design them in ways such that they represent the entire global community and not just the powerful few.

6

WINNERS AND LOSERS OF GLOBALIZATION

Introduction

Why is globalization such a controversial process? As countries have opened their borders to trade and investment, they have benefited from unprecedented levels of wealth. Virtually all economists agree that trade liberalization is a nearly certain way to increase national income. Technological advances have spread around the world. Access to the internet in even the world's poorest countries has allowed previously unimaginable communication links between people and organizations as well as connections to knowledge and resources. Millions of jobs have been created for people who once depended on subsistence-level incomes. Standards of living are up all over the globe. The number of people living in extreme poverty (defined by the World Bank as less than $1.25 a day) has declined steadily since 1990. But for all the wealth that globalization has created, it remains highly contentious. Popular understandings of globalization often portray it as a zero-sum game: in order for some to reap huge benefits, others must suffer huge losses. Alternatively, some describe globalization as a process through which everyone wins, but some win substantially more than others. A rising tide may lift all boats, but some boats may rise more or faster than the rest.

The conception of globalization as a competition that creates winners and losers may stem not entirely from popular myth, but it may be at least partially based in empirical reality. The 1980s ushered in an era of unprecedented international trade and capital mobility, but during this time income inequality has grown substantially within countries both in the developed and developing worlds (Friedman, 2000; Stiglitz, 2002; Jaumotte et al., 2007). This rise in income inequality has certainly coincided temporally with the globalization of national economies, but is globalization its true cause? If so, what aspect of globalization? This has been the subject of much research. Some studies find a link between trade openness and income inequality in developing countries

(Meschi and Vivarelli, 2007). Others point to de-unionization, demographic shifts from rural to urban areas, increased immigration into developed countries, or technological advances that advantage skilled labour rather than unskilled labour.

The demands of competition in a global economy have forced major changes in developed and developing countries alike. These changes are often very difficult and domestically unpopular. The face of small-town America, for example, has changed completely as the mom-and-pop stores that families operated for generations have had to close up shop when the big-box chains moved in, their shelves stocked with cheap imports from less developed countries. Thousands of workers in developed countries have lost their jobs as firms and entire industries have moved offshore to less costly locations. The traditional crafts and farming practices that have not only been the livelihood of tribes and ethnic groups all over the world, but also been at the core of their cultural identities, are being abandoned as the demand for these types of goods gives way to demand for cheaper, mass-produced alternatives. Why are these profound and often painful changes accepted? The most compelling justification for the disruptions imposed by the new global economy is that globalization has lifted millions out of poverty, and the hope is that it will continue to do so. Most people seem to believe that globalization, while temporarily painful for some, is the best way to bring a better way of life to the more than one billion people worldwide still living in extreme poverty.

If poverty reduction is one of the primary reasons why people accept or support globalization, is progress being made toward this goal? It is important to differentiate between measuring reductions in the *percentage* of the population living in poverty (the poverty rate), and reductions in the total *number* of people living in poverty. While the percentage of people living in extreme poverty (under $1.25 a day) has declined in every region of the world, this reduction has only been deep enough to substantially reduce the number of extremely poor people in East Asia and certain parts of South Asia, with the most dramatic poverty reduction coming mainly from China (United Nations, 2009: 6). In the rest of the world, however, the poverty reduction picture has not been so rosy. The poverty rate grew through the 1990s in Eastern Europe and Central Asia, but it has since fallen steadily. In other regions, population growth has outpaced reductions in the poverty rate, so that even though the percentage of people living in extreme poverty has declined, the total number of people living in extreme poverty may be the same or even higher. Since 1980, while the poverty rate has fallen in Latin America, the Middle East, and North Africa, there have been no significant changes in the number of poor people in Latin America, and only small reductions in the Middle East and North Africa. Sadly, the number of people living in extreme poverty has actually increased in certain world regions since 1990, most notably sub-Saharan Africa and South Asia. In addition, while there are now fewer people worldwide living on less than a dollar a day, or less than $1.25 a day, their income gains have not exactly been spectacular: there were more people living on under $2 a day in 2005 than there were in 1981 (all these figures from Chen and Ravallion, 2008: 41–4).

The poor in developing countries are not the only ones who are often characterized as 'losers' of globalization. The multi-dimensionality of globalization means that almost everyone is affected and there are many different potential winners, and many different potential losers. Some cast globalization as primarily a competition between the haves and the have-nots, in which capitalist elites win at the expense of the working masses, or developed countries of the North win at the expense of the developing countries of the South. Alternatively, some see globalization as a contest between transnational conglomerates and traditional mom-and-pop stores, the latter being steamrolled by the Wal-Marts and Starbucks that spring up on every corner. In a similar way, globalization can be viewed as a contest between the efficient and the inefficient, or between the more technologically advanced and the less advanced. It is the plight of the traditional French farmer, keeper of beloved French cultural practices, against modernized factory farms elsewhere in Europe. Still others view globalization through the lens of the worker who loses her job when it is outsourced to a cheaper labour market abroad; in this scenario, globalization creates winners and losers of workers who lose jobs or gain them at the whim of footloose capital. Finally, for many people the tons of toxic electronic waste from rich countries that are shipped offshore and dumped in developing countries like Nigeria, or in the world's largest garbage dump that floats in the middle of the Pacific Ocean, are examples of the way the natural environment is a casualty of globalization. Without global environmental standards or national-level standards that are equally high across countries, many fear that economic considerations will always win out over ecological ones.

One of the consequences of the belief that globalization creates winners and losers has been the growing number, intensity, and visibility of anti-globalization protests not only in the developing world but in the developed world as well. It seems almost taken for granted today that every major global economic summit by organizations such as the WTO, the IMF, the World Economic Forum, and the G-8 will be accompanied by massive, disruptive, and sometimes bloody demonstrations by anti-globalization protesters. The so-called Battle of Seattle surrounding a WTO summit in 1999 completely overshadowed the trade negotiations, as thousands of protesters blocked delegates' access to meetings; this led to hundreds of arrests and injuries after protesters refused to disperse, and riot police threw tear gas into the crowds. Just two years later, a meeting of G-8 leaders in Genoa triggered some of Western Europe's most violent protests in recent years, with thousands of injuries, widespread accusations of police brutality, and the fatal shooting of one protester by Genoese police. Nowadays it is commonplace for economic summits to take place in highly guarded areas barricaded by roadblocks, specially erected walls, and the protection of thousands of police, military personnel, and even snipers. The United Kingdom reportedly spent £100million on security of this sort for the meeting of G-8 leaders in

Gleneagles, Scotland, in 2005 (Shabi, 2005). If globalization made everybody better off, would things be different?

This chapter will consider why globalization is often characterized as a competition that creates winners and losers around the world. First, we will describe the dynamics of the different forms of competition introduced above. Second, we will examine the expectations generated by several leading political and economic theories about who is likely to win and who is likely to lose under conditions of globalization. Third, we will assess empirically how each group has fared thus far, arguing that as a whole, consumers, owners of capital from the developed world, and skilled labourers have been relative winners in the global economy. We also argue that unskilled labourers, developing country firms, governments, the environment, and women have as a whole lost out relative to other actors under conditions of globalization. Since anti-globalization protests have often been highly publicized and increasingly violent in recent years, the chapter will conclude with an examination of who protests against globalization, why they protest, and whether these protests have had any impact on global governance or global economic developments.

Globalization as Competition

If globalization merely reduced costs of transportation and communication, diffused technology around the world, and democratized access to knowledge, it would probably not be such a divisive subject. The problem many people have with globalization is in its capitalist power of creative destruction. As barriers to trade are brought down and markets are flooded with products from abroad, traditional markets and traditional ways of life are often destroyed. Globalization pits different models of production against each other, different technologies, different labour, and taxation policies – and the most efficient win. In this way, globalization is inherently a competitive process, with the potential to create winners and losers, and when markets are so big that they stretch across continents, the stakes are extremely high. The efficient firms that 'win' the competition will reap profits from all over the globe, and those that 'lose' will be left with a drastically smaller market share.

Globalization creates, first of all, competition among firms across national borders as national barriers to trade fall. Firms must compete not only to retain market share in existing domestic markets as foreign companies enter the fray, but also to expand market share in foreign markets. The opening of borders to international competition can be a radical adjustment for firms accustomed to operating in protected industries or in competition only with other domestic firms. Asymmetries in technology give some firms clear advantages over others and can make it impossible for firms with less advanced production processes to offer goods of equally high quality at equally low prices. Firms that are used to receiving generous subsidies and other support from government may also be ill-prepared to operate in the more *laissez-faire* economic environment that market liberalization requires. On the other hand, lax domestic regulatory environments can make it difficult for companies to succeed in more strictly regulated foreign markets. Firms from big domestic markets with larger economies of scale will also be better prepared to increase market share across national borders than firms accustomed to only a very small and local market.

Second, globalization creates competition among countries. National governments must compete to attract foreign capital in all its forms. They must compete with other countries to attract foreign direct investment that will create jobs, bring technology, and produce goods that will be consumed at home as well as exported abroad. They do this by offering incentives to foreign investors such as low corporate tax rates, low levels of regulation, secure property rights, and the privatization of state-owned firms and industries. National governments also compete to attract portfolio investment, which alleviates domestic capital shortages. They make themselves attractive for this type of investment through financial market liberalization and monetary policy designed to keep interest and exchange rates high. Finally, national governments must compete with each other to attract loans and foreign aid, and this requires them to build strong democratic political institutions and liberal economic institutions, while weeding out corruption.

Third, globalization creates competition between factors of production. The entry of the former Soviet Union, China, and India into the labour market has halved the ratio of capital to labour at the international level, making labour much more abundant relative to capital and thus driving wages downward (Freeman, 2007). The doubling of the global labour supply, combined with the mobility of capital, has for the most part increased the returns to capital and decreased the returns to labour. In an abundant labour market, business can relocate to find cheaper labour, while workers are much less mobile and hence much less able to move to markets where they can be paid higher wages. Furthermore, representatives of the factors of production compete to have their favoured policies adopted by governments, and these policies often conflict. The policies promoted by organized labour are not often the same as those promoted by business, and the policies promoted by agriculture are often different still. In a global market where capital is scarce *vis-à-vis* labour, capital enjoys a stronger bargaining position with national governments. While labour may attempt to strengthen federally mandated labour standards, social programmes, and perhaps protectionist trade rules, business often lobbies governments to do away with standards and social programmes that it views as too costly and inefficient, as well as barriers to trade and capital mobility. In this way, globalization pits capital and labour against each other in international trade negotiations as well as in domestic political battles over social protections and labour standards. However, competition exists not just between capital and labour, but between different types of capital. Multinational corporations (MNCs) from developed countries want access to markets everywhere, while small, local firms often want protection from the more competitive MNCs. In a similar way, investors in more mobile, financial capital versus more fixed industrial capital perceive different gains and losses in a globalized economy. While mobile capital benefits from the liberalization of trade and financial markets, fixed, capital often wants protection from foreign competition and privileged access to the domestic market. These conflicting demands pressure governments in opposite directions and create the potential for winners and losers.

Fourth, globalization creates competition between business and civil society. International trade and the production of goods to serve global markets create massive externalities that often turn into public problems. Environmental pollution is now a serious problem all over the world, and while industry seeks to skirt environmental regulations that it deems too costly, countless international nongovernmental organizations have sprung up to push back in the opposite direction by pressuring governments to hold business more accountable for its environmental impact. When firms themselves aren't forced to clean up their pollution, taxpayers often end up footing the bill. In the US, the Environmental Protection Agency cleans up abandoned toxic waste sites through the Superfund programme. Legal mechanisms are in place to aid the EPA in recovering cleanup costs from responsible parties, though cost recovery is not always possible. In less developed countries, governments may not have the capability to hold parties responsible for messes, large foreign firms especially, let alone the capability to clean up toxic sites with public funds. Tensions between environmental and economic concerns often erupt during trade negotiations, such as during the drafting of NAFTA, when conservation and economic growth were often portrayed as conflicting goals.

Similarly, civil society also puts the pressure on business to better protect human rights and the public interest. When industry seeks to cut costs by moving to ever cheaper labour markets, watchdog groups pressure both governments and firms themselves to provide safe, clean work environments and a living wage. Consumer safety groups pressure governments to adopt product quality standards that industry often opposes, such as the removal of lead paint from children's toys. Different countries have different safety standards, and these differences can sometimes impede international trade. The EU, for example, has banned the vast majority of American beef imports for over 20 years because cattle in the US are routinely treated with growth hormones. Concerns about the health and environmental effects of genetically modified foods have also hampered international trade, as the EU as well as several other countries have had long-standing bans on the importation of these products. These types of tensions (either real or perceived) between what is the most economically efficient mode of production and what is in the public's best interest have created a competitive environment between representatives of business and civil society who seek to institutionalize their preferred policies. Governments are lobbied hard by both sides, but the playing field may not be quite equal.

The mobility of capital in the globalized era means that if public policy strays too far from industry's preferences, firms can relocate their factories abroad, taking precious jobs with them. While workers rarely can pick up and go to another country with better labour standards, and the environment can't protect itself, INGOs and other civil society groups do find ways to successfully strengthen environmental and labour regulations, whether through domestic democratic channels or through international pressure.

Is globalization a process that benefits everyone, as many politicians claim, or is it an inherently competitive process – creating some winners but also some losers? It may be too early to tell whether or not policies can be designed that allow the economy to flourish and grow, creating jobs for millions and reducing the prices of goods for consumers everywhere, while also preventing exploitation of the natural world and its most disadvantaged inhabitants. Innovative and promising solutions to some complex problems are beginning to emerge, such as international cap-and-trade programmes for curbing emissions of pollutants, which is still a controversial method of pollution reduction but which exemplifies a creative solution meant to satisfy both business and civil society. However, at this stage in the game, there is a powerful perception among many that the globalization of the economy has been a process that disproportionately benefits certain segments of the world's population at the expense of the majority.

Theories of Winners and Losers

Theories of international trade help us understand which actors can be expected to win or lose in a competitive globalized economy, and under what circumstances. The costs and benefits of globalization will depend on a variety of considerations. In this section we will examine several leading political economic and international trade theories and their implications for which actors stand to gain or lose in a more globalized economy.

Factor-based Approaches

Factor-based approaches use factor endowments to predict which actors will be relative winners and relative losers as economies become more open to trade. The Stolper–Samuelson theorem (1941) provides a theoretical link between trade and wage levels. It is an important corollary of the Heckscher–Ohlin model of international trade, which predicts that trade patterns will reflect national endowments of factors of production (land, labour, or capital). The Stolper–Samuelson theorem predicts that trade liberalization will benefit actors associated with the abundant factor of production and harm those associated with the scarce factor. This happens through the price changes that result from international trade. As the price of a good rises when it is exported to foreign markets, the returns to the factor used most intensively in its production will also rise, primarily through the increased demand for that factor. This model builds on Ricardian theories of comparative advantage that say that countries should specialize in the production of goods in which they have a comparative advantage, relative to other countries. When a country liberalizes its trade, it will receive higher relative prices on the global market for goods that it produces more efficiently than other countries. These goods will require intensive use of the economy's abundant factor. For example, in today's economy, the advanced industrialized countries of the global North – the developed world – are rich in capital but poor in cheap labour relative to the developing world. In other words, there is a relatively greater supply of wealth and money for investment in the developed world than there is a supply of people willing to work low-paying manufacturing jobs. By contrast, in most developing nations there is an abundance of unemployed or underemployed people willing to go to work in low-paying jobs that would be considered undesirable in the developed world. There is also a shortage of capital in poor countries at earlier stages of economic development. Thus, to be most efficient, wealthy developed nations should specialize in industries that require major capital investments and advanced technology, but fewer workers, such as the production of cars or computers for export. Countries that don't have a lot of capital or advanced technology, but have a lot of workers instead, should specialize in the production of garments or textiles for export, for example, because this type of industry requires lots of workers but less capital and technology. The model can also be used with skilled labour and unskilled labour as the two factors of production. Countries with better educated workforces and lots of opportunities for skill training should export goods such as pharmaceuticals that require higher-paid, skilled workers, whereas countries with greater numbers of unskilled or poorly educated workers should export manufactured or agricultural goods that do not require a highly skilled labour force.

When countries specialize in the industries in which they have a comparative advantage, and relative prices rise on the global market, the overall returns paid to the factor used most intensively in production – the abundant factor – will also rise. This happens because as profit-seeking firms increase production for export, demand increases for the abundant factor of production, which also will drive up the price of that factor (in the form of wages if labour is the abundant factor, or in the form of interest rates if capital is the abundant factor). Returns to the abundant factor also increase simply because it is now in greater demand and more workers can be hired, or more capital can be borrowed. Trade will therefore increase the incomes of those who hold positions in relatively abundant factors, e.g. workers will gain disproportionately when labour is a relatively abundant factor, capitalists will gain when capital is relatively abundant, and so on. In economies with an abundance of labour – the developing world – Stolper–Samuelson predicts that specialization in labour-intensive goods for the international market will bring increasing returns to labour. Likewise, capital will earn higher returns than labour will in capital-rich, developed economies. This does not mean that wages will necessarily drop, but it means that inequality may grow as capital collects increasing returns.

Rogowski (1989) extends the model into the political realm, arguing that as the abundant factor gains from increasing trade, the owners of this factor will be able to translate their gains into political success. They will be able to form strong coalitions to lobby (often successfully) for their preferred economic policies, which further institutionalizes their success as long as trade continues to grow. Thus, in a world where countries are integrating more and more into the global economy, we can expect the owners of abundant factors to prosper and unite to influence the direction of policies. In the developed world, not only will the owners of capital (capitalists) increase their income through international trade, but also will workers in capital-intensive industries and other workers that possess skills and training generally unavailable in poorer, developing countries. Low-skilled workers in the developed world, however, can be expected to lose out as their jobs are increasingly outsourced to labour markets where low-skilled workers are more abundant and labour costs are thus cheaper. Similarly, the theorem predicts that the relatively abundant factor – labour – in developing countries stands to gain from trade liberalization, as jobs requiring manpower relocate to emerging markets from the developed world.

Sectoral Analysis

Sectoral theorists argue that changes in international trade are more likely to affect sectors of the economy, rather than factors of production, and because of this, Frieden argues 'political behaviour, especially with regard to economic policy, is less commonly factoral (labourers as a class, capitalists as a class) than sectoral (the steel industry, the dairy farming industry)' (Frieden, 1991: 436). Sectoral approaches expect that members of an industry that is struggling in the face of more intense international competition will unite to lobby governments whether they are executives or assembly-line workers. These sectoral coalitions will be stronger and more developed than cross-sectoral coalitions of workers or owners of capital. Additionally, the attributes of states' leading sectors determine patterns of international trade (and redistributional consequences of trade) better than factor endowments do (Shafer, 1994). Sectoral theorists justify this approach by arguing that factors are much less mobile than the Heckscher–Ohlin model assumes. Heckscher–Ohlin assumes that factors will move costlessly to the economic activity in which they are most productive; thus, unskilled workers in developed countries, finding themselves out of work once their jobs are outsourced, will soon be able to acquire skills training and get a new job in a more highly skilled sector. Stubbornly high unemployment rates in many OECD countries suggest this is not as easy as it sounds.

Sectoral theorists, on the other hand, argue that economic actors strongly resist the insecurity that comes with economic restructuring and the redeployment of factors into more productive activities; hence, they will attempt to organize as a sector and lobby government to adopt their pursued policies, whether these policies are more protectionist or more liberalizing. Sectoral attributes explain these diverging economic preferences within a state: actors associated with capital-intensive, internationally oriented firms (be they owners or workers) will support increased economic liberalization, while owners and workers in activities that are more 'stuck' in one industry and one place will be much less supportive of liberalization because of the increased competition it brings (Frieden, 1991; Milner, 1988).

Given the way different sectors are affected differently by liberalization, some expect to win in a globalized economy and some expect to lose. First, increased capital mobility will benefit internationally oriented firms and financial institutions in the developed world, like those in the banking or information technology sectors, while nationally based, less-competitive industries in these economies will suffer from increased liberalization and increased competition. The 'Made in the USA' campaign is a good example of sectoral mobilization to protect the manufacturing and garment sectors in the US, which have been hard hit by foreign competition. Second, in the developing world, globalization is likely to harm the financial sectors, which struggle to compete with the influx of foreign banks offering lower interest rates and more innovative financial products, as well as capital-intensive sectors that also fare poorly in competition with their developed country counterparts. However, at the national level, industries in developing countries may benefit from economic liberalization as a result of greater access to capital at lower interest rates.

Sectoral approaches also generate predictions of how governments may win or lose in a more globalized world. Shafer (1994) argues that sectoral attributes affect the degree to which governments are able to retain autonomous policy-making capabilities in a liberalized economic environment. As sectors find themselves winning or losing in the global economy they will attempt to persuade the government to adopt their preferred economic policies. The sectors that have been most successful in an open economy will support further liberalization; the sectors that have suffered will support a return to protectionism. If the leading sector in an economy is one with a few big, powerful firms at the forefront (such as internationally oriented banks and multinational firms), many resources, and few collective action problems, this sector is likely to hold powerful sway over government actors, constraining state capacity and autonomy. If, on the other hand, the leading sector is characterized by smaller, dispersed businesses that employ unskilled workers and face higher collective action problems (such as peasant cash croppers), the government is likely to retain higher levels of policy-making autonomy. In short, powerful industries can exert intense pressures on states to liberalize or to maintain protectionist policies, while less unified, capital-poor industries may not have the political clout to interfere with the state's pursuit of its desired socio-economic policies.

World-system Analysis/Dependency Theory

World-system or dependency theorists argue that we should look for winners and losers of globalization at the state level. A state's structural position in the global economy will determine whether it and its citizens – no matter how they earn their income – thrive in a globalized economy or fail. The primary effect of international trade will be to redistribute resources from the countries on the periphery of economic development to those at the core, and the mechanisms through which this happens are the hierarchical international division of labour and unequal exchange. By the mid-twentieth century an international division of labour was in place in which developing countries exported agricultural products, commodities, and other raw materials to the developed world, which in turn used these materials to produce manufactured goods for their domestic markets and for export (Lewis, 1978). The problem with this division of labour was that as incomes grew in the developed countries as a result of industrialization, demand for manufactured goods outpaced demand for the primary goods exported by the developing world. As demand fell for primary goods relative to manufactured goods, so did prices, leaving the developing world with lower export prices and higher import prices. Thus, the long-term effect of this division of labour is to drain resources away from the developing world to the developed, keeping developing economies poor and dependent upon their exports to the developed world (Prebisch, 1950). Furthermore, Cardoso (1973) argues that the penetration of foreign capital into emerging markets inhibits these economies from self-sustaining growth so that they will never be able to emulate the development path of the advanced industrialized economies. They will remain dependent upon the developed world for capital and technology, creating the possibility for devastating crises should the foreign capital supply dry up or move elsewhere. World-system and dependency theorists argue on these grounds that the more developing countries become integrated into the global economy, the worse they will do economically relative to other countries. Another implication of world-systems/dependency approaches is that the architecture of the global financial and trade institutions that govern the global economy will be designed to benefit the economic interests of the wealthy developed countries, with little regard given to the interests of the poor countries at the periphery.

The arguments above may have lost some of their relevance as empirical realities have changed. For example, export manufactures have surpassed primary good exports in most developing countries. The spectacular development of the East Asian tigers seems to falsify claims that developing countries will suffer from greater global integration. However, the persistent inequalities across the developed and developing worlds justify approaches that focus on how the international system may create winners and losers of entire states. Theories within the world-systems/dependency approaches expect the developed world as a whole to be the big globalization winner, while the developing world as a whole remains the big loser.

Society-centred Approaches

Society-centred approaches argue that national economic policies reflect the preferences of the politically dominant domestic interest group or class. Domestic interest groups are locked in a continual battle for the power to influence policy, and the way a state chooses to engage with the global economy depends on the outcomes of these interest group battles. Thus, these approaches expect the globalization winners to be the societal groups that have successfully influenced economic liberalization policies, while the losers are those interest groups that lost the political battle. Putnam (1988) uses a two-level game metaphor to argue that state policy in the international realm reflects bargains it has struck with powerful domestic interests. Moravcsik (1997) argues that the fundamental unit of analysis in international relations is societal actors. State foreign policy can best be understood not as an aggregation or macrocosm of societal preferences, but as representative of the preferences of those groups most successful at mobilizing, building coalitions, and marshalling resources to persuade policy-makers to adopt their preferred policies. Society-centred approaches highlight the inadequacies of purely economic models such as the factor-based models that expect economic outcomes to neatly map onto political outcomes. Factor-based approaches such as Rogowski's (1989) predict that economic winners will more often than not successfully impact policy and become political winners as well. Societal-based approaches recognize that even economic winners sometimes, as a group, face obstacles to political power. Some types of groups face huge collective action problems, mobilization problems, or coalition-building problems that frustrate their ability to influence political elites (Olson, 1982).

Van Apeldoorn (2002) develops a society-centred approach that is located at the international level rather than the national level, and seeks to explain policy choices of regional or international economic institutions rather than state governments. He argues that the transnational nature of the world economy and the institutions that govern it give a privileged position of influence to transnational interest groups. Mobile capital's experience in the transnational realm allows capitalists to develop a stronger transnational identity than other societal groups, such as labour. Multinational firms and financial institutions are also much more adept at organizing at the transnational level than are more nationally oriented societal groups, which affords them greater success at lobbying international trade and financial institutions, such as the EU, the IMF, or the WTO. Van Apeldoorn expects the winners of globalization to be those with the best mobilization and organizing capacity at the international level, and he argues that multinational capital is far and away the best situated in this capacity.

These various theories of state–society relations would lead us to expect that states will pursue trade and liberalization policies that are supported by the politically dominant domestic interest groups. These groups could be class-based, sector-based, or formed around other interests such as environmentalism. To help us understand who will win and who will lose in the globalized economy, we should look beyond pure economic theory to the outcomes of domestic (or transnational, perhaps) political battles among societal interests. The winners of these battles will succeed in persuading policy-makers to integrate with the global economy in ways that best serve their interests, perhaps at the expense of the losers.

Liberal Economic Theory

Liberal economic theory predicts that national success in the global economy will depend on the level to which states have integrated into the global economy and how well they have implemented neoliberal economic reforms (Stiglitz, 2002). Winning states will be those that have most fully liberalized their economies to global market forces, privatized their industries, and committed to fiscal austerity by downsizing the public sector and reducing social spending. Full engagement with global market forces – through opening borders to foreign trade and investment – will promote absolute gains in the living standards of all economic participants, no matter what factor, sector, or other societal group they might come from. In this way, globalization is a positive-sum game for all involved. Global market forces will drive inefficient firms and industries out of business, but capital and workers will redirect to more productive endeavours that will provide greater returns. Greater economic integration will allow countries to more fully specialize to their comparative advantage, increasing their income and helping to create a more efficient global system of supply and demand unencumbered by national boundaries. Liberals also believe that developing nations will prosper in the global economy as capital and technology flow to the poorer regions of the world, leading to convergence of living standards and an equalization of wealth (Bryan and Farrell, 1996).

Liberal economic theory makes clear predictions about who is likely to win and lose in the global economy. The winners from globalization will be those economies which have most fully integrated into the global economy through liberalization of trade and investment, privatization of industry, and stabilization of inflation (among many other political and economic reforms). Furthermore, countries must satisfy *all* neoliberal criteria: picking and choosing only the reforms that are most politically popular or palatable is not enough and may make an already weak economy worse off (Stiglitz, 2002). If national economies allow themselves to be governed by global market forces, liberals believe that everyone will be a winner in the globalized economy. Poverty will be reduced as jobs and capital penetrate the developing world; employment will become more secure in the developed world as countries specialize in production according to their comparative advantage; and capital will reap greater returns on investment as it moves to the most efficient markets. If there are losers in the global economy, it is those states that do not fully integrate. Neoliberal international financial institutions such as the IMF and the World Bank explain persistent poverty in the developing world not as a failure of neoliberal economic policies, but as a failure of governments of these countries to embark and follow through on neoliberal reforms that may be politically unpopular, such as cutting social expenditures and the size of the public sector and opening domestic markets to imports (Stiglitz, 2006). Thus, for liberals, the only losers in the global economy will be in those countries that choose not to play by the market's rules.

Who Wins Empirically?

Given the way that globalization creates competition among firms, countries, factors of production, industry, civil society, and other groups of actors, and given the various theoretical expectations about outcomes, can we tell who is actually winning and who is losing in the real world? The answer to this question is much more complex than either globalization's strongest advocates or its staunchest opponents might claim. Just as it is much too oversimplified to argue that 'everyone wins' from globalization, it is also inaccurate to say that 'only the capitalists' profit from globalization. In this section, we will attempt to identify actors and groups of actors that stand to gain, overall, from the liberalization of the global economy. This exercise is complicated by the fact that individual actors play multiple roles in the economy: a consumer who gains from lower-priced goods may also lose as a worker if her job is sent offshore or if her wages drop faster than prices do. With this in mind, we can still use theory and data to create a broad, aggregate-level classification of the groups that gain overall and those that lose overall in the global economy.

Consumers

Most broadly, consumers around the world stand to benefit from a liberalized global economy. Globalization benefits consumers in developing and developed countries alike for several reasons. First, increased levels of international trade break domestic monopolies and create stiffer competition among firms, which drives prices of goods downward while simultaneously pushing quality upwards. Prices drop as a result of the greater selection of goods available in the marketplace and firms' need to attract and retain customers. Competition makes it harder for producers to raise prices, and this keeps inflation low. Truman (2003) finds a small but significant and negative correlation between trade openness and inflation in an analysis of cross-country data. The same logic explains improved quality of goods. American carmakers were forced to improve the quality of their automobiles when US markets opened to more reliable and longer-lasting cars from foreign competitors like Japan and Germany. Globalization also allows production to migrate to its most efficient location: thus, globalization facilitates greater specialization according to comparative advantage. When countries specialize in producing the goods in which they have a comparative advantage, production is at its most efficient and the price that consumers pay for the final product falls.

At the same time, several recent studies demonstrate the way that openness to trade benefits consumers from different income groups differently. Gresser (2002) finds that in the US, tariffs disproportionately punish the poor, who are more likely to purchase manufactured goods from big-box discount stores such as Wal-Mart that keep their prices low by sourcing cheap imports from abroad. Wealthier Americans, in contrast, are more likely to 'buy American' or 'buy local' despite the higher price of these goods. Additionally, import competition keeps prices low, and this translates into lower rates of inflation. Studies have found that in the US over the past two decades the inflation rate of goods from import-competing sectors has declined relative to the inflation rate of non-traded services. This benefits consumers who purchase imports, and these consumers disproportionately come from lower-income groups. However, researchers caution that it is unclear that this disinflation is a direct result of global competition; disinflation could be a result of another process such as the appreciation of the dollar in the 1980s and 1990s (Bergsten, 2005; Clark, 2004). The benefits of lower import prices to consumers in lower-income groups may be reduced, however, if the consumer's primary income comes from an industry or firm that has been adversely affected by international competition. When wages drop faster than prices, or when a job is displaced altogether, certain consumers may find themselves worse off.

Technological change and diffusion also drive down the price of goods and services, in part because better and more widespread technology reduces the cost of long-distance transportation and communication. A good example of this process at work is in the market for international phone calls. The development of fibre-optics, communication satellites, and internet-based phone calls and the spread of these technologies around the world mean that a phone call that would have cost over $1 per minute in 1980 now might cost as little as 14 cents per minute. Technological diffusion around the world also affords workers the opportunity to increase their education and skill level and in turn increase their wages and purchasing power. The intense competition, the greater mobility of capital, and the diffusion of technology that are hallmarks of globalization all benefit consumers in both the developed and developing worlds (in the aggregate, though there are always exceptions) by pushing the prices of goods and services downwards and quality upwards.

Capitalists

Popular conceptions of globalization often portray it as a tool forced on the masses by the powerful masters of industry and finance, who stand to gain massively from liberalized, accessible markets. In this scenario, globalization is perceived as a competition of classes – capitalists versus labourers – and the capitalists always win. While this is a gross oversimplification, it is undeniably true that firms and financial institutions as a whole are among the strongest supporters of globalization, and they are also some of its biggest winners. There are several basic insights from economic theory that explain why capital (and those for whom capital is their primary source of income) benefits so significantly from globalization. First, capital is the most mobile factor of production. Land and natural resources cannot move from country to country, and workers cannot do this very easily either, even when they are legally free to do so. The great mobility of capital allows it, unlike the other factors, to seek out and move to the markets and geographic locations where it can maximize its efficiency and, subsequently, its profits. Capital mobility also gives industry-bargaining power with governments and labour unions. If industry leaders are unhappy about corporate taxation levels, trade policies, or labour and environmental standards, they may be able to have their demands met if unions or government officials believe that it is likely that the firm will close its factories and move to a cheaper location elsewhere on the globe.

Second, capital benefits from economies of scale when it can produce for a larger market, because investments in production can be spread over a larger output, and this reduces the cost per unit of output. As firms enter new product markets around the world and sales increase, the cost of producing each unit of product falls, and profits rise.

Third, at the same time that new markets can increase sales and economies of scale, the entrance of relatively capital-poor developing countries into the labour market allows wages to fall. Marginal productivity theory views the capital–labour ratio as a primary determinant of wage levels. When there are many workers competing for relatively scarce jobs, firms have the stronger bargaining position and are able to keep wages low. Capital has benefited from the liberalization of markets in China, India, and the former Soviet bloc, which alone added 1.46 billion new workers to the global work force in the 1990s. Freeman finds that this 'great doubling' of the global labour force nearly halved the capital–labour ratio (Freeman, 2007). Since these economies did not add nearly as much capital as they did labour, workers have had to compete with each other for relatively scarce capital; this drives wages down and increases the productivity of each unit of capital. Capital did see high returns on investment during this period, but Freeman is careful to note that with all the other changes attendant to trade liberalization, and without a definitive study linking the high rewards to capital during the 1990s to the doubling of the global work-force, this connection should remain hypothetical (Freeman, 2007).

Theory helps us understand why capital in general should gain from increasing economic globalization, but what has been the experience empirically? One way to answer this question is to examine what has happened to wealth during the most recent globalizing era to see if wealth has grown worldwide, and if so, where it is concentrated. There is no doubt among economists that economic liberalization has increased income globally as well as in the countries that have embraced it. However, income shares are shifting away from labour to capital across the OECD countries, and many studies have attempted to explain this phenomenon, several linking it to globalization. Guscina's (2006) analysis of cross-national OECD data from 1960 onwards finds trade openness, and trade with developing countries specifically, strongly linked to labour's declining income share in the wealthy countries. Harrison (2002) finds that trade openness reduces labour's share of income in countries across the income spectrum. Rodrik (1997b) attributes this loss to the decline in labour's bargaining power as firms realize their ability to outsource jobs. Jayadev (2007) argues that capital openness exerts a strong downward pressure on labour's share of income. Still others question the causal role of globalization in this process, instead emphasizing the effects of technology or economic cycles (Lawrence 2008; Arpaia et al., 2009). Another way capital may gain from economic liberalization is through the difficulties in taxing mobile capital. Burke and Epstein (2007) cite data indicating that corporate tax rates have indeed decreased as capital mobility has risen, and this is likely explained by the competition among countries to attract foreign direct investment. In the OECD countries, tax rates have fallen from around 40 per cent in the early 1980s to around 28 per cent in the early 2000s. Furthermore, other studies indicate that national corporate tax rates are converging, which is also likely due to tax competition (Garretsen and Peeters, 2006). However, there is no evidence that we are witnessing a 'race to the bottom' in terms of tax rates. As the varieties of capitalism literature demonstrates, some advanced capitalist countries have been able to successfully maintain relatively high corporate tax rates because firms see advantages to continuing to locate production in countries with highly skilled, stable work-forces, despite higher labour costs.

While industrial capitalists have reaped great rewards as global markets have liberalized, so have international bankers and financiers. The liberalization of international trade is only one piece of economic globalization: the liberalization of domestic financial markets to global investors has dramatically increased the flows of short-term capital in both developed and developing countries. In fact, Wall Street firms have been among the biggest lobbyists for the opening of domestic financial markets (Bhagwati, 2004). States benefit from financial liberalization as foreign financiers invest in domestic stock and bond markets. Competition among banks lowers interest rates and more funds are then available for investment in domestic enterprises. National governments gain access to much-needed capital when foreign investors buy up their bonds and currency. Banks and other investors benefit from the interest they collect on their investments, and capital flows to the places where investors expect to receive the highest return on their investments. However, the great advantage that capital has over states in the financial markets lies in capital's ability to exit a country when investments become risky or seem more lucrative elsewhere. This mobility, unfortunately, puts national economies at great risk when states are unprepared to handle a massive outflow of capital, which is what happened during the East Asian financial crisis of 1997. Foreign investors, panicking about signs of debt overextension and loan defaults in the crisis countries, began withdrawing their money, which led to currency collapses, stock market crashes, bank closures, and a severe financial crisis that undid the spectacular growth the South-east Asian 'miracle' economies (South Korea, Indonesia, Thailand, Malaysia) had experienced in the several years prior to the crash, when capital was flush. The ensuing IMF bailout package propped up the exchange rates of the troubled currencies, which encouraged more 'capital flight' out of the country at favourable rates, and the brunt of the crisis was borne by small businesses and the people of East Asia. By 1998, the GDPs of the affected countries had fallen far below their 1996 levels, unemployment soared, and per capita incomes fell to half of the 1996 levels in some countries (Stiglitz, 2002: 97; Bhagwati, 2004: 199). Foreign investors suffered too, but international capital's ability to cut its losses and exit a bad market (as well as its influence in the major international financial institutions) is one of its most advantageous characteristics, and one of the primary reasons it often emerges a relative 'winner' from crises that are devastating for individual consumers and smaller businesses.

In the recent global financial crisis that spread around the world following the US mortgage crisis of 2008, an argument could be made that developed country banks may emerge as the only clear 'winners' in the aftermath of the meltdown. The huge bailout packages cobbled together by developed country governments in 2009 were designed to rescue their biggest banks from bankruptcy. Billions of dollars flowed to the world's biggest financial institutions, many of which were soon able to turn a profit again and repay the taxpayer loans. Meanwhile, in 2010, 'Main Street' continued to suffer. While the big US banks were for the most part profitable again in 2010, millions of consumers lost their homes to foreclosure that year and millions more remained threatened by this possibility (Schwartz and Martin, 2010). Additionally, economic recovery slowed in the US because many companies that became profitable again saved money or invested it in labour-saving technologies instead of hiring. Thus, while the economy was growing again and shareholders were once again reaping gains, unemployment remained stubbornly high. Finally, voters were enraged as evidence surfaced that some banks may actually have profited from the crisis by using complex financial instruments such as credit default swaps that allow them to make money when borrowers default on their loans. These instruments were widely used by banks to insure themselves against mortgage defaults by homeowners, as well as against the credit default of entire countries. Banks across the world lent billions of dollars to Greece in the years leading up to the Greek financial meltdown, 'insuring' their loans with credit default swaps. The problem for Greece lay in the fact that the cost of these insurance schemes made it harder for Greece to borrow more money. When Greece reached the brink of default on its loans in 2010, EU governments and the IMF put together a massive rescue package, essentially bailing out the international banks whose risky lending had contributed to the crisis in the first place.

Though it is difficult to say that anyone 'wins' when a major financial crisis wreaks such havoc on national economies, multinational financial actors are at an advantage. Capital mobility in the liberalized global economy allows financial actors to exit markets when they smell trouble. In order to prevent this, governments and international financial organizations such as the IMF design bailout packages in times of crisis that primarily benefit the banks. In a sense, international capital stands to reap many gains from globalization while suffering little of the costs. Not all capitalists stand to gain from trade liberalization, however. We will discuss why firms from the developing world tend to lose out from globalization later in this section.

Skilled Labour

Globalization affects workers very differently depending on whether they live in developed or developing countries, whether they are in a tradable or non-tradable sector, whether they work in manufacturing or services, or whether they are skilled or unskilled. Though many analysts regard capital as an absolute winner from globalization, it is impossible to declare labour an absolute loser. It is more accurate to describe certain labour groups as relative winners or losers. One group of relative winners from the global labour pool is skilled workers. Skilled workers provide value to their employers by their ability to use technology in the production of higher-tech goods that command higher prices in the market. The investments skilled workers have made in their own education and specialized skills training allows them to be more productive and earn higher wages than unskilled workers. The rapid diffusion of technology around the globe as countries have liberalized their markets has greatly benefited workers in developing countries. These economies receive capital investment and technology imports that demand more skilled labour and pay higher wages (de la Dehesa, 2006). Many jobs that are considered unskilled in developed countries transfer to developing countries where they are considered skilled jobs.

Skilled labour in developed countries is often a globalization winner as well, but for different reasons. The Heckscher–Ohlin model of international trade predicts that trade patterns will reflect factor endowments. In other words, countries will specialize and trade in the products that use their abundant factors of production. Similarly, the Stolper–Samuelson theorem expects that the abundant factor will benefit from openness as the relative prices for goods using that factor increase, which in turn increases factor returns and enriches those individuals holding strong positions in these factors. Thus, in developed countries where skilled labour is the abundant factor compared to unskilled labour, wages should rise for skilled workers. Jobs in developed countries that require highly specialized training are often unlikely to move offshore because firms find it too costly and impractical to relocate production to a country or region where skilled workers are relatively scarce. These predictions are supported empirically by studies showing that exporting firms in the US use more cutting-edge technology and have higher worker productivity than similar non-exporting firms. Furthermore, since the 1980s worker wages and benefits are on average 10 to 11 per cent higher in export-oriented US firms than in similar plants that do not trade internationally, and similar patterns are found globally in other advanced economies (Bernard and Jensen, 1998; Lewis and Richardson, 2001). Developed-country firms that export are specializing in higher-tech production that both demands more productive, specialized, better-trained workers and rewards those workers with better pay.

Despite this evidence, some analysts question whether the continued wage gap between skilled and unskilled workers in advanced economies is due primarily to trade. Lawrence (2008) argues that in the 1980s, job displacement disproportionately affected unskilled US workers rather than skilled workers, but that more recent trends in job losses and wage polarization are qualitatively different. He cites evidence that since 1997, the US has lost more skilled-labour jobs to offshoring than unskilled-labour jobs, and that most goods that the US imports are from industries paying relatively high wages that should not threaten the jobs or wage levels of less-skilled US workers. He suggests that the growing wage gap between skilled and unskilled workers may now be better explained by a combination of other factors such as immigration and technological change.

Who Loses?

Unskilled Labour

The benefits to unskilled labour from globalization are much less clear than for skilled labour, in developed and developing countries alike. In fact, many analysts would consider unskilled labour to be a globalization loser. Developing countries tend to specialize in the production of unskilled, labour-intensive goods for export, because in these countries there is often an abundance of unskilled labourers. When developed countries import these low-cost goods, demand should decrease for unskilled labourers in the developed world, who are more expensive to employ than their counterparts in the developing world.

The labour market has, in fact, been described by economists as a 'disaster' for low-skilled workers in the US. The real hourly wages paid to workers with no more than a high-school education have dropped by 20 per cent in two decades (Rodrik, 1997b: 11). Total job displacement between 2000 and 2004 in the US was 1.9 million, and these jobs lost were concentrated among less skilled workers. Only 12.2 per cent were college graduates, and 28 per cent had less than a high school education (Mishel et al., 2007). In trying to measure the impact that international trade has had upon unskilled labourers in the developed world, several prominent economists that conducted studies in the 1990s concluded that the amount of trade between developed and developing countries was still not high enough to be a primary cause of the growing wage gap between skilled and unskilled workers in the developed world (Krugman, 1995; Lawrence, 1996; Cline, 1997; Borjas et al., 1997). Many economists argued that the impact of international trade on unskilled workers was modest, and that other culprits, such as immigration, were more likely to blame for downward pressure on wages. More recently, however, economists such as Krugman (2008) have observed that US importation of goods from developing countries has nearly doubled since these studies were published, and that there is now much more reason for concern about the impacts of trade on unskilled labour. Furthermore, wages in developing-country trade partners are now even lower relative to developed-country wages than they were during the 1990s, so there is renewed reason to believe that unskilled labourers in the developed world may indeed increasingly find themselves on the losing end of international trade.

The plight of unskilled workers should theoretically be different in developing countries where they are the abundant factor. Unskilled workers in these economies should enjoy increasing returns for their labour, relative to skilled workers. Domestically, goods produced by unskilled labour will be cheap, and when trade is liberalized, these goods will be exported and will command a higher price internationally from developed countries where unskilled labour is not an abundant factor. All of this should, theoretically, increase the incomes of unskilled workers in countries where their labour is abundant. However, evidence of gains from trade to unskilled workers even in developing countries that specialize in exporting unskilled labour-intensive goods is mixed. Krugman (2008) cites data indicating that since the 1990s relative prices of goods produced with unskilled labour have fallen compared to goods produced with skilled labour, even those goods produced by unskilled labour-rich developing countries. This trend runs counter to the predictions of standard trade theory, and some think that technology is to blame, rather than trade itself. As technology diffuses to liberalized developing economies, demand rises for skilled workers, and their wages rise relative to unskilled workers, even in countries where unskilled labour is the abundant factor (Arbache, Dickerson, and Green, 2004; Flanagan, 2006). The result of this 'skill-enhancing trade' is that inequality rises in developing countries and unskilled labour does not reap the rewards from trade that might be expected. In addition to the effects of technology transfers on unskilled labour, unskilled wages have for years been set very low by China. Wages have dropped in labour markets such as Central and South America that were once considered cheap labour markets, in order to compete with even-cheaper China. In 2005, hourly wages in Mexico were around 11 per cent of wages in the US, but in China, wages were a mere 3 per cent of the US level (Krugman, 2008: 108). Freeman (2007) observes that some developing countries such as Mexico, Peru, and South Africa that once produced low-wage goods simply cannot compete in this sector at all anymore and concentrate now on informal sectors and increased natural resource extraction and sales. Wage disparity among developing countries with similar factor endowments exerts downward pressure on wages in higher-priced developing-country markets. Labour markets such as Vietnam and Cambodia are now offering even lower wages than are typically paid in China, as well as more lenient regulations on the benefits foreign firms must provide to workers, keeping wages for unskilled workers down around the region, if not the globe.

Developing-Country Firms

While capital writ large is certainly a globalization winner, not all firms succeed in a globalized economy. We can generalize that certain firms are more likely to lose out than others. Firms that once benefited from protectionism or lenient regulatory environments are less likely to be prepared for competition with firms accustomed to the free market. Firms in this position tend to be from developing countries (de la Dehesa, 2006). There is typically much less market competition in newly developing countries, and government corruption may have allowed local firms to grow accustomed to special treatment and high profit margins that vanish with the liberalization of the economy and free market principles. Furthermore, most local firms in developing countries operate with technologies that are outdated in the developed world, and they also tend to be very short on capital relative to firms in the advanced economies. Thus, the playing field is often far from equal when firms from developed countries penetrate emerging markets. Not only are emerging market firms ill-prepared for competition for the reasons described above, but the foreign firms that have gone international are the ones that were most successful and most competitive in their home markets, markets characterized by tough competition, abundant capital investment, and the best technologies. Thus, home-grown businesses in developing countries are doubly disadvantaged not only for competition internationally, but for competition in their home markets as well.

Stiglitz (2002) observes that this problem is particularly true for local banks in developing countries. Large American or European banks can provide better deposit security and bigger loans than local banks often can, so they can easily drive local banks out of business and dominate the banking industry. While this is part and parcel of capitalism, banking industries dominated by foreign banks can create massive instability in an emerging economy if banks decide to pull out of an economy or significantly scale back their lending. The 'crowding out' effect, when foreign firms push smaller firms and entrepreneurs out of business, may be good for the economy as a whole, but it often pushes these entrepreneurs into the informal sectors of production (street vendors, the self-employed, and daily wage labourers, for example) where wages tend to be low and work is less stable. Stiglitz's observations, based largely on the events of the Asian financial crisis of the late 1990s, have unfortunately held true during the global financial crisis of the late 2000s as well. This crisis negatively affected capital market development in emerging economies in two important ways. First, much foreign investment dried up when the crisis hit the big banks from the US and Europe. As Stiglitz argues, this can be extremely destabilizing in countries that have grown to depend on foreign credit and sophisticated banking services provided by foreign banks. Second, local banks are unlikely to be able to provide as much credit to local businesses as the big foreign banks are able to provide, and this will curb growth. While a drop in foreign investment may present an opportunity for local banks to develop stronger, indigenous financial sectors in developing countries, if they are unable to do this they risk going under completely or being nationalized. Another way the crisis hurt companies in the developing world is that demand for exports from these countries dropped as consumers in the developed world tightened their belts and reduced their spending. 'Buy local' campaigns in the developed world take on steam during times of crisis, encouraging citizens to support their local producers, and this deepens the strain on exporting firms in emerging economies.

Governments

The debate continues to rage in the scholarly community about how exactly globalization affects government capacity. The chapter in this volume on domestic institutions is devoted to this issue. Here, however, it is worth noting that many economists and political scientists consider governments to lose, in a sense, from globalization. Certainly, most governments today support trade and financial liberalization because they understand the rewards their countries can reap in terms of increased GDP, job creation, better living standards for their citizens, and reduced poverty. Most governments today view economic liberalization as a winning strategy all around, and economists agree. However, governments themselves can lose from the globalization process when they find themselves in a weaker bargaining position with the firms that operate within their borders. Capital mobility creates the possibility that governments will be less able to collect revenue from firms, regulate firms' activity within their borders, and maintain existing social contracts with their publics. Revenue collection may be compromised by the tax competition that countries engage in to attract foreign direct investment. The high mobility of capital allows firms to engage in complex tax avoidance strategies, for example by locating their headquarters in tax havens such as Bermuda or Switzerland, or moving production itself to countries with lower corporate tax rates. Governments thus have an incentive to compete to offer the most attractive taxation structures (and lowest rates) to corporations, and corporate tax rates have fallen in most developed countries since the 1980s. Nevertheless, a 'race to the bottom' in terms of corporate taxation has not materialized, and some conclude that downward pressure on corporate tax rates as capital mobility increases is mediated by domestic political institutions, such as which political party is in power (Hallerberg and Basinger, 1998). The same logic that applies to corporate taxation also applies to government capacity to regulate firms' domestic economic activity and their adherence to labour and environmental standards: the mobility of capital and the threat of exit may – in theory – limit a government's autonomy in pursuing its preferred policies, though this is hotly debated and the evidence is not conclusive. The Greek government is currently paying a steep price for its years of financial profligacy, as it is now beholden to the demands of its foreign and domestic creditors. These creditors are not only private investors, but also governments such as Germany that contributed massively to the Greek bailout, as well as the IMF. In today's global economy, many other states have a deep interest in preventing a Greek default. In bailing out Greece, they also gained a say in how Greece restructures its economy.

Research does suggest, however, that a country's level of economic development may impact the degree to which its government is constrained by economic pressures. Mosley (2003) argues that governments in developing countries typically retain less policy-making autonomy in the face of capital market pressures than do governments of developed countries because of their need to attract foreign financing. She finds that foreign investors charge governments in emerging markets higher interest rates than governments in developed countries, even when economic fundamentals are similar. Developing countries also retrieve a higher percentage of their total revenue from tariffs and other trade taxes, so the loss of this income stream to trade liberalization disproportionately affects poorer countries (Winters, 2004). As might be expected, several studies have found that in response to globalization pressures, government spending on social programmes such as healthcare, welfare, and education has decreased on average in developing countries (Kaufman and Segura-Ubiergo, 2001; Rudra, 2002).

Conventional wisdom says that governments lose in a globalized economy because capital mobility erodes their bargaining power with firms, and makes it more difficult to achieve domestic socio-economic goals. This appears to be true in some countries and in some policy areas, but it is not true across the board. The domestic institutions chapter explores this issue in greater depth.

The Environment

The environment is widely viewed as an unequivocal globalization loser. First, the goal of economic liberalization is growth, and with economic growth comes increased natural resource depletion, energy consumption, pollution, and other forms of environmental degradation. Globalized production networks and trade networks mean that more and more products and parts are being transported all over the globe, which has had a massive effect on the environment. Environmental problems are increasing in scale, and environmental externalities are becoming truly global problems. Research suggests that 60 per cent of the world's ecosystems are already overused (Najam et al., 2007: 11). Second, firms have historically treated environmental regulations as costly burdens that reduce efficiency, although this attitude is starting to change as public awareness of the need for environmental protection grows. In a world where capital is mobile, firms can seek out countries where environmental regulations are less stringent than in other places. Third, environmental problems don't stop at national borders: they are inherently transnational issues that require international cooperation that is often difficult to secure. Climate change is the quintessential example, since the developed world is responsible for the vast majority of polluting gases, yet the world's poorest populations (primarily in the tropics) are likely to disproportionately bear the damaging impacts (Schaeffer, 2005: 294). Fourth, the development of the advanced industrialized economies was built on the burning of fossil fuels, and efforts from the West to restrict pollutant emissions in today's developing world are met with resentment from these countries, stalling the adoption of international agreements that would begin the process of addressing environmental degradation.

International institutions have had very mixed success in dealing with environmental problems, and there is little regulation at the global level. Complex environmental problems such as climate change require the cooperation of a very wide, transnational array of actors from government, the private sector, and civil society. While some argue that economic growth cannot continue indefinitely in a world of finite resources, the diffusion of ideas, knowledge, and technology that is also inherent to globalization is likely to accelerate the adoption of solutions to the world's most pressing environmental problems. Market-based solutions are likely to be the way forward. More and more firms now realize they can save money through the adoption of energy-efficient technologies, and they also recognize marketing value in being labelled as 'environmentally responsible' by an increasingly environmentally aware global public. There may even be a 'climb to the top' if environmental best practices from the developed world diffuse globally through foreign direct investment (Prakash and Potoski, 2007). Finally, if big, lucrative markets such as those in Western Europe and Japan adopt stronger environmental standards, firms may find it in their interest to standardize all their production to meet these standards, rather than using a 'patchwork' of production processes to meet different national standards. This is known as the 'California Effect' (Vogel 1995).

Women

An increasing number of studies are focusing on the ways that globalization is gendered, affecting men and women differently. A strong case can be made that traditional prejudices against women that prevail in most of the world, women's lower levels of education and skills training, and women's limited access to financial and capital resources put them at a disadvantage in a more globalized economy. First, in the globalized era, employment in the informal economy is growing throughout the world, in all regions of the developing world and in much of the developed world as well (Carr and Chen, 2002). Jobs in informal sectors are characterized by low wages, low capital, low skills, unregulated work conditions, and significant insecurity. These 'invisible' jobs are jobs such as street peddlers, domestic workers, and casual wage labourers, and they often pass under the radar of government oversight entirely. Workers are pushed into the informal sector through some of the economic processes described earlier in this chapter: through outsourcing of jobs; through the 'crowding out' of small, local businesses by multinational firms; through 'jobless' capital-intensive growth and technological progress that replaces humans with machines; and through the transfer of technology to the developing world that increases jobs for skilled workers but not for the unskilled. The growth of low-wage informal economic sectors is problematic because it means that people are being pushed out of the formal, skilled, regulated economy, and it is especially problematic because women are over-represented in the informal sectors. More women work in informal sectors than men, and the number of women in this sector relative to the number of men has been growing for several decades, as men use their education to take advantage of the growing demand for skilled workers in the formal economy (Anglin and Lamphere, 2007; Desai 2009). Chen estimates that over 90 per cent of women in India, Indonesia, and much of sub-Saharan Africa working non-agricultural jobs are employed in the informal sector, and over half of women in several Latin American and East Asian countries (Chen, 2001). As the informal sector grows as a result of economic restructuring and global economic processes, more women than men are being pushed into the least desirable, most unsafe, lowest-paying jobs on the planet.

Second, disparities in skill levels between men and women mean that globalization can disproportionately disadvantage women. Women make up more than 80 per cent of the unskilled labour force involved in the production of transnational goods and services (Gunewardena and Kingsolver, 2007: 6), a group of workers that we have argued suffers from trade liberalization and technology transfers in both developed and developing economies. Additionally, when jobs in the developed world that may employ equal numbers of men and women are outsourced to the developing world, men are more likely to be the recipients of these jobs if technical skills or other professional education are required. The higher skill and education levels of men in the developing world mean that outsourcing jobs to emerging economies is likely to have the aggregate effect of displacing more women from jobs than men.

Third, gender inequality in most countries means that women are largely excluded from the benefits that male workers and entrepreneurs reap from globalization and economic growth. Women have more difficulty obtaining credit than men, and their mobility and access to transportation is often limited. Thus, they are more prone to specialize in trade in low-profit food products – selling food on the streets or in markets. Men, by contrast, are more likely to have cars and access to credit; they can more successfully engage with the formal economy (Desai, 2009: 19). Women conduct the majority of informal cross-border trade, so they benefit from trade liberalization at borders, but this type of trade is overlooked in the scholarship, which focuses overwhelmingly on formal trade involving large multinational firms and banks.

All this being said, there are many ways that economic globalization has affected women positively. At minimum, it has brought jobs – even if they are not the best jobs – to millions of women (and men) who were formerly unemployed or underemployed. It may also lead to more equal pay in the formal sectors of the economy. Black and Brainerd (2004) analysed US wage data from 1976 to 1993 and argued that globalization had reduced the gender wage gap by increasing competition and forcing firms to cut unnecessary spending, including discriminatory pay favouring men. In a closed economy where all domestic firms were equally prejudiced, there would be no incentive to reduce the gender wage gap. Since 70 per cent of the world's poor are women, globalization's role in reducing global poverty is very important for women. Women may not be winners relative to men in the globalized economy, and in fact they may be losers, but they are likely be winners in absolute terms, especially as their access to education improves.

Who Protests, and Why?

Because of the profound ways that globalization has reshaped societies in every corner of the world, it has become a subject that inspires passionate and often violent dissenters that fear neither imprisonment nor bodily harm as they stage massive and disruptive protests from Seattle to Genoa. Every meeting of the G-8 or the WTO is now met with massive public demonstrations demanding major revisions to the global trading regime. Economic globalization specifically has become a popular scapegoat for a plethora of social ills – whether or not scholars can confirm a direct causal link – from environmental destruction to Third World poverty to the so-called death of the welfare state. Globalization is also said to destroy local cultures, creating a homogeneous McWorld where everyone wants their Big Macs, Coca-Cola, and American TV shows. While different groups of activists focus on a wide range of issues from environmentalism to poverty to labour standards to consumer protection, most share a common belief that the guilty parties involved in all the injustices are multinational corporations and the advanced capitalist governments and international financial institutions that support their hegemony. Anti-globalization movements generally view the capitalist enterprise not only as morally bankrupt but as profoundly unjust as it glorifies the pursuit of private profits at the expense of workers, consumers, communities, and the environment.

Why Protest?

Sklair (2006) divides the movement into three spheres: economic challenges to multinational corporations, political challenges to the power of the developed countries over the developing world, and cultural-ideological challenges to rampant consumerism. The anti-corporate strains within the movement contend that globalization has ceded too much power to corporations and that corporations do not use this power responsibly. Rather, corporations devastate communities across the world economically, politically, socially, and environmentally in the relentless drive for profits. Politically, the anti-globalization movement charges that the advanced capitalist economies have pursued a form of integration tailored to their own interests, making much-needed aid to the poor countries conditional on the developing world's acceptance of the wealthy world's global economic plans. Culturally, many activists oppose the diffusion of the consumer culture to all corners of the earth, arguing that cultural exports from the developed world are destroying indigenous lifestyles and replacing them with a culture of limitless consumption that is ecologically unsustainable.

Bhagwati (2004) argues that there are two main groups of anti-globalization activists. The first consists of radical groups that organize hard-core protests against the evils of global capitalism and multinational corporations. They view global capitalism as a zero-sum game that will increasingly impoverish all but the owners of capital and finance, but fail to provide realistic and promising alternatives. The second main type of globalization protesters are located well within the bounds of the political and economic mainstream and accept the huge benefits that globalization can bring but criticize the way it has been managed. These critics contend that globalization has been mismanaged by the international financial institutions such as the IMF and the World Bank that guide developing countries as they integrate into global markets, as well as the WTO, which designs international trade rules. Many dissenters contend that these institutions have put the interests of capital and financial markets ahead of the interests of the general public (Stiglitz, 2002). This is evidenced, according to the dissenters, by the rise of world income inequality, by the crippling debt that developing-country governments owe creditors from the developed world, and by the short-sighted destruction of the world's finite natural resources to support unsustainable consumption. In redesigning globalization to better fit the needs of the majority rather than the rich and powerful, developed-country governments and international financial institutions need to recognize that the one-size-fits-all development and integration policies of the Washington Consensus will not work in many developing countries and regions. Rather, the developing countries need to be allowed to play a greater role in tailoring their economic development to their unique national strengths and weaknesses, and they also need to be given a greater role in the design and management of the international economic architecture.

Many opponents of globalization charge that it encourages countries to turn a blind eye to human rights in order to attract and retain foreign investment. Klein (2000) argues that rather than improving human rights, trade encourages the erosion of human rights because corporations are continually looking to build factories in places where governments will not object to (or will pretend not to notice) appalling labour standards in factories and the employment of young children at near slave labour. Developing-country governments have also become less democratic, Klein argues, as they crack down on peaceful globalization protests that governments view as 'destabilizing' (Klein, 2000: 338–9). Critics decry the increases in crime, corruption, and police abuse that integration with global markets has brought to countries with weak states and feeble democratic institutions (Brysk, 2002). Many anti-globalization groups concerned with human rights are opposed to the neoliberal insistence on deregulation, and they advocate the development of strong global labour standards to accompany the spread of low-wage jobs to the developing world.

In addition to these economic and political concerns, many opponents of globalization focus on the environmental effects of international trade and the spread of American-style consumerism around the globe. Environmentalist activists are enraged by the way corporations treat national environmental safety standards as 'non-tariff barriers to trade'. Canadians were horrified that the Ethyl Corporation of the US successfully used NAFTA regulations to sue the Canadian government to overturn its ban on a toxic chemical that Ethyl used in its gasoline. Ethyl won the right to sell its gasoline in Canada, and Canada found its sovereignty over its own environmental and health standards compromised by a free trade agreement (Swenarchuk, 2003). Environmentalist challengers to globalization demand greater transparency in the creation of global trade and investment agreements, in order to reclaim some popular control over a process that has such profound implications for national environmental and health regulations. Because of the challenges that trade presents to national environmental standards, many environmentalists advocate the development of a global environmental governance regime, adopting a similar tactic to labour activists who seek the creation of a global labour standards regime. Environmentalists also believe that since environmental problems are increasingly becoming global in scale – the hole in the ozone, climate change, and deforestation are good examples – there needs to be greater global oversight to enforce existing agreements and national regulations.

Who Protests?

The anti-globalization movement stretches from the global North to the global South, and it includes near-terrorist fringe groups as well as well-financed and well-respected international non-governmental organizations. Friedman argues that the most likely opponents of globalization are 'the used-to-bes': people in the middle and lower-middle classes who benefited from the security offered by protectionism and generous welfare states, and who now face a much more uncertain future as jobs and capital relocate around the planet (Friedman, 2000 [1999]: 274). As this argument would predict, many trade unions and labour organizations in the developed world are outspoken critics of unfettered inter-national trade, as their members face greater job insecurity than ever before and increasing wage inequality. In the developing world, government leaders themselves have at times taken a bold stance against some elements of the glo-bal economic regime. While not threatening to disengage from the global economy, groups of developing countries have banded together under names such as the G-77 to emphasize the undemocratic nature of a global economic regime that is designed and run by a mere eight developed countries (the G-8). Leaders of developing states have fought hard in WTO trade rounds and other economic negotiations to hold the developed 'free trading' world accountable for the billions of dollars of subsidies they provide to their agricultural (and other) industries to keep out imports from the developing world, while at the same time insisting that the emerging economies open their borders to imports from the developed world. This unfair and hypocritical practice is one of the developing world's primary objections to the current global trading system. That said, the vast majority of leaders of developing countries recognize that integration into the liberalized international economy is the best chance their economies have for ending the long-standing cycles of poverty, corruption, and marginalization in the international sphere.

Social activists have found a renewed purpose in the globalized era: champions of human rights, environmentalism, poverty reduction, and labour rights con-stitute a large part of the anti-globalization contingency. Many activist organ-izations that once had national focuses have scaled up their scope of advocacy to the international level. In addition, large and long-standing international nongovernmental organizations are also playing a major role in the debate on the future of globalization. Amnesty International, one of the most respected human rights groups, is now not only holding governments accountable for human rights violations, it is also monitoring multinational corporations as well. The Jubilee movement is dedicated to securing debt forgiveness for the world's least developed countries. Oxfam International organizes massive protests at G-8 conferences and other summits of world leaders under the banner of their 'Make Poverty History' campaign, which wants to amend trade rules to give developing countries more flexibility over trade liberaliza-tion. The World Social Forum brings together anti-globalization groups of all stripes from all over the world in summits designed to mimic the World Economic Forum of business and finance leaders. Participants share ideas about alternatives to neoliberalism.

Effecting change in the global economic system will require the collabora-tion of governments, the private sector, and civil society. Successful proposals for making the global economy more just and even-handed in the benefits it brings will require creative solutions grounded in an unwavering commitment to market principles.

Conclusion

This chapter has illustrated some of the reasons why globalization remains a highly controversial process. While its benefits are well known, they do not necessarily extend to all social groups everywhere, to all industries every-where, or even to all countries in the same way. The unevenness in the rewards globalization bestows on different countries and social actors is the main rea-son why it is often fiercely protested. Leading theories make different predic-tions about winners and losers of globalization, and trying to test theories about globalization empirically is notoriously difficult because of the massively complicated nature of large-scale structural changes such as globalization. In the real world, it is difficult to isolate globalization as a causal factor, when glo-balization itself is so complex and multi-dimensional, and when other major socio-economic changes (population ageing, de-industrialization, etc.) are hap-pening at the same time. What is clear is that social, economic, and environ-mental processes associated with globalization – offshoring of jobs, high levels of foreign capital movement in (and out of) countries, increased transport of products, parts, and materials across borders – do create real externalities that affect social groups, national economies, and the environment. The way that globalization redistributes wealth is extremely unjust in the minds of many people, laypeople and economists alike, and when global financial crises occur, many argue that the costs are borne by everyone except global capital. We have used insights from political and economic theories to argue that those who lose out from globalization processes, at least relative to other actors, are likely to be unskilled labour, firms from developing countries, governments, and women. The environment – though not an actor – is also likely to suffer in the quest for profit and economic growth. Although the world's poorest could be considered absolute winners from globalization in the sense that millions have been lifted out of poverty, and the number of people living on less than $1 a day is less than it was 30 years ago, they are relative losers in the sense that inequality is increasing and wealth is becoming more and more concentrated in the hands of the world's wealthiest. The creation of a global economy that benefits as many people as possible will require management and cooperation at the global level.

7

CONCLUSION

We have stressed three themes in this book. First, we have argued that globalization can be an engine of growth and development. Since globalization provides the opportunity for bringing together capital, labour, and resources from any location on the planet, it makes sense that a global scale of opportunities is more efficient than local or even national ones. More broadly, the chance to travel and work in different countries, to read books published anywhere in the world, and to watch 'foreign' movies are all examples of added consumption possibilities that globalization offers. Our second theme tells us that these additional choices, attractive as they are from the standpoint of the consumer, do not come without a price, a price that may be denominated in terms of lost jobs, industrial decline, diminished autonomy, growing inequality, and shifts in income among different classes within society. In short, our second theme is that globalization creates winners and losers. Third, we have repeatedly stressed the importance of institutions in this book. Indeed, there are three chapters where institutions play a central role: Chapter 3 on domestic politics and institutions, Chapter 4 on globalization and governance (where institutions form the most important part of governance structures), and Chapter 5 on global institutions. Institutions perform diverse roles, even in their benign form: they constitute the basic framework of the global political economy, they regulate activities within it, and both domestic and international institutions allow for the pursuit of social objectives (e.g. equality, solidarity, autonomy) not inherent in the market.

Instead of summarizing the main arguments and perspectives of the book, we comment on the prospects for the global system in the future. The first thing to acknowledge is that there is an ongoing geographic shift in the core of the world economy. We have emphasized throughout that a static view of the global North and global South is hopelessly inadequate to describe, let alone explain, our complex and changing global economy. During the last forty years, we have witnessed the decline of manufacturing activity in the advanced capitalist world (the rich countries in the OECD), the rise of a small group of newly industrializing countries, the expansion of this group to a much larger set of countries, the spectacular growth of India and China, the impressive development of Brazil under 'Lulu', and the modest yet hopeful growth of countries in South America, Asia, and Africa. We do not wish to give the impression that our planet has become an economic paradise with plenty for all. Indeed, chronic scarcity, disease, civil and international war, ethnic violence, predation (by governments and private groups), and inequality still exist and in some cases are worsening. All we are arguing is that, from an economic point of view, there are hopeful signs and that the term 'Third World' is now inadequate to describe our complex and differentiated global system.

To add flesh to this abstract point, consider the following. *The Economist* (Oct. 9 15, 2010: 3) points out that just 10 years ago, around the turn of the twenty-first century, about 30 rich countries accounted for about two-thirds of global output. Since that time, the share for the same countries has fallen to just over 50 per cent, and could, on current projections, decline to 40 per cent by 2020. This is a remarkable figure, given the short duration in question. Shifts in the economic cores and peripheries of the world are normal, but it is also normal for these shifts to take place over many decades if not centuries. British hegemony lasted a century and a half. The United States has been a major economic actor, if not *the* major actor, since the turn of the twentieth century. These shifts also involve the composition of output – not just the total volume. Rich countries in North America, Europe, and Asia are no longer the only industrial powers. Indeed, most of the advanced capitalist world (Germany being a key exception) is de-industrializing, especially if one measures this by percentage of the work force engaged in manufacturing rather than in terms of output. The trends have been away from production of hard goods (cars, refrigerators, electronics) to knowledge intensive production and services.

While we notice today the spectacular rise of India and China, the foundation for this geographical shift has been taking place since the 1960s and 1970s. During these decades, the Asian tigers (South Korea, Taiwan, Hong Kong, and Singapore) began their decades-long ascent into sustained economic growth. Powered by Japan as a strong regional power, these countries took advantage of changes in the global economy such as growing labour costs in the capitalist core, the growing obsolescence of certain kinds of capital (heavy industries, cars, consumer durables), and hence the export of this capital to 'offshore' locations. The United States unloaded its old growth industrial capital to Mexico and South America; Japan exported its capital to the four tigers; and Northern and Western Europe carried out the same task by shifting production to Southern Europe and North Africa.

The first wave of NIC (newly industrializing country) activity was limited to a handful of countries, but the process expanded to include others in Asia (Thailand, Malaysia, Indonesia, and the Philippines), in Europe (Portugal, Spain, Turkey, even Yugoslavia before it broke into several separate states), and in Latin America (Brazil, Argentina, and Chile) as well as Mexico in North America. The rise of the NICs was not a purely national phenomenon. True, these countries adopted a successful mix of policies: export promotion, low taxes on foreign capital, a cheap work force, and market-friendly policies all the way around. Nevertheless, there was a strong foreign component to NIC industrialization, both in terms of the provision of markets for their goods as well as the capital needed to produce these goods.

A second focus for the future has to do with recurrent crises that seem to attack the global capitalist system. The changes in the global economy are not without negative consequences, quite serious ones judging from the past several years. And these problems are not confined to the less developed world or to relations between the less developed world and the richer countries. Many of the most serious crises have taken place, and continue to play out, within and among the richest members of the globe.

The twin crises at the end of the 2000s moved at a startling pace. The first one started in the United States in 2007 and the second one started in Greece and Europe more broadly in 2009. The first crisis was triggered by cheap money, low interest rates, the overleveraging of investments, and inadequate regulation of financial services. The question of whether regulation was too much or not enough is the wrong question. The more important issue was and continues to be whether the regulations in existence are the right ones. If the goal was to prevent excessive risks with 'other people's money', then the regulatory structure was not satisfactory. The second crisis was triggered by poor and non-transparent accounting procedures on the part of the government of Greece. This crisis quickly generalized to Ireland, Spain, Portugal, and Italy. Here the issue was not so much weak regulations of private sector actors but rather the dishonest practices of governments attempting to hide their debt, practices which resulted in the explosion of sovereign debt. The two crises were related but also very different and they call for different solutions. It is likely that in the case of Greece, and possibly Ireland and Spain too, there will be closer supervision and more intrusive investigation of budgetary practices by external actors, i.e. the EU Commission and Eurostat, the EU's statistical office. Member states of the EU are now required to submit their national budgets to the European Commission before they are approved by national parliaments.

The years ahead will tell the story but our prediction is that it will take years for many countries to recover – not just the weaker ones like Greece, Ireland, and Portugal, but also perennially strong countries such as the United States, France, and Germany. Germany seems to have a good start by lowering unemployment and raising output but Germany's strategy relies to a large extent on increasing its manufacturing exports. This is a strategy that can't be pursued by just any other country, especially in the short to medium term. First of all, Germany continues to be a manufacturing country – not just a manufacturing exporter. Germany has not seen its manufacturing base decline as many other advanced countries have. German leaders continue to pour a lot of resources into the education and training of workers, developing skills that allow German firms to find export niches in the global economy. As a result, Germany's favourable balance of trade is not the result of cyclical factors or temporary currency alignments. Second, not all countries can run balance-of-trade surpluses. That is of course impossible in a pure accounting sense but this kind of trade competition could quickly deteriorate into a downward spiral of 'beggar they neighbour' policies. Other adaptive solutions are available. Short-term fixes either of a Keynesian kind, emphasizing demand management, or supply side solutions such as tax cuts are not likely to be effective in the long term. This is not to say they should not be pursued. Global Keynesians such as Krugman (2009 [1999]) argue for large infusions into the economy as a precursor to longer-range policies of a supply side nature. However, the cascading crises that started in 2007 are on a scale unseen since the Great Depression. It will take a long time, even with luck, to recover the level of economic performance that existed prior to 2007, especially with regard to employment.

The longer-run challenges are formidable. It is easy to say that we should spend more on education, infrastructure, job training, and active labour market policies. Perhaps all countries should do these things. However, there are many supply side problems that will be difficult to address, not because we don't understand them but because they are not amenable to easy political solutions. One structural problem that will be difficult to solve has to do with the supply of workers. The population, including the working age population, of most advanced countries is in decline. Less children and more retired people on pensions spell trouble for any economy. Governments may be able to change these figures at the margins (allowances for children, maternity and paternity leaves, job guarantees when leaves are used up) but they are unlikely to change things enough to solve the long-term problems. Despite the anger at taxes and big government in the United States, grass roots movements are unlikely to alter the upward trends of government spending, since these trends are driven by a few very costly programmes that are increasingly treated as entitlements. Migration policy may provide the short- and long-term solution to finding workers but there is already a high level of citizen hostility to migrants in many countries, including those most in need of workers, foreign or domestic.

A third issue for the future concerns the relationship between globalization and governance. We have argued throughout the book that globalization implies governance. It is impossible to put a market in place without political institutions and public policies and it is impossible for those markets to work without creating consequences that people will want to control: pollution, job losses, security concerns, trade wars, and erosion of national economic autonomy, to name a few. Whether one is trying to maximize the positive effects of globalization, minimize its negative effects, or level the playing field for global exchange, politics is unavoidable. Global markets, as national markets, are not self-organizing.

What form will global governance take? This is the difficult question. We have tended to think about governance in conventional ways, focusing on global institutions such as the United Nations, the Food and Agricultural Organization, and the International Labour Organization. We have also naturally awarded a major role in global governance to the existing nation states, since states are still the chief repositories of authority in today's world. Authority is not easily outsourced, and if someone (some institution) is to take a major decision 'on behalf of others', it has to draw on some reservoir of legitimacy. Even in the EU, the most advanced regional organization in terms of the strength and autonomy of institutions, the member states retain their role as important actors as members of the European Council and the Council of Ministers. States are still the actors with the most clout in terms of administrative capacity, extractive (tax) capacity, and ability to pursue autonomous goals within the global system as a whole.

Without denying the continuing importance of states, we also want to draw attention to other forms of governance. Regional trading associations (RTAs) are proliferating, especially since the end of the Cold War (1990) and completion of the single market in the EU (1993). The Asia Pacific Economic Cooperation was set up in 1989, and the Association of South-east Asian Nations (ASEAN), created in 1967, made the move to a free trade area in 1992. Since the East Asian financial crisis of 1997, China, Japan, and South Korea are now included in ASEAN summit meetings.

Apart from RTAs, there are some *ad-hoc* or loosely institutionalized groupings such as the G-20, which is a body composed of advanced as well as emerging countries. The G-20 has become an important forum for dealing with trade and development issues, as well as the environment. Yet, representation of the less developed world is weak. Brazil and Argentina are part of the G-20, as are India, Russia, and China. However, there is only one country from Africa (Republic of South Africa) and one from the Middle East (Saudi Arabia) if one does not count Turkey.

Finally, we can think of governance in the global system quite apart from nation states, universal organizations such as the UN, regional organizations, and multilateral institutions such as the G-20 which are neither comprehensive in membership nor completely general in terms of the scope of issues addressed. Governance in the global system is also 'private', strange as that may sound at first. The making of rules and the management of conflict also occur through subsidiaries of MNCs, and among banks and corporations. Sassen (2001 [1991]) has argued that global cities play a key role in the management and control of globalization while Hatch and Yamamura (1996) have argued for the importance of political control through coordination among subsidiaries of capital-exporting firms, particularly Japanese firms. Clearly, it is best not to limit our vision to the usual suspects when it comes to questions of governance.

Globalization clearly has a technological dynamic. The ability to traverse wide distances, both physically and in terms of communications, has certainly lowered the costs of moving people, goods, and symbols worldwide. In addition, structural changes in the international system have altered the opportunities for cooperation and conflict. The end of the Cold War has changed the relationships among countries in the global North and South, not always to the liking of all countries involved. Our goal in this book has been less to provide an overall balance sheet of a very complicated process, and more to impart a sense of the interplay among economic, political, and cultural forces at the global level, hopefully providing a sense of the available political choices for governments attempting to maximize the gains from globalization while minimizing its costs.

REFERENCES

Abdelal, R. (2007). *Capital Rules*. Cambridge, MA: Harvard University Press.

Abdelal, R., Blyth, M., & Parsons, C. (2010). Introduction. In R. Abdelal, M. Blyth, & C. Parsons (Eds.), *Constructing the International Economy*. Ithaca, NY: Cornell University Press.

Adserà, A., & Boix, C. (2002). Trade, Democracy and the Size of the Public Sector: The Political Underpinnings of Openness. *International Organization, 56*(2), 229–62.

Alcacer, J., & Ingram, P. (2008). *Spanning the Institutional Abyss: The Intergovernmental Network and the Governance of Foreign Direct Investment* (Working Paper No. 09-045). Harvard Business School. Retrieved from http://hbswk.hbs.edu/item/6049.html.

Anderson, B. (1991). *Imagined Communities: Reflections on the Origin and Spread of Nationalism* (rev. ed.). New York: Verso.

Anglin, M., & Lamphere, L. (2007). Complex Negotiations. In N. Gunewardena & A. Kingsolver (Eds.), *The Gender of Globalization*. Santa Fe, NM: School for Advanced Research Press.

Arbache, J. S., Dickerson, A., & Green, F. (2004). Trade Liberalization and Wages in Developing Countries. *Economic Journal, 114*, F73–96.

Arpaia, A., Pérez, E., & Pichelmann, K. (2009). *Understanding Labour Income Share Dynamics in Europe* (MPRA Working Paper No. 15649). University of Munich. Retrieved from http://mpra.ub.uni-muenchen.de/15649/.

Avelino, G., Brown, D. S., & Hunter, W. (2005). The Effects of Capital Mobility, Trade Openness, and Democracy in Latin America. *American Journal of Political Science, 49*(3), 625–41.

Axelrod, R. (1984). *The Evolution of Cooperation*. New York: Basic Books.

Axelrod, R., & Keohane, R. O. (1985). Achieving Cooperation under Anarchy: Strategies and Institutions. *World Politics, 38*(1), 226–54.

Baldwin, D. (1985). *Economic Statecraft*. Princeton, NJ: Princeton University Press.

Barnett, M., & Finnemore, M. (1999). The Politics, Power and Pathologies of International Organizations. *International Organization, 53*(4), 699–732.

Barnett, M., & Finnemore, M. (2004). *Rules for the World*. Ithaca, NY: Cornell University Press.

Bartolini, S. (2005). *Restructuring Europe*. Oxford: Oxford University Press.

Bastasin, C. (2009). *Another Greek Lesson: As Always Hard But Inspiring*. Washington, DC: Peterson Institute for International Economics.

Baumol, W. J., Litan, R. E., & Schramm, C. J. (2007). *Good Capitalism, Bad Capitalism, and the Economics of Growth and Prosperity*. New Haven, CT: Yale University Press.

Benhabib, S. (2005). Borders, Boundaries, and Citizenship. *PS: Political Science and Politics, 38*(4), 673–677.

Berger, S. (1996). Introduction. In S. Berger & R. Dore (Eds.), *National Diversity and Global Capitalism*. Ithaca, NY: Cornell University Press.

Berger, S. (2000). Globalization and Politics. *Annual Review of Political Science, 3*, 43–62.

Berger, S. (2002). French Democracy Without Borders: Anti-globalization Movements in France. *French Politics, Culture and Society, 20*(1), 1–10.

Bergsten, C. F. (2005). *The United States and the World Economy*. Washington, DC: Institute for International Economics.

Berkovitch, N. (2000). The Emergence and Transformation of the International Women's Movement. In F. J. Lechner & J. Boli (Eds.), *The Globalization Reader*. Malden, MA: Blackwell Publishers.

Bernard, A., & Jensen, J. B. (1998). *Understanding the US Export Boom* (NBER Working Papers No. 6438). National Bureau of Economic Research. Retrieved from http://www.nber.org/papers/w6438.

Bhagwati, J. N. (1992). Regionalism versus Multilateralism. *The World Economy, 15*(5), 535–56.

Bhagwati, J. N. (2004). *In Defense of Globalization.* New York: Oxford University Press.

Bhagwati, J. N. (2008). *Termites in the Trading System: How Preferential Trading Agreements Undermine Free Trade.* Oxford: Oxford University Press.

Black, S., & Brainerd, E. (2004). Importing Equality? The Impact of Globalization on Gender Discrimination. *Industrial and Labor Relations Review, 57*(4), 540–59.

Borjas, G. J., Freeman, R. B., Katz, L. F., DiNardo, J., & Abowd, J. M. (1997). How Much Do Immigration and Trade Affect Labor Market Outcomes? *Brookings Papers on Economic Activity, 1997*(1), 1–90.

Bové, J., Dufour, F., & Luneau, G. (2000). *Le Monde n'est pas une marchandise: Des paysans contre la malbouffe.* Paris: La Decouverte.

Boyer, R. (2005). How and Why Capitalisms Differ. *Economy and Society, 34*(4), 509–57.

Braudel, F. (1980). *On History.* Chicago: University of Chicago Press.

Bryan, L., & Farrell, D. (1996). *Market Unbound: Unleashing Global Capitalism.* New York: John Wiley & Sons.

Brysk, A. (2002). *Globalization and Human Rights.* Berkeley, CA: University of California Press.

Burke, J., & Epstein, G. (2007). Bargaining Power and Distributional Equity and the Challenge of Offshoring. In E. Paus (Ed.), *Global Capitalism Unbound.* New York: Palgrave Macmillan.

Cabrera, L. (2004). *Political Theory of Global Justice: a Cosmopolitan Case for the World State.* London and New York: Routledge.

Cameron, D. (1978). The Expansion of the Public Economy: A Comparative Analysis. *American Political Science Review, 72*(4), 1243–61.

Caporaso, J. A. (1993). Global Political Economy. In A. Finifter (Ed.), *Political Science: The State of the Discipline* (pp. 451–81). Washington, DC: American Political Science Association.

Caporaso, J. A (2003). Democracy, Accountability and Rights in Supranational Governance. In M. Kahler & D. A. Lake (Eds.), *Governance in a Global Economy.* Princeton, NJ: Princeton University Press.

Caporaso, J. A., & Tarrow, S. (2009). Polanyi in Brussels: Supranational Institutions and the Transnational Embedding of Markets. *International Organization, 63*(4), 593–620.

Cardoso, F. H. (1973). Associated Dependent Development: Theoretical and Practical Implications. In A. Stepan (Ed.), *Authoritarian Brazil: Origins, Policies, and Future.* New Haven, CT: Yale University Press.

Cardoso, F. H., & Faletto, E. (1979). *Dependency and Development in Latin America.* Berkeley, CA: University of California Press.

Carr, M., & Chen, M. A. (2002). *Globalization and the Informal Economy: How Global Trade and Investment Impact on the Working Poor* (Employment Sector Working Paper on the Informal Economy No. 2002/1). Geneva: International Labour Organization. Retrieved from http://www.wiego.org/publications/wiego.php.

Checkel, J. (1993). Ideas, Interests, and the Gorbachev Foreign Policy Revolution. *World Politics, 45*(1), 271–300.

Checkel, J. T. (1998). The Constructivist Turn in International Relations Theory. *World Politics, 50*(2), 324–48.

Chen, M. A. (2001). Women and Informality: A Global Picture, the Global Movement. *SAIS Review, 21*(1), 71–82.

Chen, S., & Ravallion, M. (2008). *The Developing World Is Poorer Than We Thought, But No Less Successful in the Fight Against Poverty* (Policy Research Working Paper No. 4703). The World Bank Development Research Group. Retrieved from http://ideas.repec.org/p/wbk/wbrwps/4703.html.

Choi, Y. J., & Caporaso, J. A. (2002). Comparative Regional Integration. In W. Carlsnaes, B. A. Simmons, & T. Risse (Eds.), *Handbook of International Relations*. London: Sage Publications.

Chwieroth, J. M. (2007). Testing and Measuring the Role of Ideas: The Case of Neoliberalism in the International Monetary Fund. *International Studies Quarterly*, *51*(1), 5–30.

Chwieroth, J. M. (2008). Normative Change from Within: The International Monetary Fund's Approach to Capital Account Liberalization. *International Studies Quarterly*, *52*(1), 129–58.

Clark, T. E. (2004). An Evaluation of the Decline in Goods Inflation. *Federal Reserve Bank of Kansas City Economic Review*, *89*(2), 19–52.

Cline, W. (1997). *Trade and Income Distribution*. Washington, DC: Institute for International Economics.

Coase, R. A. (1960). The Problem of Social Cost. *Journal of Law and Economics*, *3* (Oct.), 1–44.

Coglianese, G. (2000). Globalization and the Design of International Institutions. In J. S. Nye, Jr, & J. D. Donahue (Eds.), *Governance in a Globalizing World*. Washington, DC: Brookings Institution Press.

Cohn, T. H. (2005). *Global Political Economy: Theory and Practice*. London: Pearson Longman.

Culpepper, P. A. (2006). Capitalism, Coordination, and Economic Change: The French Political Economy since 1985. In P. A. Culpepper, P. A. Hall, & B. Palier (Eds.), *Changing France*. Basingstoke, UK: Palgrave Macmillan.

Curtin, D. (1993). The Constitutional Structure of the Union: A Europe of Bits and Pieces. *Common Market Law Review*, *30*, 17–63.

Dahl, R. A. (1985). *A Preface to Economic Democracy*. Berkeley, CA: University of California Press.

Dahl, R. A. (1999). Can International Organizations be Democratic? A Skeptic's View. In I. Shapiro & C. Hacker-Cordón (Eds.), *Democracy's Edges*. London: Cambridge University Press.

Dasgupta, A. K. (1985). *Epochs of Economic Theory*. New York: Blackwell.

Davies, G. (2005). 'Any Place I hang My Hat?' or: Residence is the New Nationality. *European Law Journal*, *11*(1), 43–56.

Davis, C. L. (2004). International Institutions and Issue Linkage: Building Support for Agricultural Trade Liberalization. *American Political Science Review*, *98*(1), 153–69.

de la Dehesa, G. (2006). *Winners and Losers in Globalization*. Malden, MA: Blackwell.

Desai, M. (2009). *Gender and the Politics of Possibilities: Rethinking Globalization*. Lanham, MD: Rowman & Littlefield.

Deutsch, K. W., et al. (1957). *Political Community and the North Atlantic Area: International Organization in the Light of Historical Experience*. Princeton, NJ: Princeton University Press.

Domar, E. (1946). Capital Expansion, Rate of Growth, and Employment. *Econometrica*, *14*, 137–47.

Dreher, A. (2004). A Public Choice Perspective of IMF and World Bank Lending and Conditionality. *Public Choice*, *119*(3/4), 445–64.

Easterly, W. (2001). *The Elusive Quest for Growth*. Cambridge, MA: MIT Press.

Economist, The. (2009, Feb. 13). The Return of Economic Nationalism. *390*(8617), 9–10.

Economist, The. (2010, Jan. 16). Immigration in Italy: Southern Misery. *393*(8665), 1–2.

Economist, The. (2010, Oct. 9). How to Grow. *397*(8703), 3–30.

Eichengreen, B., & Leblang, D. (2008). Democracy and Globalization. *Economics & Politics*, *20*(3), 289–334.

Evangelista, M. (1999). *Unarmed Forces: The Transnational Movement to End the Cold War.* Ithaca, NY: Cornell University Press.

Fearon, J., & Wendt, A. (2002). Rationalism and Constructivism: A Skeptical View. In W. Carlsnaes (Ed.), *Handbook of International Relations* (pp. 52–72). London: Sage Publications.

Feldstein, M. (1998). Refocusing the IMF. *Foreign Affairs*, *77*(2), 20–33.

Ferrera, M. (2005). *The Boundaries of Welfare*. Oxford: Oxford University Press.

Finnemore, M. (1996). *National Interests in International Society*. Ithaca, NY: Cornell University Press.

Finnemore, M., & Sikkink, K. (1998). International Norm Dynamics and Political Change. *International Organization*, *52*(4), 887–917.

Flanagan, R. J. (2006). *Globalization and Labor Conditions*. New York: Oxford University Press.

Follesdal, A., & Hix, S. (2006). Why There is a Democratic Deficit in the EU: A Response to Majone and Moravcsik. *Journal of Common Market Studies*, *44*(3), 533–62.

Frank, A. G. (1968). *Sociology of Development and Underdevelopment of Sociology*. Stockholm: Zenit.

Frankel, J. (2000). Globalization of the Economy. In J. S. Nye, Jr. & J. D. Donahue (Eds.), *Governance in a Globalizing World* (pp. 45–71). Washington, DC: Brookings Institution.

Freeman, R. B. (2007). The Challenge of the Growing Globalization of Labor Markets to Economic and Social Policy. In E. Paus (Ed.), *Global Capitalism Unbound*. New York: Palgrave Macmillan.

Frieden, J. A. (1991). Invested Interests: The Politics of National Economic Policies in a World of Global Finance. *International Organization*, *45*(4), 425–51.

Friedman, T. L. (2000 [1999]). *The Lexus and the Olive Tree*. New York: Anchor Books.

Garretsen, H., & Peeters, J. (2006). *Capital Mobility, Agglomeration and Corporate Tax Rates: Is the Race to the Bottom for Real?* (DNB Working Papers No. 113). Netherlands Central Bank. Retrieved from http://ideas.repec.org/p/dnb/dnbwpp/113.html.

Garrett, G. (1995). Capital Mobility, Trade, and the Domestic Politics of Economic Policy. *International Organization*, *49*(4), 657–87.

Garrett, G. (1998). *Partisan Politics in the Global Economy*. New York: Cambridge University Press.

Garrett, G. (2001). Globalization and Government Spending around the World. *Studies in Comparative International Development*, *35*(4), 3–29.

Garrett, G., & Lange, P. (1991). Political Responses to Interdependence: What's 'Left' for the Left. *International Organization*, *45*(4), 539–64.

Garrett, G., & Weingast, B. (1993). Ideas, Interests and Institutions: Constructing the European Community's Internal Market. In J. Goldstein & R. O. Keohane (Eds.), *Ideas and Foreign Policy*. Ithaca, NY: Cornell University Press.

Geyer, R. (1998). Globalisation and the (Non-) Defence of the Welfare State. *West European Politics*, *21*(3), 77–102.

Gilpin, R. (2000). *The Challenges of Global Capitalism*. Princeton, NJ: Princeton University Press.

Gilpin, R. (2001). *Global Political Economy*. Princeton, NJ: Princeton University Press.

Gomme, P., & Rupert, P. (2004). *Measuring Labor's Share of Income* (Policy Discussion Paper No. 7). Federal Reserve Bank of Cleveland. Retrieved from http://ssrn.com/abstract =1024847.

Gordon, P. H., & Meunier, S. (2001). *The French Challenge: Adapting to Globalization*. Washington, DC: Brookings Institution Press.

Gould, E. R. (2003). Money Talks: Supplementary Financiers and International Monetary Fund Conditionality. *International Organization, 57*(3), 551–86.

Grant, R. W., & Keohane, R. O. (2005). Accountability and Abuses of Power in World Politics. *American Political Science Review, 99*(1), 29–43.

Gresser, E. (2002). *Toughest on the Poor: Tariffs, Taxes, and the Single Mom* (Policy Report). Progressive Policy Institute. Retrieved from http://www.ppionline.org/documents/Tariffs_Poor_0902.pdf.

Grieco, J. M. (1988). Anarchy and the Limits of Cooperation: A Realist Critique of the Newest Liberal Institutionalism. *International Organization, 42*(3), 485–507.

Grimm, D. (1995). Does Europe Need a Constitution? *European Law Journal, 1*(3), 282–302.

Guillen, M. (2006). *Mauro Guillen's Indicators of Globalization*. Retrieved from http://www-management.wharton.upenn.edu/guillen/files/Global.Table.1980-2003.pdf.

Gunewardena, N., & Kingsolver, A. (2007). *The Gender of Globalization*. Santa Fe, NM: School for Advanced Research Press.

Guscina, A. (2006). *Effects of Globalization on Labor's Share of National Income* (IMF Working Paper No. 06/294). International Monetary Fund. Retrieved from http://ideas.repec.org/p/imf/imfwpa/06-294.html.

Haas, E. B. (1958). *The Uniting of Europe: Political, Social, and Economic Forces, 1950–1957*. Palo Alto, CA: Stanford University Press.

Haas, E. B. (1964). *Beyond the Nation-State: Functionalism and International Organization*. Palo Alto, CA: Stanford University Press.

Haggard, S., & Kaufman, R. R. (1992). Institutions and Economic Adjustment. In S. Haggard & R. R. Kaufman (Eds.), *The Politics of Economic Adjustment*. Princeton, NJ: Princeton University Press.

Hall, P. A. (2006). Introduction: The Politics of Social Change in France. In P. A. Culpepper, P. A. Hall, & B. Palier (Eds.), *Changing France*. Basingstoke, UK: Palgrave Macmillan.

Hall, P. A., & Soskice, D. (2001). An Introduction to Varieties of Capitalism. In P. A. Hall & D. Soskice (Eds.), *Varieties of Capitalism*. Oxford: Oxford University Press.

Hallerberg, M., & Basinger, S. (1998). Internationalization and Changes in Tax Policy in OECD Countries: The Importance of Domestic Veto Players. *Comparative Political Studies, 31*(2), 321–53.

Harrison, A. E. (2002). *Has Globalization Eroded Labor's Share: Cross-Country Evidence*. Unpublished MS. UC Berkeley and NBER. Retrieved from http://cdi.mecon.gov.ar/biblio/docelec/gr1042.pdf.

Hatch, W. F. (2010). *Asia's Flying Geese: How Regionalization Shapes Japan*. Ithaca, NY: Cornell University Press.

Hatch, W. F., & Yamamura, K. (1996). *Asia in Japan's Embrace*. Cambridge: Cambridge University Press.

Hawkins, D. G., Lake, D. A., Nielson, D. L., & Tierney, M. J. (2006). Delegation under Anarchy: States, International Organizations, and Principal–Agent Theory. In D. G. Hawkins (Ed.), *Delegation and Agency in International Organizations*. Cambridge: Cambridge University Press.

Held, D. (1995). *Democracy and the Global Order: From Modern State to Cosmopolitan Governance*. Stanford: Stanford University Press.

Hendriks, G., & Morgan, A. (2001). *The Franco-German Axis in European Integration*. Cheltenham, UK: Edward Elgar.

Hirschman, A. O. (1945). *National Power and the Structure of Foreign Trade*. Berkeley, CA: University of California Press.

Hirschman, A. O. (1970). *Exit, Voice, and Loyalty: Responses to Decline in Firms, Organizations, and States*. Cambridge, MA: Harvard University Press.

Hix, S. (2008). *What's Wrong with the European Union and How to Fix it.* Cambridge: Polity.

Huber, E., & Stephens, J. D. (2001). Welfare State and Production Regimes in the Era of Retrenchment. In P. Pierson (Ed.), *The New Politics of the Welfare State.* Oxford: Oxford University Press.

Iversen, T. (2001). The Dynamics of Welfare State Expansion: Trade Openness, De-industrialization, and Partisan Politics. In P. Pierson (Ed.), *The New Politics of the Welfare State.* Oxford: Oxford University Press.

Jacobs, A., & Helft, M. (2010, Jan. 13). Google May End Venture in China over Censorship. *New York Times,* 1.

Jaumotte, F., Lall, S., & Papageorgiou, C. (2008). *Rising Income Inequality: Technology, or Trade and Financial Globalization* (IMF Working Paper No. 08/185). International Monetary Fund. Retrieved from http://ideas.repec.org/p/imf/imfwpa/08-185.html.

Jayadev, A. (2007). Capital Account Openness and the Labour Share of Income. *Cambridge Journal of Economics, 31,* 423–43.

Kahler, M. (1992). The US and the International Monetary Fund: Declining Influence or Declining Interest? In M. P. Karns & K. A. Mingst (Eds.), *The United States and Multilateral Institutions: Patterns of Changing Instrumentality and Influence.* London: Routledge.

Kahler, M., & Lake, D. A. (2003). Globalization and Governance. In *Governance in a Global Economy* (pp. 1–30). Princeton, NJ: Princeton University Press.

Kapur, D. (1998). The IMF: a Cure or a Curse? *Foreign Policy, 111,* 114–129.

Katzenstein, P. (1985). *Small States in World Markets: Industrial Policy in Europe.* Ithaca, NY: Cornell University Press.

Kaufman, R. R., & Segura-Ubiergo, A. (2001). Globalization, Domestic Politics, and Social Spending in Latin America. *World Politics, 53*(4), 553–87.

Keohane, R. O. (1984). *After Hegemony.* Princeton, NJ: Princeton University Press.

Keohane, R. O. (1988). International Institutions: Two Approaches. *International Studies Quarterly, 32*(4), 379–96.

Keohane, R. O. (2001). Governance in a Partially Globalized World: Presidential Address, American Political Science Association. *American Political Science Review, 95*(1), 1–13.

Keohane, R. O., & Martin, L. L. (1995). The Promise of Institutionalist Theory. *International Security, 20*(1), 39–51.

Keohane, R., O., & Milner, H. (1996). *Internationalization and Domestic Politics.* Cambridge: Cambridge University Press.

Keohane, R. O., & Nye, J. S., Jr. (1977). *Power and Interdependence.* Glenview, IL: Scott Foresman.

Keohane, R. O., & Nye, J. S., Jr. (2000). Introduction. In J. S. Nye, Jr. & J. N. Donahue (Eds.), *Governance in a Globalizing World* (pp. 1–41). Washington, DC: Brookings Institution Press.

Keohane, R. O., & Nye, J. S., Jr. (2003). Redefining Accountability. In M. Kahler & D. A. Lake (Eds.), *Governance in a Global Economy.* Princeton, NJ: Princeton University Press.

Kimmelman, M. (2010, Jan. 17). When Fear Turns Graphic: Populist Parties in Europe Mobilize Posters as Weapons in Their Culture Wars. *New York Times,* 1.

Kindleberger, C. P. (1973). *The World in Depression, 1929–1939.* Berkeley, CA: University of California Press.

Kindleberger, C. P., & Aliber, R. (2005 [1978]). *Manias, Panics, and Crashes: A History of Financial Crises* (5th edn). New York: John Wiley and Sons.

Klein, N. (2000). *No Logo: Taking Aim at the Brand Bullies.* New York: Picador Press.

Knorr, K. (1975). *The Power of Nations: The Political Economy of International Relations.* New York: Basic Books.

Krasner, S. D. (1991). Global Communications and National Power: Life on the Pareto Frontier. *World Politics, 43*(3), 336–66.

Krasner, S. D. (1999). *Sovereignty: Organized Hypocrisy*. Princeton, NJ: Princeton University Press.

Krugman, P. (1995). Growing World Trade: Causes and Consequences. *Brookings Papers on Economic Activity*, (Spring 1995), 327–77.

Krugman, P. (2002, Jan. 1). Crying with Argentina. *New York Times*.

Krugman, P. (2008). Trade and Wages, Reconsidered. *Brookings Papers on Economic Activity*, (Spring 2008), 103–54.

Krugman, P. (2009 [1999]). *The Return of Depression Economics*. New York: W. W. Norton & Co.

Krugman, P. (2010, Feb. 15). The Making of a Euromess. *New York Times*, 19.

Lasswell, H. D. (1971 [1958]). *Politics: Who Gets What, When, How?* New York and Cleveland: World Publishing Co.

Lawrence, R. Z. (1996). *Single World, Divided Nations? International Trade and OECD Labor Markets*. Washington, DC: Brookings.

Lawrence, R. Z. (2008). *Blue-Collar Blues: Is Trade to Blame for Rising US Income Inequality?* Washington, DC: Peterson Institute for International Economics.

Lewis, H., & Richardson, J. D. (2001). *Why Global Commitment Really Matters!* Washington, DC: Peterson Institute for International Economics.

Lewis, W. A. (1978). *The Evolution of the International Economic Order*. Princeton, NJ: Princeton University Press.

Lindblom, C. E. (1988). *Democracy and the Market System*. New York: Oxford University Press.

Manow, P. (2001). Comparative Institutional Advantages of Welfare State Regimes and New Coalitions in Welfare State Reforms. In P. Pierson (Ed.), *The New Politics of the Welfare State*. Oxford: Oxford University Press.

Mansfield, E. D., & Bronson, R. (1997). The Political Economy of Major-Power Trade Flows. In E. D. Mansfield & H. V. Milner (Eds.), *The Political Economy of Regionalism*. New York: Columbia University Press.

March, J. G., & Olson, J. P. (1989). *Rediscovering Institutions: The Organizational Basis of Politics*. New York: Free Press.

Martin, L. L., & Simmons, B. A. (1998). Theories and Empirical Studies of International Institutions. *International Organization, 52*(4), 729–57.

Maxfield, S. (2000). Capital Mobility and Democratic Stability. *Journal of Democracy, 11*(4), 95–106.

McNamara, K. (1998). *The Currency of Ideas: Monetary Politics in the European Union*. Ithaca, NY: Cornell University Press.

Mearsheimer, J. J. (1994/1995). The False Promise of International Institutions. *International Security, 19*(3), 5–49.

Meschi, E., & Vivarelli, M. (2007). *Trade Openness and Income Inequality in Developing Countries* (Working Paper Series No. 232/07). University of Warwick Centre for the Study of Globalisation and Regionalisation. Retrieved from http://www2.warwick.ac.uk/fac/soc/csgr/research/abstracts/232/.

Meunier, S. (2003). France's Double-Talk on Globalization. *French Politics and Society, 21*(1), 20–34.

Milner, H. (1988). Trading Places: Industries for Free Trade. *World Politics, 40*, 350–76.

Mishel, L., Bernstein, J., & Allegretto, S. (2007). *The State of Working America: 2006–2007*. Ithaca, NY: ILR Press.

Mitrany, D. (1943). *A Working Peace System: An Argument for the Functional Development of International Organization*. London: Royal Institute of International Affairs.

Mitrany, D. (1948). The Functional Approach to World Organisation. *International Affairs, 24*, 350–63.

Mitrany, D. (1965). The Prospect of Integration: Federal or Functional. *Journal of Common Market Studies, 4*(2), 119–49.

Moravcsik, A. (1997). Taking Preferences Seriously: A Liberal Theory of International Politics. *International Organization, 51*(4), 531–53.

Moravcsik, A. (1998). *The Choice for Europe*. Ithaca, NY: Cornell University Press.

Mosley, L. (2000). Room to Move: International Financial Markets and National Welfare States. *International Organization, 54*(4), 737–73.

Mosley, L. (2003). *Global Capital and National Governments*. Cambridge: Cambridge University Press.

Mosley, L., & Uno, S. (2007). Racing to the Bottom or Climbing to the Top? Economic Globalization and Collective Labor Rights. *Comparative Political Studies, 40*(8), 923–48.

Najam, A., Runnalls, D., & Halle, M. (2007). *Environment and Globalization: Five Propositions*. Winnipeg, Canada: International Institute for Sustainable Development.

Nielson, D. L., & Tierney, M. J. (2003). Delegation to International Organizations: Agency Theory and World Bank Environmental Reform. *International Organization, 57*(2), 241–76.

North, D. C. (1981). *Structure and Change in Economic History*. New York: W. W. Norton.

North, D. (1989). Institutions and Economic Growth: An Historical Introduction. *World Development, 17*(9), 1319–32.

OECD. (2008). *OECD Factbook 2008: Economic, Environmental and Social Expenditures*. OECD Publishing.

Ohmae, K. (1990). *The Borderless World: Power and Strategy in the Interlinked Economy*. New York: Harper Business.

Olson, M. (1982). *The Rise and Decline of Nations*. New Haven, CT: Yale University Press.

Olson, M. (2000). Big Bills Left on the Sidewalk: Why some nations are rich and others poor. In M. Olson & S. Kahkonen (Eds.), *A Not-So-Dismal Science* (pp. 37–60). Oxford: Oxford University Press.

Ostrom, E. (1990). *Governing the Commons: The Evolution of Institutions for Collective Action*. Cambridge and New York: Cambridge University Press.

Parsons, C. (2003). *A Certain Idea of Europe*. Ithaca, NY: Cornell University Press.

Pierson, P. (Ed.). (2001). *The New Politics of the Welfare State*. Oxford: Oxford University Press.

Polanyi, K. (1944). *The Great Transformation: The Political and Economic Origins of Our Time*. Boston, MA: Beacon Press.

Pontusson, J. (2005). *Inequality and Prosperity*. Ithaca, NY: Cornell University Press.

Prakash, A., & Potoski, M. (2007). Investing Up: FDI and the Cross-National Diffusion of ISO 4001 Management Systems. *International Studies Quarterly, 51*(3), 723–44.

Prasad, M. (2006). *The Politics of Free Markets*. Chicago: University of Chicago Press.

Prebisch, R. (1950). *The Economic Development of Latin America and Its Principal Problems*. New York: United Nations.

Przeworski, A. (2004). Economic History and Political Science. *Political Economist, 12*(2), 1–13.

Przeworski, A., Alvarez, M. E., Cheibub, J. A., & Limongi, F. (2000). *Democracy and Development*. Cambridge: Cambridge University Press.

Putnam, R. D. (1988). Diplomacy and Domestic Politics: The Logic of Two-Level Games. *International Organization, 42*(3), 427–60.

Quinn, D. (1997). The Correlates of Change in International Financial Regulation. *American Political Science Review, 91*(3), 531–52.

Ricardo, D. (1817). *The Principles of Political Economy and Taxation*. London: Everyman's Library.

Risse, T. (2002). Transnational Actors and World Politics. In W. Carlsnaes, B. A. Simmons, & T. Risse (Eds.), *Handbook of International Relations* (pp. 255–74). London: Sage.

Risse, T. (2010). *A Community of Europeans? Transnational Identities and Public Spheres*. Ithaca, NY: Cornell University Press.

Risse-Kappen, T. (1995). Ideas Do Not Float Freely: Transnational Coalitions, Domestic Structures, and the End of the Cold War. In R. N. Lebow & T. Risse-Kappen (Eds.), *International Relations Theory and the End of the Cold War* (pp. 187–222). New York: Columbia University Press.

Rodrik, D. (1997a). Sense and Nonsense in the Globalization Debate. *Foreign Policy, 107* (Summer), 19–36.

Rodrik, D. (1997b). *Has Globalization Gone Too Far?* Washington, DC: Institute for International Economics.

Rodrik, D. (1998). Why Do More Open Economies Have Larger Governments? *Journal of Political Economy, 106*(5), 997–1032.

Rodrik, D., Subramanian, A., & Trebbi, F. (2004). Institutions Rule: The Primacy of Institutions over Geography and Integration in Economic Development. *Journal of Economic Growth, 9*(2), 131–65.

Rogowski, R. (1989). *Commerce and Coalitions*. Princeton, NJ: Princeton University Press.

Rokkan, S. (1999). *State Formation, Nation Building and Mass Politics in Europe*. Oxford: Oxford University Press.

Rudra, N. (2002). Globalization and the Decline of the Welfare State in Less-Developed Countries. *International Organization, 56*(2), 411–45.

Rudra, N. (2005). Globalization and the Strengthening of Democracy in the Developing World. *American Journal of Political Science, 49*(4), 704–30.

Rudra, N., & Haggard, S. (2005). Globalization, Democracy and Effective Welfare Spending in the Developing World. *Comparative Political Studies, 38*(9), 1015–49.

Ruggie, J. (1982). International Regimes, Transactions and Change: Embedded Liberalism in the Postwar Economic Order. *International Organization, 36*, 379–415.

Samuelson, P. A. (1948). *Economics: An Introductory Analysis*. New York: McGraw-Hill.

Sandholtz, W., & Stone Sweet, A. (Eds.) (1998). *European Integration and Supranational Governance*. Oxford: Oxford University Press.

Sassen, S. (2001 [1991]). *The Global City: New York, London, Tokyo*. Princeton, NJ: Princeton University Press.

Schaeffer, R. K. (2005). *Understanding Globalization*. Lanham, MD: Rowman & Littlefield.

Scharpf, F. W. (1999). *Governing in Europe: Effective and Democratic?* Oxford: Oxford University Press.

Schimmelfennig, F. (2001). The Community Trap: Liberal Norms, Rhetorical Action, and the Eastern Enlargement of the European Union. *International Organization, 55*(1), 47–80.

Schmidt, V. A. (2007). Trapped by their Ideas: French Elites' Discourses of European Integration and Globalization. *Journal of European Public Policy, 14*(7), 992–1009.

Schwartz, N. D., & Martin, A. (2010, Oct. 18). Largest Bank Will Resume Foreclosure Push in 23 States. *The New York Times*, 1.

Servan-Schreiber, J.-J. (1968). *The American Challenge*. New York: Athenaeum Press.

Shabi, R. (2005, July 2). The War on Dissent. *The Guardian*.

Shafer, D. M. (1994). *Winners and Losers: How Sectors Shape the Development Prospects of States*. Ithaca, NY: Cornell University Press.

Shane, S. (2009, Dec. 5). The War in Pashtunistan. *The New York Times*.

Shapiro, M., & Stone Sweet, A. (2002). *On Law, Politics, and Judicialization*. Oxford: Oxford University Press.

Shklar, J. N. (1984). *Ordinary Vices*. Cambridge, MA: Harvard University Press.

Shklar, J. N. (1989). The Liberalism of Fear. In N. L. Rosenblum (Ed.), *Liberalism and the Moral Life* (pp. 21–38). Cambridge, MA: Harvard University Press.

Simmons, B. A. (2000). Legalization and World Politics. *International Organization, 54*(3), 573–602.

Singer, P. (2002). *One World: the Ethics of Globalization* (2nd edn). New Haven, CT: Yale University Press.

Sklair, L. (2006). Capitalist Globalization and the Anti-Globalization Movement. In S. Dasgupta & R. Kiely (Eds.), *Globalization and After*. New Delhi: Sage Publications.

Slaughter, A. (2004). *A New World Order*. Princeton, NJ: Princeton University Press.

Smith, T. B. (2004). *France in Crisis*. Cambridge: Cambridge University Press.

Soros, G. (2002). *On Globalization*. New York: PublicAffairs.

Steinberg, R. H. (2002). In the Shadow of Law or Power? Consensus-Based Bargaining and Outcomes in the GATT/WTO. *International Organization, 56*(2), 339–74.

Stiglitz, J. (2002). *Globalization and its Discontents*. New York: W. W. Norton.

Stiglitz, J. (2006). *Making Globalization Work*. New York: W. W. Norton & Co.

Stolper, W. F., & Samuelson, P. A. (1941). Protection and Real Wages. *Review of Economic Studies, 9*, 58–73.

Stone, R. W. (2004). The Political Economy of IMF Lending in Africa. *American Political Science Review, 98*(4), 577–91.

Stone Sweet, A. (2002). Islands of Transnational Governance. In M. Shapiro & A. Stone Sweet (Eds.) *On Law, Politics, and Judicialization*. Oxford: Oxford University Press.

Stone Sweet, A., & Caporaso, J. A. (1998). From Free Trade to Supranational Polity: The European Court and Integration. In W. Sandholtz & A. Stone Sweet (Eds.), *European Integration and Supranational Governance* (pp. 92–133). Oxford: Oxford University Press.

Sunkel, O. (1973). Transnational Capitalism and National Disintegration in Latin America. *Social and Economic Studies, 22*(1), 132–76.

Swank, D. (2001). Political Institutions and Welfare State Restructuring: The Impact of Institutions on Social Policy Change in Developed Democracies. In P. Pierson (Ed.), *The New Politics of the Welfare State*. Oxford: Oxford University Press.

Swank, D. (2005). Globalisation, Domestic Politics, and Welfare State Retrenchment in Capitalist Democracies. *Social Policy and Society, 4*(?), 183–95.

Swenarchuk, M. (2003). Protecting the Environment from Trade Agreements. In R. Sandbrook (Ed.), *Civilizing Globalization*. Albany, NY: State University of New York Press.

Thelen, K. (2001). Varieties of Labor Politics in the Developed Democracies. In P. A. Hall & D. Soskice (Eds.), *Varieties of Capitalism*. Oxford: Oxford University Press.

Truman, E. M. (2003). *Inflation Targeting in the World Economy*. Washington, DC: Institute for International Economics.

United Nations. (2009). *Millennium Development Goals Report*. New York: United Nations.

Van Apeldoorn, B. (2002). *Transnational Capitalism and the Struggle over European Integration*. London: Routledge.

Vaubel, R. (1991). The Political Economy of the International Monetary Fund. In R. Vaubel & T. D. Willett (Eds.), *The Political Economy of International Organizations: A Public Choice Approach*. Boulder, CO: Westview.

Vernon, R. (1971). *Sovereignty at Bay: The Multinational Spread of U.S. Enterprises*. New York: Basic Books.

Vogel, D. (1995). *Trading Up: Consumer and Environmental Regulation in a Global Economy*. Cambridge, MA: Harvard University Press.

Vreeland, J. R. (2003). Why Do Governments and the IMF Enter into Agreements? Statistically Selected Cases. *International Political Science Review*, *24*(3), 321–43.

Waever, O. (1995). Identity, Integration, and Security: Solving the Sovereignty Puzzle in EU Studies. *Journal of International Affairs*, *48*, 389–429.

Walker, J. A. (2008). Union Members in 2007: A Visual Essay. *Monthly Labor Review*, *131*(10), 28–39.

Waltz, K. N. (1959). *Man, the State, and War: A Theoretical Analysis*. New York: Columbia University Press.

Waltz, K. N. (1979). *Theory of International Politics*. Reading, MA: Addison-Wesley.

Waltz, K. N. (1999). Globalization and Governance. *PS: Political Science and Politics*, *32*(4), 693–700.

Watters, E. (2010). *Crazy Like Us: The Globalization of the American Psyche*. New York: Free Press.

Weiler, J. (1995). *The State 'über alles' Demos, Telos and the German Maastricht Decision* (Working Paper No. 95/6). New York: NYU School of Law, Jean Monnet Center.

Wendt, A. (1994). Collective Identity Formation and the International State. *American Political Science Review*, *88*(2), 384–96.

Wendt, A. (1995). Constructing International Politics. *International Security*, *20*(1), 71–81.

Wendt, A. (2003). Why a World State is Inevitable. *European Journal of International Relations*, *9*(4), 491–542.

Wibbels, E. (2006). Dependency Revisited: International Markets, Business Cycles, and Social Spending in the Developing World. *International Organization*, *60*(2), 433–68.

Wibbels, E., & Arce, M. (2003). Globalization, Taxation, and Burden-Shifting in Latin America. *International Organization*, *57*(1), 111–36.

Winters, L. A. (2004). Trade Liberalisation and Economic Performance: An Overview. *The Economic Journal*, *114*(493), F4–F21.

Wolf, M. (2001). Will the Nation-State Survive Globalization? *Foreign Affairs*, *80*(1), 178–90.

Wolf, M. (2004). *Why Globalization Works*. New Haven, CT: Yale University Press.

Woods, N. (2001). Making the IMF and the World Bank More Accountable. *International Affairs*, *77*(1), 83–100.

Woods, N. (2006). *The Globalizers: The IMF, the World Bank, and their Borrowers*. Ithaca, NY: Cornell University Press.

Woods, N., & Lombardi, D. (2006). Uneven Patterns of Governance: How Developing Countries Are Represented in the IMF. *Review of International Political Economy*, *13*(3), 480–515.

INDEX